REVI OTHER BOOKS ABOUT GHOSTS & HAUNTINGS BY TROY TAYLOR

How does Troy Taylor continue to produce one quality book after another? Perhaps only the spirits know for sure! HAUNTED ILLINOIS is truly another top-notch, in-depth look at the Land of Lincoln. I recommend this book to anyone interested in Illinois ghost stories, as it goes to show that ghosts can be found anywhere throughout the state!
Dale Kaczmarek author of **Windy City Ghosts**

Troy Taylor has done it yet again. In HAUNTED ILLINOIS, the author has hit that rare (and delightful) middle ground between fascinating paranormal research and compelling storytelling. His stories will put you on the edge of your seat and his insights into the supernatural will keep you there. A rare and delightful find and an absolute must-read from one of the best ghost authors writing today!
Mark Meriman author of **Haunted Indiana** and **School Spirits**

We have read all the books on Civil War haunts and SPIRITS OF THE CIVIL WAR is the best one ever! It has it all from the history to the hauntings and both familiar and little-known ones. This is a must-read for any Civil War buff and for anyone who believes the war continues on in the afterlife! We're not sure how Troy Taylor's going to top this one... but we'll be waiting!
Rob and Anne Wlodarski authors of **Haunted Alcatraz** and **Southern Fried Spirits**

HAUNTED ILLINOIS is a generous introduction to the resident wraiths of one of the nation's most haunted states, from its most prolific ghost writer. This book is a must for natives, ghost hunters and aficionados of Americana and it will hold captive anyone with an interest in the wonderful experiences so often omitted from the "proper" historical record.
Ursula Bielski author of **Chicago Haunts**

THE GHOST HUNTER'S GUIDEBOOK offers a wealth of modern and really valuable information regarding sophisticated detection equipment, investigation procedures and methods... should be essential reading for anyone in the field of paranormal research, whatever their level of interest or knowledge in the subject.
Andrew Green author of **500 British Ghosts & Hauntings**

OTHER BOOKS BY
TROY TAYLOR

HAUNTED ILLINOIS (1999)
SPIRITS OF THE CIVIL WAR (1999)
GHOST HUNTER'S GUIDEBOOK (1999)
SEASON OF THE WITCH (1999)
HAUNTED ALTON (2000)
HAUNTED NEW ORLEANS (2000)

THE HAUNTED DECATUR SERIES
HAUNTED DECATUR (1995)
MORE HAUNTED DECATUR (1996)
GHOSTS OF MILLIKIN (1996)
WHERE THE DEAD WALK (1997)
DARK HARVEST (1997)
**HAUNTED DECATUR REVISITED
(2000)**

GHOSTS OF SPRINGFIELD (1997)
GHOST HUNTER'S HANDBOOK (1997)
**NEW GHOST HUNTER'S HANDBOOK
(1998)**
GHOSTS OF LITTLE EGYPT (1998)

BEYOND THE GRAVE

THE HISTORY OF AMERICA'S MOST HAUNTED GRAVEYARDS

· A WHITECHAPEL PRODUCTIONS PRESS BOOK ·

This book is dedicated solely to my wife Amy, who continues to be the inspiration for all that I do and who makes me realize that just about anything is possible. While just about everything else in my life remains a constant mystery, my love for her is the one thing that I never have to question.

Original Cover Artwork Designed by

Michael Schwab, M & S Graphics & Troy Taylor
Visit M & S Graphics at www.manyhorses.com

This Book is Published by

- WHITECHAPEL PRODUCTIONS PRESS -
A DIVISION OF THE HISTORY & HAUNTINGS BOOK CO.
515 EAST THIRD STREET - ALTON, ILLINOIS - 62002
(618) 465-1086 / 1-888-GHOSTLY
Visit us on the Internet at www.prairieghosts.com

First Printing - January 2001
ISBN: 1-892523-12-4

Printed in the United States of America

BEYOND THE GRAVE

REMEMBER ME AS YOU PASS BY,
AS YOU ARE NOW, SO ONCE WAS I.
AS I AM NOW, SO YOU MUST BE,
PREPARE FOR DEATH AND FOLLOW ME.
EARLY AMERICAN EPITAPH

THERE IS NO SINGLE LOCATION THAT CAN CHILL THE HEART LIKE A
DESERTED OLD GRAVEYARD CAN... THERE IS SOMETHING ABOUT THE
FACT THAT WE ALL MAY END UP IN SUCH A PLACE ONE DAY THAT
SENDS A COLD SHIVER UP THE MOST HARDENED SPINE...

TO THINK THAT WE MIGHT END UP AS A GHOST IN SUCH A PLACE,
WELL, THAT MAY EVEN BE WORSE!
THE HAUNTING OF AMERICA

IT IS WONDERFUL THAT FIVE THOUSAND YEARS HAVE NOW ELAPSED
SINCE THE CREATION OF THE WORLD, AND STILL IT IS UNDECIDED
WHETHER OR NOT THERE HAS EVER BEEN AN INSTANCE OF THE
SPIRIT OF ANY PERSON APPEARING AFTER DEATH.
ALL ARGUMENT IS AGAINST IT... BUT ALL BELIEF IS FOR IT.
SAMUEL BOSWELL

I BELIEVE THAT THOSE APPARITIONS AND GHOSTS OF DEPARTED
PERSONS ARE NOT THE WANDERING SOULS OF MEN BUT THE
UNQUIET WALKS OF THE DEVIL... NOT AT REST IN THEIR GRAVES...
THOSE PHANTASMS APPEAR OFTEN, AND DO FREQUENT CEMETERIES,
CHARNEL HOUSES AND CHURCHES, BECAUSE THOSE ARE
DORMITORIES OF THE DEAD...
SIR THOMAS BROWNE

BEYOND THE GRAVE
- TABLE OF CONTENTS -

BEYOND THE GRAVE
INTRODUCTION

There is not a single person among us who has not contemplated the mystery of death at one time or another. We all wonder, no matter what we believe in, what will happen to us after we pass on from this world. Some believe that everything comes to an end, that life in this world is our only existence. Others feel that we are born again, as an old soul in a new body, while others believe that our spirits pass on to another place... or perhaps even remain behind as ghosts.

We all wonder about such things... and perhaps this is the reason that we have dreamed up so many rituals and practices dealing with death. Death has been celebrated and feared since the beginning of time itself. We have immortalized it with cemeteries, grave markers and of course, with our darkest and most frightening legends and lore.

And such is the subject of this book.... The darkest side of death.

Within these pages, you will read of not only the most haunted cemeteries in America, but also the fabulous lore of such forgotten places... tales of ghosts, vampires and of nightmarish visions beyond the human imagination. But this book is not a work of fiction! All of the stories contained here are "real" stories... real tales that have been passed along by real people about events they claim have happened to them. These are genuine encounters with phantoms, mysterious creatures, strange deaths, premature burial and much more.

stories have been discovered in historical documents or have been recorded as true-life encounters... and are not always for the faint of heart!

But what attracts such dark elements to what should be places of rest?

It is a common belief among experts of the occult that cemeteries are not usually the best places to find ghosts. While most would fancy a misty, abandoned graveyard to be the perfect setting for a ghost story, such stories are not as common as you might believe. A cemetery is meant to be the final stop in our journey from this world to the next, but is it always that way?

Nearly every ghost enthusiast would agree that a place becomes haunted after a traumatic event or unexpected death occurs at that location. History is filled with stories of houses that have become haunted after a murder has taken place there, or after some horrible event occurs that echoes over the decades as a haunting.

But what of a haunted cemetery? Do such places really exist? Most assuredly they do, as you will soon discover, but ghosts who haunt cemeteries seem to be a different sort than those you might find lingering in a haunted house. Most of these ghosts seem to be connected to the cemetery in some way that excludes events that occurred during their lifetime. As most spirits reportedly remain in this world because of some sort of unfinished business in life, this seems to leave out a cemetery as a place where such business might remain undone.

Graveyard ghosts seem to have a few things in common. These spirits seems to be connected to the burial ground because of events that occurred after their deaths, rather than before. In other cases, the ghosts seem to be seeking eternal rest that eludes them at the spot where their physical bodies are currently found. Cemeteries gain a reputation for being haunted for reasons that include the desecration of the dead and grave robbery, unmarked or forgotten burials, natural disasters that disturb resting places, or sometimes event because the deceased was not properly buried at all!

In the pages of the book to follow, we will explore all of these tragedies, and many others, and will perhaps some of the mysteries of the haunted cemetery. Having said that, I do want the reader to know that I don't claim to have all the answers to these mysteries, nor do I claim to have documented very haunted graveyard in America. What I have done though, is collect stories from the most haunted cemeteries that have ever been whispered about on dark and stormy nights! I have also collected tales of ghosts, hauntings and dark history that will hopefully have you leaving a light on next to your bed at night.

If nothing else, I do believe this book will have you whistling self-consciously as you pass by the local graveyard after dark!

But what about those readers who do not believe in ghosts? Sure, you must believe that spirits and hauntings are merely figments of our imagination. Such stories, you insist are the creations of fools, drunkards and folklorists. You will most likely finish this book and will still be unable to consider the idea that ghosts might exist. In your case, I can only hope to entertain you with the history and horrific tales of America's graveyards.

But I ask that you not be too sure that you have all of the answers...

Can you really say for sure that ghosts aren't real? Are you totally convinced that spirits do not wander the old and mysterious burial grounds of America? Those are questions that you should ask yourself, but before you immediately reply, try answering them while standing in some fog-shrouded cemetery at midnight.

Is the moaning sound that you hear really just the wind whispering in your ear, or could it be the voices of the dead, crying for eternal peace?

Is that merely a patch of fog on the hill, or could it be the ethereal form of a girl in a wedding gown, still searching for the spirit of her murdered lover?

Are those lights in the distance simply the reflections of passing headlights, or are they the souls of the forgotten searching for the graves in which their bodies are buried?

Is that rustling in the leaves really just the passing breeze, or is it the ominous sound of footsteps coming up behind you?

If you suddenly turn to look, then you just might realize that, despite the fact there is no living person around you, you just might not be alone! Perhaps you are not as sure as you thought you were about the existence of ghosts. Perhaps they are not simply a part of fanciful fiction after all? Perhaps no one person among us has all of the answers....

The unknown still beckons to us today and in spite of the hurried world around us and the hard reality of modern life, the unknown remains difficult for us to ignore. Death and the spirit world continue to remain a part of that mysterious unknown and no matter how hard we try, we are unable to completely explain either one. There are stranger things, to paraphrase the poet, than are dreamt of in our philosophies. In this book, you will confront some of them face-to-face....

Are you ready?

Troy Taylor
Holidays 2000

- CHAPTER ONE -
THE GRAVEYARD IN AMERICA

Death is the final darkness at the end of life. It has been both feared and worshipped since the beginnings of history. For this reason, our civilization has dreamed up countless practices and rituals to deal with and perhaps understand it. We have even personified this great unknown with a semi-human figure, the "Grim Reaper", and have given him a menacing scythe to harvest human souls with. Yet, death remains a mystery.

Maybe because of this mystery, we have chosen to immortalize death with stones and markers that tell about the people who are buried beneath them. We take the bodies of those whose spirits have departed and place them in the ground, or in the enclosure of the tomb, and place a monument over these remains that speaks of the life once lived. This is not only out of respect for the dead because it also serves as a reminder for the living. It reminds us of the person who has died... and it also reminds us that someday, it will be our bodies that lie moldering below the earth.

The stone monuments became cemeteries, or repositories of the dead, where the living could come and feel some small connection with the one that passed on. The earliest of the modern cemeteries, or what is referred to as a "garden" cemetery, began in Europe in the 1800's. Such cemeteries are common today, but in times past, graveyards were sometimes hellish and frightening places.

Before the beginning of the Garden cemetery, the dead were buried strictly in the churchyards of Europe. For the rich, burial within the church itself was preferred. Princes, clerics and rich benefactors of the church came to regard such entombment as a right rather than a privilege and soon the buildings began to fill. The Church tried hard to limit such burials but the abuse of the arrangements (usually after a large sum of money had changed hands) soon had the churches packed with the bodies of the dead. The accompanying health risks for the living forced officials to stop the practice. From that point on, only bishops, abbots and "laymen of the first distinction" could be entombed within the church building. The interpretation of "first distinction" was left to the local clergy to decide upon and this decision could normally be influenced by a large donation to the church funds. Most considered the extorted cash to be a small price to pay for the security of an interior tomb and a place safe from the elements.

For those who could not be buried inside of the church, the churchyard became the next best thing. Even here, one's social status depended on the section of the ground where you were buried. The most favored sites were those to the east, as close as possible to the church. In such a location, the dead would be assured the best view of the rising sun on the Day of Judgment. People of lesser distinction were buried on the south side, while the north corner of the graveyard was considered the Devil's domain. It was reserved for stillborns, bastards and strangers unfortunate enough to die while passing through the local parish.

Suicides, if they were buried in consecrated ground at all, were usually deposited in the north end, although their corpses were not allowed to pass through the cemetery gates to enter. They had to be passed over the top of the stone wall. During the late Middle Ages, the pressure of space finally "exorcized" the Devil from the north end of the churchyard to make way for more burials.

As expected, it soon became nearly impossible for the churchyards to hold the bodies of the dead. As towns and cities swelled in population during the 1700's, a chronic shortage of space began to develop.

The first solution to the problem was simply to pack the coffins more closely together. Later on, coffins were stacked atop one another and the earth rose to the extent that some churchyards rose twenty feet or more above that of the church floor. Another solution was to grant only limited occupation of a grave site. However, it actually got to the point that occupancy of a plot was measured in only days, or even hours, before the coffin was removed and another was put in its place.

Not surprisingly, with so many bodies crammed into the churchyards, a protest began to arise from the people who lived nearby. The decaying bodies and the vile stench coming from the graveyard were considered a great risk to local health and doctors began penning stern warnings about the unsanitary conditions. One solution to this was to begin "cycling" the bodies through the cemetery, whereby fresh corpses were deposited on top of coffins long since rotted away by natural decomposition. The burial cycle would begin and then ten or twenty-year gaps would take place between subsequent burials at the same site. Two factors continued this cycling for some time, population and profit. The death rate had stripped the land available for burial and now the churches needed income from whatever space they could create.

It became impossible for the churchyards to hold the dead and by the middle 1700's, the situation had reached crisis proportions in France. Dirt and stone walls had been added around the graveyards in an attempt to hold back the bodies but they often collapsed, leaving human remains scattered about the streets of Paris. The government was finally forced into taking action. All of the churchyards in Paris were closed down for at least five years and cemeteries were established outside of the city to serve the needs of the parishes within the city itself.

Closure of the city graveyards was still not enough though. In 1786, it was decided to move all of the bodies from the Cemetery of the Innocents and transport them to catacombs that had been carved beneath the southern part of the city. It was a massive undertaking. On the night of April 7, a long procession of funeral carts, carrying the bones of tens of thousands of people, made its way to the catacombs. The wagons were escorted by torchlight and buoyed by the chanting of priests. There was no was to identify the individual remains, so it was decided to arrange the bones into rows of skulls, femurs and so on. It has been estimated that the Paris catacombs contain the bodies of between 3 and 6 million people.

In addition to the catacombs, four cemeteries were built within the confines of the city. They were Montmartre, Vaugiard, Montparnasse and Pere-Lachaise, the latter of which has become known as the first of the "garden" cemeteries. It was named after the confessor priest of Louis XIV and is probably the most celebrated burial ground in the world. As it was, the cemetery began in debt and caused a great amount of concern for the investors who created it. If Napoleon had been buried there, as he originally planned, the businessmen would have rested much easier. As it was, they were forced to mount a huge publicity campaign to persuade Parisians to be buried there. They even dug up the bones of famous Frenchmen who had been buried elsewhere and moved them to Pere-Lachaise.

Ironically, it was the burial of people who never lived at all that gained the cemetery its popularity. The novelist Honore de Balzac began burying many of the fictional characters in his books in Pere-Lachaise. On Sunday afternoons, readers from all over Paris would come to the cemetery to see the tombs that Balzac described so eloquently in his novels. Soon, after business began to boom and today, the walls of this graveyard hold the bodies of the most illustrious people in France, and a number of other celebrities as well. The dead include Balzac, Victor Hugo, Colette, Marcel Proust, Chopin, Oscar Wilde, Sarah Bernhardt and Jim Morrison of the Doors (if you believe he's dead, that is).

Pere-Lachaise became known around the world for its size and beauty. It covered hundreds of acres and was landscaped and fashioned with pathways for carriages. It reflected the new creative age where art and nature could combine to celebrate the lives of those buried there.

Paris set the standard and America followed, but London was slow to adopt the new ways. The risks to public health came not only from the dank odors of the churchyards but from the very water the people drank. In many cases, the springs for the drinking supply tracked right through the graveyards. Throughout the early 1800's, the citizens of London still continued to be buried in the overflowing churchyards or in privately owned burial grounds within the city limits. The call for the establishment of cemeteries away from the population center became louder.

In 1832, the London Cemetery Company opened the first public cemetery at Kensal Green. It was made up of fifty-four acres of open ground and was far from the press of the city. From the very beginning, it was a fashionable place to be buried and in fact, was so prestigious that it can still boast the greatest number of royal burials outside of Windsor and Westminster Abbey. The dead here also include novelists Wilkie Collins, James Makepeace Thackery and Anthony Trollope, among others.

But if Kensal Green is London's most fashionable cemetery, then Highgate is its most romantic... and its most legendary. Over time, the cemetery has crumbled and has fallen into gothic disrepair but for many years, it was considered the "Victorian Valhalla".

Highgate did not start out as a cemetery. In fact, in the late 1600's, the grounds were part of an estate owned by Sir William Ashhurst, who had built his home on the outskirts of a small, isolated hilltop community called Highgate. By 1836, the mansion had been sold, demolished and then replaced by a church. The grounds themselves were turned into a cemetery that was consecrated in 1839.

Perhaps the most famous person buried here is Karl Marx, but he does not rest here alone. Other notables include Sir Ralph Richardson, George Eliot and several members of the Charles Dickens and Dante Rossetti families.

For years, it was a fashionable and desirable place to be buried, but as the decades passed, hard times came to Highgate. The owners steadily lost money and the monuments, statues, crypts and markers soon became covered with undergrowth and began to fall into disrepair. By the end of World War II, which saw an occasional German bomb landing on the burial ground, the deterioration of the place was out of control.

If there was ever a location that was perfect for a Gothic thriller, Highgate was the place. Dark visions were created from the crumbling stone angels, lost graves and the tombs ravaged by both time and the elements. As the cemetery continued to fall, trees grew slowly through the graves, uprooting the headstones. Dense foliage and growth gave the place the look of a lost city. Although paths were eventually cleared, nature still maintained its hold on Highgate and in such a setting, occultists and thrill seekers began to appear.

In the early 1970's, the legendary Hammer Films company discovered Highgate's moody setting and used it as a location for several of their horror films. Other companies began using the setting as well, attracting public interest to a place that had been largely forgotten. Soon, stories of grave robbing and desecration began to appear in local news reports.

Not long after, rumors circulated that Highgate was a haven for real vampires, as many claimed to see a particular creature hovering over the graves. Scores of "vampire hunters" regularly converged on the graveyard in the dead of night. Tombs were broken open and bodies were mutilated with wooden stakes driven into their chests. These stolen corpses, turning up in strange places, continuously startled local residents. One horrified neighbor to the cemetery discovered a headless body propped behind the steering wheel of his car one morning!

Bizarre activity reached its peak with the 1974 trial of David Farrant, who the press called the "High Priest and President of the Occult Society". He was tried on five charges connected with activity inside the cemetery.

Highgate Cemetery

Stories of weird rituals and naked women cavorting on desecrated graves filled the newspapers. When he was arrested, photographs of the nude women lying in open graves were found. He had also placed salt around all of the doors and windows of his house and slept with a large, wooden cross under his pillow. Possible witnesses against him in the trial were sent dolls with pins stuck through their chests.

Farrant acted as his own defense at trial. He admitted to occasionally visiting the cemetery but denied ever damaging any of the graves. He was eventually convicted on two criminal counts and sentenced to two-and-a-half years in prison.

Highgate Cemetery continues to hold a fascination for visitors, including for ghost hunters. There have been a number of spirit sightings here, including that of a skeletal figure seen lurking near the main entrance. There is also a white, shrouded figure that has been seen staring into the distance, seemingly oblivious to the surroundings. However, if anyone tries to approach it, it vanishes and reappears in a nearby spot. Witnesses also claim to have seen a tall, thin figure in a black, wide-brimmed hat. This phantom has been seen fading into the high wall that surrounds the grounds. Another, more elusive ghost, is said to be that of a madwoman who prowls among the graves searching for the resting places of the children she murdered.

In spite of the ghost stories though, Highgate's greatest supernatural connections concern the vampires. A television program, which explored the lore of the real and the literary Dracula, was broadcast live from Highgate a number of years ago. A guest on the program was Bernard Davies of the British Count Dracula Society, who stated that Highgate was "the setting for one of the only confirmed sightings of a Twentieth Century vampire".

According to his story, in the winter of 1970-1971, a tall, shadowy figure was seen lurking about the graves and crypts of Highgate Cemetery. The figure was seen vanishing into one of the tombs and footsteps were discovered leading up to it. Inside of the tomb was found an extra casket containing the remains of a body that could not be accounted for, as well as a few drops of blood on the floor nearby.

A vampire expert named Sean Manchester was called investigate and in 1975, he filed a written account of the incident. A short time after his investigation, a missing man was found unconscious in the cemetery. Someone had attacked him and an open wound was found on his throat. He died a few days later, never regaining consciousness, and was never able to tell who, or what, had attacked him. Manchester later published an updated account of his investigations of Highgate in 1985. This embellished account stated that the additional body found in the tomb had been much less decomposed than the others. It also had, he wrote, long, pointed teeth and there had been dried blood around its mouth. According to his story, the tomb had been sealed up with bricks and cement that had been sprinkled with garlic.

While the story remains beyond the bounds of the fantastic, if there ever was a place where a vampire might take up residence, it would certainly be Highgate Cemetery. Thankfully today, the cemetery is under restoration by a group called the Friends of Highgate. They have been working hard to preserve this historic spot and tours are regularly conducted of the grounds.

In America, the churchyard remained the most common burial place through the end of the 1800's. While these spots are regarded as picturesque today, years ago, they varied little from their European counterparts. The colonists viewed them as foul-smelling, unattractive eyesores and in 1800, Timothy Dwight described the local burial ground as "an unkempt section of the town common where the graves and fallen markers were daily trampled upon by people and cattle". This view of the local churchyard intensified by the middle 1800's, when public health reformers began to regard graveyards as a source of disease. As a result, most burials were prohibited from taking place within city limits after the Civil War.

After the founding of the Pere-Lachaise Cemetery in Paris, the movement toward creating "garden" cemeteries spread to America. The first of these was Mount Auburn Cemetery in Cambridge, Massachusetts, which was consecrated in 1831. Proposed by Dr. Jacob Bigelow in 1825 and laid out by Henry A.S. Dearborn, it featured an Egyptian style gate and fence, a Norman tower and a granite chapel. It was planned as an "oasis" on the outskirts of the city and defined a new romantic kind of cemetery with winding paths and a forested setting. It was the opposite of the crowded churchyard and it became an immediate success, giving rise to many other similar burial grounds in cities across the country. In fact, they became so popular as not only burial grounds, but as public recreation areas as well. Here, people could enjoy the shaded walkways and even picnic on weekend afternoons. The Garden cemetery would go on to inspire the American Park movement and virtually create the field of landscape architecture.

The idea of the Garden cemetery spread across America and by the early 1900's was the perfect answer to the old, overcrowded burial grounds. Many of these early cemeteries had been established closer to the center of town and were soon in the way of urban growth. Small towns and large ones across the country were soon hurrying to move the graves of those buried in years past to the new cemeteries, which were always located outside of town.

There are several examples of wonderful Garden cemeteries scattered across America, but two of them are located virtually side-by-side in St. Louis, Missouri. Both cemeteries were created by the need to move a number of smaller burial grounds from out of the way of urban progress.

In March 1849, a banker and church leader named William McPherson and a lawyer and St. Louis Mayor named John Darby incorporated a new burial ground outside of the city. Together, they gathered a group of men, regardless of religious affiliation, and purchased 138 acres of land (which later grew to 327 acres) that became the "Rural Cemetery Association". That spring, the state of Missouri issued a charter to the men for the land along Bellefontaine Road and the graveyard later changed its name from "Rural" to "Bellefontaine".

The cemetery today is largely the work of its first superintendent, Almerin Hotchkiss, a landscape architect and the former caretaker of famed Greenwood Cemetery in Brooklyn, New York. He remained at Bellefontaine for more than 46 years, creating a forested burial ground with over fourteen miles of roads.

The cemetery grew rapidly, mostly because of a terrible cholera epidemic that hit

St. Louis later in June 1849. At the height of the epidemic, there were more than thirty burials each day. Thanks to a law that went into effect forcing all burial grounds to be located outside of the city for health reasons, Bellefontaine began to receive internments from most of the churches in St. Louis.

Today, Bellefontaine has become the resting place of governors, war heroes, writers and adventurers and noted residents include Thomas Hart Benton, General William Clark, Sara Teasdale, William S. Burroughs, the infamous Lemp Family and others. One notable monument here is that of the Adolphus Busch family of beer brewing fame. Their mausoleum has been designed to resemble a French cathedral, right down to the gargoyles. Another famous tomb belongs to the Wainwright family. It was designed by architect Louis Sullivan, who refused to put the family name on the exterior of the crypt. He wanted cemetery visitors to look inside out of curiosity. When they do, they discover a domed ceiling and walls that are completely covered with intricate mosaic tile designs.

Located on the other side of the roadway from Bellefontaine is Calvary Cemetery, another beautiful example of the classic Garden burial ground. Calvary was started in 1857 and also came about because of the epidemic of 1849. After the death of so many St. Louis citizens from cholera, most of the city's cemeteries, including all of the Catholic cemeteries were filled. In addition, many of these burial grounds stood in the way of new development. There was no question that St. Louis Catholics were in need of a larger burial ground, and thanks to the new law, one located outside of the city limits.

In 1853, Archbishop Peter Richard Kenrick purchased a 323-acre piece of land called "Old Orchard Farm" on the northwest side of the city. Kenrick established his own farm on half of the property and gave the other half for use as a cemetery. The ground had already been used for burials in the past, as a portion of the land had once been an ancient Indian burial site. In addition, Native Americans and soldiers from nearby Fort Bellefontaine had also buried the dead here. After Kenrick purchased the ground, all of these remains were exhumed and moved to a mass grave. A large crucifix was placed on top of the site and it is located at one of the highest points in the cemetery today.

Kenrick lived in a mansion on the western edge of the grounds for many years, even after the Calvary Cemetery Association was incorporated in 1867. Archbishop Kenrick became its first president. Around this same time, many of the smaller Catholic cemeteries in the area were moved to Calvary, which now contains over 315,000 graves on 477 acres of ground.

Like Bellefontaine Cemetery, Calvary also takes advantage of the natural wooded setting and rolling hills. It also features amazing displays of cemetery artwork and the final resting places of many notable people like Dred Scott, William Tecumseh Sherman, Dr. Thomas A. Dooley, Tennessee Williams, Kate Chopin, and many others.

Strangely, while neither of these cemeteries boasts a single ghost story, there is a spirited tale connected to Calvary Drive, the road that runs between the two burial grounds, connecting Broadway and West Florissant Road.

There are actually two different versions of the story, but each concerns a phantom that appears along this gloomy stretch of road. The first is a classic "Vanishing Hitchhiker" story (see Chapter 3) about a girl who is sometimes picked up along the road but who then vanishes from the car. A writer named Mike Schrader, who tried to track down the story, said that it started back in the 1940's when she was referred to as "Hitchhike Annie". He also wrote that she limits her appearances to the time of day when the sun is setting and that she also sometimes appears on different roads in the same general vicinity. Schrader found that he was unable to verify the story, although he encountered a number of second hand accounts of "Annie". He also ran across a Sixth District police officer that introduced him to the second version of the "hitchhiker" story.

In this version, the phantom is a boy who is dressed in old-fashioned clothing from the late 1800's. He is said to appear in the middle of Calvary Drive when there are cars coming, causing the vehicles to swerve and slam on their brakes to avoid hitting what they think is a flesh and blood child. When the drivers try to look for him, they always discover that he has simply vanished.

In Chicago, Illinois, one burial ground actually created several Garden Cemeteries, although the most spectacular of them is undoubtedly Graceland Cemetery. Graceland and several others came about thanks to the closure of the old Chicago City Cemetery around 1870.

The City Cemetery was located exactly where Chicago's Lincoln Park is located today. Before its establishment, most of the early pioneers simply buried their dead out in the back yard, leading to many gruesome discoveries as the downtown was developed years later. Two cemeteries were later set aside for both Protestants and Catholics, but both of them were located along the lake shore, leading to the frequent unearthing of caskets whenever the water was high. Finally, the city set aside land at Clark Street and North Avenue for the Chicago City Cemetery. Soon, many of the bodies were moved from the other sites.

Within ten years of the opening of the cemetery, it became the subject of much criticism. Not only was it severely overcrowded from both population growth and cholera epidemics, but many also felt that poorly carried out burials here were creating health problems and contaminating the water supply. To make matters worse, both the city morgue and the local Pest House, a quarantine building for epidemic victims, were located on the cemetery grounds. Soon, local families and churches were moving their loved ones to burial grounds considered to be safer and the City Cemetery was closed down.

One cemetery that benefited from the closure of the graveyard was Graceland

Cemetery, located on North Clark Street. When it was started in 1860 by real estate developer Thomas B. Bryan, it was located far away from the city and over the years, a number of different architects have worked to preserve the natural setting of its 120 acres. Two of the men largely responsible for the beauty of the place were architects William Le Baron Jenney and Ossian Cole Simonds, who became so fascinated with the site that he ended up turning his entire business to landscape design. In addition to the natural landscape, the cemetery boasts a number of wonderful monuments and buildings, including the cemetery chapel, which holds city's oldest crematorium, built in 1893.

There are a number of Chicago notables buried in Graceland, including John Kinzie, regarded by some as the "first white settler" of Chicago and regarded by others as the first crook; Marshall Field of department store fame; Phillip Armour, the meat packing magnate; Gorge Pullman, the much-maligned railroad car manufacturer; Potter Palmer, dry goods millionaire; Allan Pinkerton, of the Pinkerton National Detective Agency; Vincent Starrett, writer and creator of the "Baker Street Irregulars"; architect Louis Sullivan; and many others.

Graceland is also home to several ghost / supernatural stories, some of which will be discussed later in the chapter. One story however, remains puzzling to both cemetery buffs and ghost hunters alike. It involves the strange story of the ghost who has been seen in the vicinity of the underground vault belonging to a man named Ludwig Wolff. The tomb has been excavated from the side of a mildly sloping hill at the south end of the cemetery and according to local legend, it is supposedly guarded by the apparition of a green-eyed dog that howls at the moon. There are those who believe this creature is some form of supernatural entity, while others dismiss it as nothing more than a story created from the name of the man buried in the crypt. Who can say for sure?

The cemeteries of America have taken a long strange trip in the course of their evolution and through the pages of this book, we will be visiting all sorts of burial grounds, from Garden Cemeteries to churchyards to rural cemeteries nestled deep in the woods. One thing remains certain with all of these various cemeteries though. It seems that no matter what different type of graveyard you mention, all of them seem to have one thing in common.... each of them has the potential to be haunted!

· GRAVE MARKERS & TOMBSTONES ·

The tombstone, or grave marker, underwent much the same type of transformation as the cemetery did. The graveyards changed from the crowded churchyards and charnel houses to the tranquil, park-like settings of the early 1900's. Tombstones also started out as crude items that were used more because of superstition than for remembrance of the dead.

The first grave markers were literally stones and boulders that were used to keep the dead from rising out of their graves. It was thought, in these primitive times, that if heavy rocks were placed on the grave sites of the deceased, they would not be able to climb out from underneath them. As time went on, a need came for the living to mark the graves of the dead with a reminder of about the person who was buried there. Many of the markers were made from wood, or rough stone, and did not last long when exposed to the elements.

Early monuments and grave stones in Europe and in old New England were crude and were carved with frightening motifs like winged skulls, skeletons and angels of death. The idea was to frighten the living with the very idea of death. In this way, they were apt to live a more righteous life after seeing the images of decay and horror on the markers of the dead. It would not be until the latter part of the 1800's that scenes of eternal peace would replace those of damnation.

Early grave markers invited the Living to preview Death with Skulls and Dark Imagery.

Eventually, grave markers, monuments and tombs became a craft, as well as an art form. In those days, many brick layers and masons began to take up side jobs as gravestone carvers but soon demand became so great that companies formed to meet the needs of this new trade. Stone work companies formed all over the country, especially in Vermont, where a huge supply of granite was readily available. Many stones and monuments that were carved and cut in Vermont were done by Scottish and Italian immigrants. The most delicate carving was done by the Italians though. As children, many of them had trained in Milan, going to school at night to be carvers. Despite the thousands of statues and mausoleums that were created, only a few dozen carvers could handle the most intricate work.

A Heartbroken Angel Mourns for the Dead.

The peak for the new funeral industry and for graveyard art and mausoleums came in the last part of the 1800's, the Victorian era. During these years, American cemeteries were packed with massive and beautiful statues and tombs. This was a time when maudlin excess and ornamentation was greatly in fashion. Funerals were extremely important to the Victorians, as were fashionable graves and mausoleums. The skull and crossbones tombstones had all but vanished by this time and now cemeteries had become very survivor-friendly. ... and of course, heartbreakingly sad. Scantily dressed mourners carved from stone now guarded the doors of the tombs and angels draped themselves over monuments in agonizing despair.

The excessive ornamentation turned the graveyards into a showplace for the rich and the prestigious. Many of them became inundated with artwork and crowded with crypts as the society folk attempted to outdo one another.

Gaudy and maudlin artwork like furniture, carved flowers and life-size (and larger) statues dominated the landscape. Realistic representations of the dead began to appear, as did novelty monuments like that of the Di Salvo family in Chicago's Mount Carmel Cemetery. This marker portrays the entire family on a round dais... that spins 360 degrees!

There was nothing as elaborate in the Victorian cemetery as the mausoleum however. Tombs for the dead had been around already for thousands of years. The pyramids are the largest and most famous but even ancient man entombed their leaders and chieftains in subterranean and aboveground structures. Most of these were domed chambers created from circular mounds of earth, although some of the stone structures still exist today.

The word *mausoleum* comes from the name of Mausolus, who was the king of

Halicarnassus, a great harbor city in Asia. When Mausolus died in 353 B.C., his grief-stricken wife, Artemisia (who also happened to be his sister), constructed a huge fortress to serve as his tomb. Inspiration for what would become the world's first mausoleum is believed to have come from the Nereid Temple, which boasted statues and friezes of battling warriors and female statues standing between Ionic columns.

The tomb at Halicarnassus was similar to the temple, but much larger, standing a full five stories and having hundreds of statues decorating all quarters. It was said to be surrounded by a colonnade of 36 columns and a pyramid-like structure that climbed 24 steps to the summit. Here was located a four-horse chariot, all made from marble.

Nothing remains of the tomb today save for a few stones from the foundation. It was most likely damaged during earthquakes and by the Knights of St. John of Jerusalem, who plundered the structure in the late fifteenth and early sixteenth centuries. They took the stones to strengthen their own castles and destroyed the underground tomb chambers.

During its heyday though, the tomb attracted many sightseers, including Alexander the Great, who conquered Halicarnassus. The tomb is still considered one of the Seven Wonders of the Ancient World. The Greeks adopted the tomb of Mausolus as the new standard and began building their own "mausoleums" and coining the word. The Romans emulated the Greeks and influenced the modern styles of the nineteenth century, thanks to the fact that many great archaeological finds were uncovered during this period.

The rise of the American mausoleum came with the founding of Mount Auburn, the first Garden cemetery, near Boston. The arrival of this cemetery meant the end of the horrifying graveyards of the past and a new era for burial grounds. Although grave markers dominated the cemeteries, mausoleums experienced a Golden Age, starting in the mid-1800's and ending around the time of the Great Depression. They became the most desired burial spots in any cemetery and bankers, industrialists, robber barons, entrepreneurs and anyone else with plenty of money to spend committed their mortal remains to a mausoleum. They became like the pharoahs of Ancient Egypt, who if they were not remembered for their accomplishments, would be remembered for their tombs.

The best architects were hired and extravagant amounts of money were spent. Most mausoleums of the era were made from granite, marble and various types of stone and often the imaginations of the designers ran wild. They created everything from gothic cathedrals to classic temples to even Egyptian pyramids. One can find just about everything imaginable decorating the tombs of the period, from nude women to macabre animals and the sphinx.

Not surprisingly, many of these bizarre structures have given birth to stories of ghosts and assorted strangeness. We will be exploring many tombs and their related decorations in the pages to follow.

The gravestones themselves have proven to be just as fascinating to cemetery enthusiasts. As mentioned previously, the earliest American stones were copies of the old European ones with skulls, crossbones and death's heads decorating their surfaces. Later, carvings on the stone began to represent the grief of the family and began to make a statement about the life of the person buried beneath it. As time passed, even the plainest of illustrations began to take on a new significance.

A variety of different images were used to symbolize both death and life, like angels, who were seen as the emissaries between this world and the next. In some cases they appeared as mourners and on other graves, as an offer of comfort for those who are left behind.

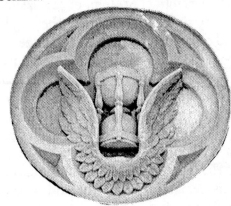

Broken columns, inverted torches, spilled flower pots and funeral urns were meant as simple images of lives that were ended too soon. Some graves were marked with the image of an hour glass with wings that represented the fleeting passage of time or with ferns and anchors that were meant to give hope to grieving loved ones. Much the same can be said of clasped hands, bibles and pointing fingers. These symbols direct the mourners to look toward heaven and know that the worries of the world are now past.

Flowers, like roses or lilies, were common symbols that represented love and purity or that life is like a blooming flower, never meant to be permanent. There are other monuments where depictions of discarded clothing, opened books or forgotten tools have been etched or carved. Such items are meant to symbolize the fact that the dead have left behind the burdens of life. The depiction of wheat or a sickle would show the reaping of the soul and the gathering of the harvest to the next world.

Suns, moons, planets and stars have various meanings in the cemetery, from that of rising saints to that of glorified souls. They can also signify that heaven is the abode of the stars and the planets.

Trees, and most especially the famous "willow tree" motif, stood for human life and the fact that man, like a tree, must reach for the heavens. The willow itself often stood for mourning. Trees could also have other meanings, especially when the monuments were made to look like wood. Cemetery visitors can often find examples of chairs, centerpieces and even entire monuments that are designed to look like the rough wood of a tree. These markers symbolize the fact that the tree has died, its life has been taken away, just like the life of the person the stone honors.

Perhaps the most heartbreaking, and often most eerie, monuments mark the graves of children. These images include the images of disembodied hands from heaven reaching down to pluck flowers from the earth and small lambs, lost and alone. Cribs and beds are sometimes seen, holding the images of sleeping children, or are often empty, symbolizing that these little ones are gone forever. Most disconcerting of all are the life-size images of the children themselves. They stare out at the cemetery visitor with lifeless, and occasionally frightening, eyes.

Gravestones and markers have a myriad of meanings and symbolize both comfort and grief... but are they all what they appear to be? Throughout this book so far, I have suggested the idea that cemeteries and burial grounds can become haunted. But what about the grave markers that exist within these haunted cemeteries? Do some of these monuments actually become haunted by the ghosts who are unable to rest within the bounds of the graveyard?

The annals of ghostlore contain a number of stories about burial markers that may possibly be more frightening than the tales of the cemeteries where these stones reside!

· SPIRITS IN STONE ·

Grave markers and simple tombstones can play host to a surprising number of stories and legends. There are stones across America that people claim to have been not only cursed, but literally move on their own! Is the supernatural at work, or the darker devices of man's own imagination? You be the judge...

THE DEVIL'S CHAIRS

Growing up in the Midwest, I was fascinated by the strange tales and stories that seemed to be unique to our region. One of the most enduring supernatural tales seems to be that of the "Devil's Chairs", stone seats that can be found in scattered graveyards across the midwestern states. Many people accept the stories connected to these chairs as factual, offering second-hand reports and accounts as proof. Often hearing such tales repeatedly, the listener begins to wonder if these fantastic stories might just have a basis in fact?

The story of the "Devil's Chair", or at least the modern version of it, began in the Appalachian Mountains of the middle 1800's. Legend had it that on certain nights, a chair would rise from the ground in the local graveyard. Anyone who sat down in this chair could make a pact with the Devil and receive his or her heart's desire for the next seven years. At the end of that time, the Devil would return and take the hapless victim's soul.

The legend has changed and modified over the years, taking on a more simple mythology. The stories now state that if you sit down in one of these chairs, you are sure to die within the next year. Whether or not such a statement is true is not for me to say, although most of the chairs that are mistaken for "Devil's Chairs" have nothing to do with the supernatural. Most of these chairs are simply what were called "mourning chairs" during the Victorian era. They were usually placed next to the grave of the recently deceased by a relative, creating a more comfortable place to sit when visiting the grave site.

Most of these chairs were of simple design, but there were a few that were almost throne-like in appearance. It was this type of chair that may have accidentally resurrected the legend of the "Devil's Chair". Many of the throne-type chairs have been destroyed in recent years, creating a legend in itself. In these apocryphal tales, the chairs are alleged to have been destroyed by the grieving parents or friends of the luckless teenager who sat in a chair and then was killed a short time later, usually in an auto accident.

The cemeteries of the Midwest boast a number of these so-called "Devil's Chairs" and nearly every one is surrounded by a story of death. The stories are almost always unsubstantiated and on only one occasion have I met someone who was actually present when a person sat in a chair and then later died. Most of the stories involve the fabled "friend of a friend" or some distant cousin. The stories have remained popular throughout the years and are often the first anecdotes to come up when people start telling me their local ghost stories. I usually urge the tellers to take the tale with a grain of salt. However, that doesn't always work!

"We used to get people coming here every night to see the thing. The cemetery is closed after dark but that didn't stop them, they'd just climb the fence... finally we moved it to a storage shed," a cemetery superintendent in Illinois told me.

Apparently, a local "Devil's Chair" stirred up such a fuss with the teenagers in the area that they were making nightly treks to the graveyard to get a look at it. The story started making the rounds that a local boy, who had recently been killed in a car accident, had sat in the chair the previous Halloween. The teenagers began climbing the fence and sneaking into the cemetery to see the chair in question. First, the caretakers moved the chair to make it more difficult to find and then finally, with the family's permission, removed the chair from the grounds and placed it in storage. It now sits in a dusty warehouse somewhere, its legend fading with time.

But the question remains, with all of the stories of "Devil's Chairs" that have been told, is there any truth to these tales? Most likely there isn't... but the story had to get started somewhere, right?

THE STONES THAT WOULDN'T STAY STILL

In the Oak Hill Cemetery of Taylorville, Illinois, there stands a "haunted" monument that seems to have a life of its own. The monument was constructed around 1910 and bears the family names of Richardson and Adams. It is not an unusually unique monument, as there are many like it in cemeteries across America. It is simply a large marble ball that has been placed on top of a pedestal at the center of a family plot. It is so nondescript that it has been a forgotten ornament in this cemetery for many years.

Then, local people began to notice that it moved.

The stone ball, which weighs several hundred pounds, is set into a granite base and is not designed to rotate. Somehow though, it has managed to move and has turned to expose the rough bottom of the sphere. It was at this spot where workmen attempted to seal the stone to the base. Caretakers were puzzled. It would take several men with pry bars to move the granite ball and yet somehow, it has happened... and it continues to move today. Visitors to the cemetery can see where the rough, round area at the bottom of the sphere has become visible, thanks to the movement of the stone. They can also return to the cemetery on another occasion and see the rough spot facing in another direction.

This moving monument is not the only one of its kind either. In his book *Strange World*, author Frank Edwards told about another similar stone, this one located in Marion, Ohio. This sphere can be found marking the grave site of Charles Merchant and his family. The monument was built in 1887 and is a white stone column that is topped with a granite ball.

In July 1905, workmen discovered that this sphere seemed to rotate on its own accord. The ball, like the Taylorville stone, could not have been moved without a number of workmen and a block and tackle. Perplexed, the officials at the cemetery poured concrete into the stone base and set the sphere back into position. Two months later, it was discovered to have moved again and the rough bottom patch was once again visible.

Curiosity seekers began traveling to the cemetery. One geologist theorized that the movement of the stone occurred because of unequal expansion caused by resting in the sun on one side and shade on the other. Others believed that weather might be the culprit. If moisture on the stone froze at night and then thawed in the daylight hours, the ball might shift slightly in its base as the dampness lubricated it. This theory seemed to hold up in the winter months, but what about in the summer, when the stone was also reported to move? The rotation was first noticed in July and has continued to turn ever since. And, how do the stones turn at all if they were designed and fixed to stay in place?

Both mysteries remain unsolved to this day.

THE UNCOOPERATIVE GRAVESTONE

Another moving gravestone seems to be influenced by the spirit of the man who is buried beneath it. It is located in a cemetery in Bardstown, Kentucky and it has acquired a rather unusual legend over the last 150 years.

This stone is placed over the grave of John Rowan, one of historic America's most prominent men. He was a state judge in Kentucky, served seven terms in the legislature and was elected to the United States Senate. He was also Kentucky's Secretary of State and the chief justice for the court of appeals. His cousin, Stephen Foster, is probably the best remembered songwriter of the 1800's and Rowan's former mansion, Federal Hill, is now a popular tourist attraction. It was at Federal Hill that foster wrote "My Old Kentucky Home" and the house was given this nickname many years ago.

Tragedy plagued Rowan throughout his life. When he was a boy, he was so sickly that his family never expected him to live very long. Hoping that the robust country might invigorate the puny child, Rowan's father, William Rowan, moved the family west to Kentucky. Here, enrolled in Dr. James Priestly's school, John began to thrive and not only improved physically but intellectually as well. He became a brilliant scholar and studied law in Lexington and was a well-known lawyer by 1795. A few years earlier, Rowan met Ann Lytle and the two married. The land on which Federal Hill was constructed was deeded to Rowan by his father-in-law in 1794. Throughout the early 1800's, the Rowans hosted a number of dignitaries, including Henry Clay, James K. Polk, James Monroe and others.

The house was also the scene of Rowan's greatest heartbreak. It was here in 1801 that Rowan was forced into a duel with an acquaintance, Dr. James Chambers. Their disagreement began during a card game where the men argued over which one of them was more conversant in Latin. Witnesses stated that the spat deteriorated to the point that Rowan made a disparaging remark about Chambers' wife. Chambers then challenged Rowan to a duel. Rowan admitted that he behaved ungentlemanly and made a public apology, but Chambers insisted on the duel anyway. The two men met on the field of honor, but only John Rowan walked away.

Tragedy came to Federal Hill again in July 1833 when four members of the Rowan family and 26 slaves died during a cholera epidemic. Rowan's oldest son, John, had just been appointed as Secretary of State for President Andrew Jackson. He had stopped at Federal Hill to pay a visit to his family on the way to Washington. Unfortunately, he came down with cholera and died with the others.

When Rowan died in July of 1843, he expressly stated that he wished to have no monument or stone placed on his grave site. He felt that since his parents had been buried without grave markers, he would be disrespecting their memories if he were given an honor they had not received. He felt that his home at Federal Hill stood as more than enough monument to his memory. His family and friends ignored this request however, believing that such a great and prominent man deserved a suitable marker to grace his final resting place. He was buried in Bardstown Cemetery and a tall, obelisk-shaped stone was placed at the site.

A short time after work was completed and the monument was placed at the site, it suddenly toppled over for no apparent reason. Members of the family, already disturbed by the talk that had gone around about the controversial marker, quickly summoned a stonemason to repair the marker and put it back into place. The workmen were puzzled by how the stone could have fallen. Someone suggested that perhaps the ground had settled or that tree roots had knocked the stone over. They hesitantly agreed, but remained unconvinced. Soon after, rumors began to circulate about the stone's mysterious movements.

Within a month or two, the masons received word that their services were needed once more. John Rowan's gravestone had again fallen over. Several of the workmen refused to return to the cemetery. The stone was fixed, but soon after, it fell over again. It tumbled off its base and fell directly onto the ground where Rowan lay. More rumors began to spread that the unhappy spirit of John Rowan had returned and was knocking over the marker that he had not wanted placed there in the first place. It continued to fall over on a regular basis and finally, frightened stone masons refused to return to the cemetery at all. Repair of the stone was left in the hands of the cemetery workers.

Inexplicably, workmen and caretakers are still trying to keep the stone in place today. It continues to fall over for no apparent reason. Why? No one seems to know, but it's just possible that John Rowan meant exactly what he stated in his will... that he forbid a monumental stone of any kind to be placed on his grave!

THE MIRACLE CHILD OF CHICAGO

Another grave, located in the Chicago suburb of Worth and at Holy Sepulchre Cemetery, has much more benevolent properties. In fact, it is said be able to heal the sick and the dying. Many people feel that this is a sacred place and is made so because the grave holds the final remains of a young girl named Mary Alice Quinn.

Over the years, hundreds have claimed to experience miraculous healings here, while others speak of strange occurrences that can only be paranormal in nature. Because of this, Mary's grave and tombstone have been the subject of visits by religious pilgrims and supernatural enthusiasts alike.

Mary was a quiet child who died suddenly in 1935, when she was only 14. She was a devoutly religious girl, devoted to St. Theresa, who claimed to have a mystical experience when she saw a religious image appear on her wall. After that, she became known in her neighborhood for curing the sick. While on her deathbed, Mary told her parents that she wanted to come back and help people after her death. The faithful say that she has done just that. Soon after her death, she was said to have mysteriously appeared to a number of people in the Chicago area. Throughout the 1930's and 1940's, it was not uncommon to hear of new Mary Alice Quinn sightings.

Today, her healing powers are said to have taken on another manifestation and one that surrounds her grave marker. When she passed away, she was secretly buried in a cemetery plot that belonged to the Reilly family. It was thought that this might keep her burial place a secret and prevent the graveyard from being overrun by curiosity seekers intent on finding her resting place. Word soon spread though and a gravestone was eventually cut with her name on it. Since that time, thousands have come to the site, many of them bringing prayer tokens, rosaries, coins and photos to leave as offerings and to ask that Mary intercede for them in prayer. Many claim to have been healed of their afflictions after visiting the grave and others have been healed by extension. They claim to have found relief from one of the many spoonfuls of dirt that has been taken from Mary's grave.

Strangely, the phantom scent of roses has been reported filling the air around the gravestone, even when there are no roses anywhere around. The smell is said to be especially strong in the winter months, when the scent of fresh roses would be impossible to mistake. Many visitors have alleged this smell over the years and some of them even say that it is overwhelming. The faithful claim that this unexplainable odor is proof that Mary's spirit is still nearby and interceding on their behalf. Her love and charity continues, even decades after her death.

THE FACE ON THE TOMBSTONE

One grave marker, this one located in Washta, Iowa, has a more sinister tale to tell. The story of this tombstone dates back to the early 1900's and centers around an elderly couple named Heinrich and Olga Schultz and their mysterious farm hand, Will Florence.

The old couple owned and operated a small farm outside of town and they were well liked in the community. Schultz had hired Will Florence during the haying season, despite the fact that many of his friends and neighbors were suspicious of the stranger. They had already turned him down when he asked for work and prodded Schultz to do the same. The kindly old man hated to see anyone down on their luck, so he hired Florence anyway, providing him with food and board and a small salary.

There was no clue as to where Florence had come from and the man revealed little information about himself. He did say that he had been recovering from some medical problems in Texas and while he claimed to have worked outdoors in the past, he was clumsy and obviously inexperienced at farm work. Schultz continued to show the man kindness though and he patiently instructed him with his chores.

Unfortunately, Florence repaid that kindness with murder.

One day, word came to the farm that failure was eminent at the bank in town. These were uncertain days and banks closed all over the country. Fearing for his savings, Schultz went into Washta and withdrew most of his money. He felt that it would be much safer at home until the bank crisis had passed. On his way out of town, Schultz waved a friendly greeting to one of his neighbors and that was the last time he was seen alive.

Three days later, a friend decided to check on the old couple because no one recalled seeing them for several days. He stopped by the house and opened the front door to find

Heinrich and Olga lying on the kitchen floor in a huge pool of blood. Both were dead and their heads had been split open by an ax. The house had been wrecked and all of the money withdrawn from the bank was gone. And so was Will Florence!

The authorities were quickly notified and Florence was tracked down a few days later in Nebraska. He was arrested and returned to Washta for questioning. Convinced of his guilt, the local prosecutor convened a grand jury and pushed for an indictment. Sadly, there was just not enough evidence to hold him for the crime and the officials were forced to let him go. He vanished from town and was never seen again.

A short time later, a strange story began making the rounds in Washta. It was said that a face was starting to appear on the tombstone of Heinrich and Olga Schultz. Many believed that it was the face of their murderer. To make matters even more intriguing, those who saw it swore that it was the face of Will Florence!

The story was told and re-told and people flocked to the cemetery to see the gravestone. More and more of them, some grudgingly, admitted that the cloudy face that was forming in the stone appeared to be that of Florence. Was it the power of suggestion, or was the tombstone somehow changing to show the face of the man who killed the elderly couple?

A marble dealer was brought to the cemetery to examine the stone and try to explain what was happening to it. He reported that the features were developing because of "atmospheric influences of the rust and veins in the marble". He predicted that the face would grow plainer, and it did. He believed that the strange event was caused by perfectly natural means, but local folks weren't so sure.

Finally, after much urging, two police detectives agreed to visit the cemetery and examine the stone. They soon returned with other officers. Even the most skeptical of them agreed that the face in the marble did resemble Will Florence. That was enough to convince them to take a closer look at the case. When they did, they discovered new evidence that had been overlooked the first time. The new evidence solidly implicated Will Florence and a warrant was put out for his arrest. He was never found though... Florence simply vanished from the pages of history. I would like to think that he got just what he deserved. I'd also like to think that whatever happened to him took place at just about the same time that his face was being stamped on the tombstone of Heinrich and Olga Schultz.

THE WITCH'S MARK

The town of Bucksport is truly a part of old Maine and a historical, and sometimes spooky, place. The Bucksport Cemetery is haunted by a spirit from an event that happened long ago and it is said this spirit left her mark on the tombstone of the man who allegedly condemned her to death.

The tombstone is extremely hard to miss in this cemetery. It stands nearly fifteen feet high and is clearly visible from the gates to the graveyard. An inscription on the side marks this as the final resting place of Col. Jonathan Buck, who founded the city of Bucksport, and who lived between 1719 and 1795. Apparently, soon after Colonel Buck's descendants erected this monument in 1852, a strange image appeared on the stone. It seemed to be the image of a human leg and it marked the monument just below the name "Buck". Despite attempts to remove it, the mark remained vivid to anyone who came to the cemetery.

How this mark came to be on the grave of Colonel Buck is a part of the lore and legend of the area and will forever be a mystery. There are several versions of the story and all of them end with Colonel Buck being cursed for his alleged misdeeds. What is presented here is perhaps the most popular of the stories but the reader is asked to judge the veracity of this tale for himself. What we do know is that Colonel Buck was born in Massachusetts and gained his military title during the American Revolution. He moved to Maine before the war and founded the city of Bucksport around 1762.

One version of the Buck legend, the "Witch's Curse", comes from his earlier life in Massachusetts. A woman had been accused of being a witch and Colonel Buck was asked to preside over her trial. It was a quick and dirty affair that ended with the woman being found guilty and sentenced to death. The woman, whose name was Ida Black, swore to Colonel Buck before she was hanged that she would return from the grave. She vowed that her ghost would come back to dance on the grave of the man who had accused her of the crime. Colonel Buck, apparently a superstitious man, took this threat very seriously and never forgot it.

Years passed and Colonel Buck died in 1795. A half century later, the large marker was constructed for him in the cemetery. The stories say that a short time after, on the anniversary of Ida Black's death, the blood-red image of a woman's dancing leg first appeared on the grave marker. Where it had come from, no one knew. The stone was sanded and cleaned over a dozen times.... but it was no use, the image remained. Rumors started that Ida Black had fulfilled her promise after all.

According to local lore, the Buck family had the tombstone replaced two times, but the macabre blemish always appeared on the new stone. Finally, his descendants gave up and allowed the final stone to remain. The grave marker of Jonathan Buck can still be seen today, resting in the Bucksport Cemetery... and still bearing the mark of Ida Black's dancing foot.

While tombstones and grave markers can certainly be strange, and even frightening at times, they cannot compare with the dark shadows and delightful chills that can be experienced when peering into the window of a tomb. Mausoleums and crypts have been a part of the American way of death since the beginning. They were the burial place of choice for the rich and powerful and for those who did not wish for their remains to be placed in the ground.

Instead of dank holes in the earth, the dead were placed inside of interior crypts, usually set into the floor or the side walls. Some have dozens of such crypts, enough for several generations of the family clan. The interiors of the tombs vary in size and shape and today, many are seldom used. Tombs range in condition from tidy chapels to dark, decaying rooms that have remained unvisited for decades. Such mausoleums often make fitting subjects for tales of horror... and ghost stories.

THE MOVING COFFINS

Perhaps one of the greatest unsolved mysteries of all time concerned an old burial vault that was located on a high, windswept hill overlooking the Caribbean. The mystery occurred at Christ Church, Barbados, near the village of Oistin.

During the days of the slave trade, in the early 1800's, rum and sugar created huge fortunes in the West Indies. Home and government buildings here were constructed on a grand scale by wealthy plantation owners who believed that their displays of power should extend beyond their homes and offices and to their final resting places.

Such was the vault near Christ Church. It was hewn from stone and constructed from coral and concrete. The large stone blocks were firmly cemented together, creating walls that were nearly two feet thick. The floor space inside measured twelve feet by six feet and was reached by several descending steps. The entrance was closed off by a huge slab of blue marble, effectively sealing the vault until it was required to admit another coffin.

It should be carefully noted that there was no way to enter into this tomb, save for the removal of the slab. Regardless, between the years of 1812 and 1820, someone, or something, managed to enter the tomb and wreak havoc on the contents... without leaving a single clue behind. The events were completely inexplicable to the Chase family, who owned the tomb and abandoned it in 1820, and they remain inexplicable today.

The tomb was built in 1724 and even the first burial here remains somewhat of a mystery. It was constructed by a man named James Elliot and on May 14 of that same year, the remains of his wife, Elizabeth, were allegedly placed inside. This is according to records, which also state that the tomb was not re-opened until 1807, when it was found to be empty. What ever became of the body of Elizabeth Elliot it unknown.

In 1807, the Walrond family purchased the vault and body of Mrs. Thomasina Goddard was placed inside.

The Chase family purchased the vault a year after this interment. They were wealthy plantation owners on the island. On February 22, 1808, the vault was opened for the first time by the family to admit the body of Mary Ann Maria Chase, the infant daughter of

Thomas Chase. At that time, the Goddard coffin was found to be undisturbed. A few months later, in July, another of the Chase daughters, Dorcas, also died. There was nothing out of the ordinary reported about the vault until August 8, 1812, when it was opened again for the burial of Thomas Chase himself.

A startling sight greeted the mourners and a workman, who had actually been the first to enter the tomb. He cried out when he saw the coffins of the two Chase daughters standing on end against the northeast wall. There was no sign that anyone had entered the vault, or that the door had been disturbed. The children's coffins were placed beside that of Thomasina Goddard, which lay undisturbed. The heavy, lead-enclosed casket belonging to Thomas Chase was then carried inside by eight men and deposited on the floor. The mourners then left and the stone masons cemented the marble slab back into place.

Four years passed and on September 22, 1816, the vault was opened again to admit the small coffin of a boy named Samuel Ames. The stone slab was removed and a vivid memory of four years before immediately sprang to mind. The interior of the vault was in wild disarray. The coffins were scattered about and tipped over, including the immense coffin of Thomas Chase, which was found standing against one wall.

Once again, the vault was sealed, only to be opened again just eight weeks later to admit the body of Samuel Brewster, who had been killed in a slave uprising. The slab was pulled aside and mourners lined the area around the doorway, hoping for a glimpse inside of the now infamous tomb. They discovered another gruesome sight. The coffins were scattered about and stacked on top of one another. Only the original Goddard coffin was undisturbed but in the confusion around it, the old wood had broken apart, scattering her bones onto the floor. They were carefully collected and wrapped and then placed near the wall as the rest of the vault was again organized into some semblance of order.

The unexplained desecration of the tomb caused "great astonishment" on the island, wrote an early chronicler of the events, Sir Robert H. Schombaugh. He wrote that "no signs were observed that the vault had been opened without knowledge of the family". The Chase family naturally launched an inquiry into the events, but nothing could be found. The vault appeared to have been sealed the entire time.

Many of the plantation owners blamed the desecrations on the slaves. It was thought that many of them were restless, as proven by the recent disturbance that had taken the life of Samuel Brewster, and now were vandalizing the graves of their masters. This still did not explain why the door slab showed no signs of being opened.

Others suggested flooding, although there was no indication of this outside of the tomb. In addition, the vault had purposely been constructed on high ground. It was also suggested that earthquakes might have inflicted the damage, but there was no sign of this in any of the other tombs on the island.

Three years later, the vault was opened again. On July 17, 1819, the body of

Thomassina Clarke, another member of the family, was scheduled to be interred there. By now, the weird story of the vault was known all over the island and even attracted the attention of the Governor, Lord Combermere, who went out of his way to make sure he was present for the service. Predictably, the vault was once again disturbed. All of the leaden coffins were tipped over and scattered about. Only the Goddard remains were undisturbed. Thomas Chase's coffin stood against one wall while the others were thrown about the chamber.

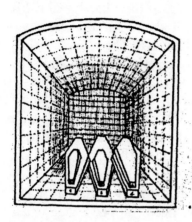 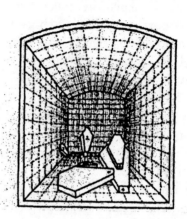

The drawings made by Nathan Lucas to show how the coffins appeared in the vault both before and after it was opened. The drawing at left was made in July 1819 and shows the children's coffins stacked on top of the adults. The sketch at right shows the chaos discovered in the vault in April 1820.

Lord Combermere was so fascinated with the mystery that he personally led a search of the tomb. They investigated every inch, looking carefully for secret passages, underground doors or any signs of digging. They finally gave up, still finding nothing to explain the phenomenon.

Finally, Miss Clarke's coffin was brought in and all of the coffins were rearranged with those of the adults on the floor and the children's stacked atop them. Then, at Lord Combermere's direction, fine sand was spread on the floor so that if anyone entered the vault, his or her footprints would be seen. The slab was then sealed back into place and the Governor's personal seal was affixed to it in front of witnesses.

In April 1820, Lord Combermere ordered that the vault be opened again. There was no one to be buried at that time, but as he was traveling nearby, he asked the local rector, Reverend T. Orderson, to have it opened for his inspection. According to Nathan Lucas, a witness who was present at the time and who drew "before and after" sketches of the chamber, the coffins were again scattered about.

The cement was broken from the door and then they attempted to remove the slab.

Unfortunately, it refused to budge. It eventually took ten slaves to get the door open and when entry was forced, they discovered what was causing the difficulty. Thomas Chase's huge casket was turned upside-down and was jammed against the marble slab. The other coffins were also strewn about the room but to the amazement of the men who entered the tomb.... not a single footprint marred the sand on the floor!

Shortly after, the Chase family removed their relatives from the vault and it has been abandoned ever since.

What explanation could there be for the moving coffins? Earthquakes? Retreating waters? The restless spirits of those interred within? Obviously, natural explanations have been attempted to explain the bizarre disturbances. However, these explanations were all eliminated decades ago. All that we seem to have left to us is the supernatural.

Author Sir Arthur Conan Doyle, who embraced the unexplainable, suggested that the disturbances were created by "forces" that reacted to the lead in the Chase family coffins. While it is true that the wooden Goddard coffin was always undisturbed, it has never been quite clear what these "forces" may have been. Doyle suggested that perhaps they were the spirits of the Chase family, unable to pass on to the other side because of the lead chambers.

Sir Arthur also considered the idea that perhaps energy expelled by the workers who moved the heavy coffins into the vault may have been trapped inside when the door was sealed. If this was the case, perhaps this electrical-type energy was able to move the coffins around inside of the vault.

So, what are the answers behind this strange mystery? It is certain that we will never really know for sure and the vault today is not providing any answers. It remains there on Barbados, its black, open mouth swallowing the daylight that attempts to pierce the shadows below. The stone interior is still cool and dry to the touch but nothing rests inside save for the dust of the centuries and the eerie memories of yesterday's strange events.

THE BLOOD-STAINED MAUSOLEUM

Located in the southeastern Tennessee city of Cleveland is the Saint Luke's Episcopal Church, a historic chapel built in the 1870's. At the rear of the church is a marble mausoleum that, over the years, has attracted curiosity seekers from all over the region. The tomb is the burial place for the Craigmiles family, four members of who died tragically. The white surface of the stone is marred with streaks of crimson stain... the dark color of blood.

John Henderson Craigmiles came to Cleveland from Georgia around 1850. He and his brother, Pleasant, operated a successful mercantile business but John soon grew restless with small town life and traveled west to the California gold fields. He soon discovered that prospecting held little appeal for him, but out west, he did make a discovery that would both change his life and create his fortune. He realized the travel and supply needs of the western territory and soon discovered that a large amount of money could be made in the shipping business. He managed to purchase a small fleet of six ships and began a shipping line between California and Panama. Not only could he trade back and forth between Central America and the West Coast, but he could also carry passengers from the eastern United States who booked passage to Panama and then on to California.

The shipping business prospered for some time, then disaster struck. Mutinous crews hijacked five of John's ships at sea and made off with the vessels and cargo. Claims from his creditors soon wiped out his fortune, but Craigmiles refused to give up. He borrowed $600 from his brother, Green, and set out to rebuild his business with the one ship that he had left. By 1857, he returned in Tennessee, once again a very wealthy man.

Soon after his return, John began courting a young woman named Adelia Thompson, the daughter of local doctor, Gideon Blackburn Thompson, and on December 18, 1860, they were married.

A few months after the wedding, the Civil War began. The Secretary of State for the Confederacy, Judah P. Benjamin, recognized John's head for business and appointed him the chief commissary agent for the South. He held this position throughout the entire war and reportedly used it to great advantage. Buying cattle and speculating in cotton, he sold goods to the Confederacy at a profit and made a fortune from the war. He was also wise enough to know that paper money was of little value and only traded in gold. After the defeat of the Confederacy, when the paper money printed in Richmond turned out to be worthless, John was not ruined as many other southern businessmen were.

In August 1864, Adelia gave birth to the couple's first daughter, Nina. John soon became absolutely devoted to the little girl and along with her mother, grandparents and uncles, she became wonderfully spoiled. Perhaps no one loved the little girl more than her grandfather, Dr. Thompson. He took long walks with her in downtown Cleveland, where she was popular with the shopkeepers, and often took her on medical calls in his buggy. They would spend entire afternoons enjoying the fresh air and journeying about town.

It was during one of these outings that tragedy came to the Craigmiles family. The day was October 18, 1871 and Nina and her grandfather were off on a short jaunt in the buggy. No one knows how the accident happened, but somehow, Dr. Thompson steered the carriage in front of an oncoming train. He was thrown clear but Nina was instantly killed.

The whole town grieved for the little girl. John, Adelia and the entire family were crushed by the loss and could barely function during the funeral services. When it was over, John began making plans to build a church in memory of his daughter. The Episcopal congregation in town had no permanent meeting place and John felt that a new church in Nina's honor would be fitting. The ground was broken the following August and Saint

Luke's was completed on October 18, 1874, the third anniversary of Nina's death.

Almost as soon as the brick and stone church was completed, the family began construction on a mausoleum for Nina's body. It was placed at the rear of the church and was built from expensive marble with walls that were four feet thick. A cross tops the marble spire of the tomb and rises more than thirty-seven feet off the ground. Inside of the tomb, six shelves were built into the walls and in the center was a marble sarcophagus, into which Nina's body was placed.

As time passed, the other members of the family followed Nina to the grave. The first to die was an infant son who was born to John and Adelia, but only lived a few hours. He was never named but his body lies in peace next to his sister.

John Craigmiles died in January 1899 from blood poisoning. Apparently, he had been walking downtown one day and slipped and fell on the icy street. An infection developed and turned into blood poisoning. He died a short time later.

Adelia, who married Charles Cross some time after John's death, was also tragically killed in September 1928. She was crossing Cleveland Street when she was struck and killed by an automobile. She was laid to rest with the other members of her family in the mausoleum.

The stories say that the bloody stains first began to appear on the Craigmiles mausoleum after Nina was interred there. With the death of each family member, the stains grew darker and more noticeable. Some of the locals began to believe that the marks were blood, coming from the stone itself, in response to the tragedies suffered by the family.

To this day, the bloody marks remain. What may have caused them, and why they refuse to be washed away, remains a mystery.

VOICES FROM THE GRAVE

Greenwood Cemetery in Decatur, Illinois has long been a place known for its ghost stories and hauntings (see later chapter on "Graveyards of the Heartland"). Growing up in Central Illinois, I visited the place often, intrigued by its history and its eerie tales. Older acquaintances often told me of a place in the graveyard that had been destroyed many years before. It is long gone now.... but its legacy remains.

Located in the heart of the cemetery is a low, flat area where the Greenwood Community Mausoleum was once located. It was constructed in 1908 and for decades held the bodies of several hundred of Decatur's former residents. The structure was a long, narrow, stone building that was fitted with individual crypts along both interior walls. An open hallway ran down the center and opened at both ends. Overhead glass skylights provided dim lighting for the usually shadowy chamber. The only security provided for the building was a set of iron gates located at each end of the center corridor. They were locked at night with a steel padlock and while this may have kept the curious out, it certainly didn't keep some pretty strange tales from being told about the place.

The mausoleum deteriorated rapidly, whether because of poor construction or harsh weather, no one really knows. It did however, begin to crumble and fall apart. The skylights began to leak and it became common to find puddles of water on the floor after it rained. It also became a place to which neighborhood children would only go to on a dare and a spot about which visitors began to tell stories of shadows and strange noises. The most often repeated stories recalled the sounds of screaming that could be heard bellowing out from both ends of the empty building.

The interior of the Greenwood Mausoleum

Soon, the old mausoleum began to be avoided and interments dropped off rapidly. By the early 1950's, they had ended completely and the tomb became a forsaken place. The cemetery itself had fallen into abandonment and disrepair by this time and the community tomb had followed along with it.

In 1957, Greenwood Cemetery was taken over by the local township and plans were made to restore the burial ground. One of the first items on the new agenda was the destruction of the Community Mausoleum. It was declared to be unsafe by city inspectors and scheduled for demolition. Since then, many have argued that it could have been repaired. Some believe the mausoleum was torn down more because of the stories of disembodied voices inside, than because of it was structurally unsound. Of course, we will never really know for sure.

Once plans were made to destroy the building, caretakers began the long and time consuming process of trying to locate family members of the people interred in the mausoleum. Permission was needed from these family members to rebury their loved ones in other locations in the cemetery. This search took nearly ten years and by the time it was finished, there would remain about a dozen sets of remains that would be unclaimed, as their families could not be located. They had either moved out the area, or had died themselves, leaving no one to pay the costs of moving the bodies.

The crypts inside of the building had been broken open over the past decade, leaving gaping holes in the walls. By the middle 1960's, the last of the bodies were removed and the mausoleum was left with nothing inside save for empty crypts and floors that were covered with dust, stones and plaster. The area around the building was barricaded off and no one was allowed near it as the last of the unclaimed bodies were taken out. These remains were moved to a common grave directly across the cemetery road from the mausoleum site. They were placed in the ground in random order and it is believed that no one ever took the time to identify the individual remains. The common grave can still be seen today, directly east of the mausoleum site. The building itself was finally torn down in 1967.

The building was gone, but it was not forgotten, and neither were the ghosts said to linger there. While the empty building was still standing, witnesses reported the cries of people coming from inside of it, even though it was clearly empty. Strange energy and physical sensations have also been reported around the site of the common grave across the road. Ghost researchers conducted experiments around this area in the summer of 1996, using Geiger counters and devices that measure fluctuations in the earth's energy. All of the equipment picked up abnormal amounts of activity around the common grave and on the site of the mausoleum itself. Apparently, energy has lingered here for over 30 years and may be responsible for the unusual reports that still come from this area today.

I happened to be in the cemetery with a group of people one night in October 1998. It was a very warm night in the early part of the month and as we walked down a hill and onto the mausoleum site, everyone in the group noticed that the air temperature dropped at least 30 degrees. It became so cold that we could literally see the vapor from our breath in the air. The really strange thing was that this only happened in the area were the mausoleum once stood. We could cross the road and feel the air immediately grow warmer!

Why was this so strange? Most paranormal researchers believe that unexplainable energy drops often point to the presence of ghosts, or some sort of spirit energy. That's why you often hear mention of "cold spots" in ghost stories and accounts of haunted houses. Did we encounter the restless ghosts of the mausoleum that night in Greenwood Cemetery? I don't know, but I certainly can't tell you what we did encounter that night either!

THE FLAMING TOMB

Located on the outskirts of New Orleans is a place called Metairie Cemetery and it has always been known as the most fashionable burial ground in the city. It became the epitome of the classic Victorian graveyard, which was far removed from the jumbled chaos of St. Louis Cemetery No. 1. and the other graveyards like it in New Orleans. Originally a racetrack, the grounds were converted to their present use in 1873 by Charles T. Howard, president of both the New Orleans Racing Association and the Louisiana State Lottery. The circle of the racecourse became the main drive of the cemetery and other roads were laid out, ponds were dug and flowers and trees were planted. Metairie remains an opulent park-like cemetery and holds the grave and tombs of the wealthiest people in the city. It now serves as the final resting place as not only famous local citizens but also a number of Confederate leaders as well, including General Pierre Beauregard, General Richard Taylor, General Fred N. Ogden and General John Bell Hood. At one time, Jefferson Davis was also buried here, but his body was removed.

The most interesting tomb in Metairie does not belong to any Confederate leader or wealthy politician. However, it does belong to 'royalty'.... to Josie Arlington, the once reigning Queen of Storyville.

For years, the tomb of Josie Deubler, also known as Josie Arlington, has attracted more people to Metairie than any other monument in the cemetery. In fact, curious crowds have sometimes forced police officers to remain all night on the spot to maintain order.

During the heyday of the Storyville district, Josie was the most colorful and infamous madam of New Orleans. In this center of vice is where Josie operated her house of ill repute and became very rich. The house was known as the finest bordello in the district, stocked with beautiful women, fine liquor, wonderful food and exotic drugs.

The women were all dressed in expensive French lingerie and entertained the cream of New Orleans society. Many of the men who came to Josie's were politicians, judges, lawyers, bankers, doctors and even city officials. She had the friendship of some of the most influential men in the city, but was denied the one thing she really wanted... social acceptance.

She was shunned by the families of the city and even publicly ignored by the men she knew so well. Her money and charm meant nothing to the society circles of New Orleans. But what Josie could not have in life, she would have in death. She got her revenge on the society snobs by electing to be buried in the most fashionable cemetery in New Orleans, Metairie Cemetery.

She purchased a plot on a small hill and had erected a red marble tomb, topped by two blazing pillars. On the steps of the tomb was placed a bronze statue that ascended the staircase with a bouquet of roses in the crook of her arm. The tomb was an amazing piece of funerary art, designed by an eminent architect named Albert Weiblen, and cost Josie a small fortune. Although from the scandal it created, it was well worth it in her eyes.

Tongues wagged all over the city and people, mostly women, complained that Josie should not be allowed to be buried in Metairie. There was nothing they could do to stop her though and nothing was ever said to Josie's face. The construction of the tomb had achieved just what she had wanted it to do... it had gotten the people's attention!

No sooner had the tomb been finished in 1911, than a strange story began making the rounds. Some curiosity-seekers had gone out to see the tomb and upon their arrival one evening, were greeted with a sight that sent them running. The tomb seemed to burst into flames before their very eyes! The smooth red marble shimmered with fire, and the tendrils of flame appeared to snake over the surface like shiny phantoms. The word quickly spread and people came in droves to witness the bizarre sight. The cemetery was overrun with people every evening, which shocked the cemetery caretakers and the families of those buried on the grounds. Scandal followed Josie even to her death.

Josie passed away in 1914 and was interred in the "flaming tomb", as it was often referred to. Soon, an alarming number of sightseers began to report another weird event, in addition to the glowing tomb. Many swore they had actually seen the statue on the front steps move. Even two of the cemetery gravediggers, a Mr. Todkins and a Mr. Anthony, swore they had witnessed the statue leaving her post and moving around the tomb. They claimed to follow her one night, only to see her suddenly disappear. There were also two occasions when the statue may have traveled about the graveyard! According to records, she was found both times in other parts of the cemetery. Most blamed vandals, but the legends say otherwise.

There were also stories told by people who lived in the vicinity of the cemetery. They claimed that the statue of the "Maiden" would sometimes become angry and begin pounding on the door of the crypt. This spectral pounding would create a din that could be heard for blocks. Anyone who asked about the noises would be told that it was the Maiden "trying to get in." The story was that Josie had lived by a certain rule regarding her bordello in Storyville. The rule was that no virgins would ever be allowed to enter her establishment. The stories say that she placed the statue of the Maiden on the steps of the tomb to symbolize this lifelong code of honor.

Others say that the statue is Josie herself. As a young girl, she stayed out too late, the stories say, and her father locked her out of the house. Even though she pounded on the door and pleaded with him, he would never allow her to enter again. After that, she went away and began a career that made her one of the richest women in New Orleans. Still other agree that the statue may be Josie Arlington, but they say it symbolizes Josie as an outsider to the society circles that she always wanted to be inside of. They say that no matter hard she "knocked", the doors would never open for her.

The tradition of the flaming tomb has been kept alive for many years, although most claim the phenomena was created by a nearby streetlight that would sway in the wind. Regardless, no one has ever been able to provide an explanation for the eyewitness accounts of the "living" statue.

Perhaps Josie was never accepted in life... but she is certainly still on the minds of many in New Orleans long after her death!

From the preceding pages, the reader can easily see that are many ghostly legends involving haunted and moving gravestones and mysterious tombs and crypts in America.

While these objects can certainly be strange, and even downright spooky, few of them can provide as eerie an experience as encountering the baleful stare of a piece of graveyard statuary. Many of these monuments are nothing more than the peaceful, angelic forms of heavenly messengers.... but look into their cold, stone eyes.

Does there seem to be something hidden there, lurking just below the surface? Or is that shadowed gaze just the result of the elements beating down on this figure year after year? There is no doubt about it. Graveyard statuary runs the entire gamut between beautiful and frightening. During the early part of the century, craftsmen were allowed to express themselves in cemetery art and create sculptures that included seductive angels, surrogate mourners and even the deceased themselves. Many of these sculptures have gained a reputation for being something other than just the ordinary artwork of a cemetery.... something which may not be of this world at all!

Even when I was young, I heard about such strange statues in some of the local cemeteries. One of them was a surrogate mourner that was located in a small cemetery in Maroa, Illinois. According to the local stories, the statue was said to weep real tears on occasion. The story dates back many years and I have spoken to people who claim to have witnessed this first hand. An examination of the sculpture does reveal some odd streaks on the stone of the statue's face. Natural or supernatural?

Another mysterious sculpture is dedicated to Mrs. Bishop Rayburn and can be found in Oak Ridge Cemetery in Springfield, Illinois. The statue, intended to be a life-size rendition of Mrs. Rayburn, tops a very tall pillar in the cemetery, making a rather unusual monument. It is so high that you have to peer pretty closely to even make out the features on the statue's face. Legends circulated for many years that when Mrs. Rayburn died, her husband constructed this memorial in her honor. When he did so, he had her diamond engagement ring placed on the statue's finger, then had the tall pillar built to protect it from thieves. The stories maintained that upon his death, his ghost took up guard around the pillar and that visitors to the cemetery have reported his apparition here over the years.

Near Oak Ridge is Springfield's Catholic burial ground, Calvary Cemetery. Here, the sculpture of an angel is said to turn on its base on certain nights of the year. For more than four decades, Springfield residents have talked of the mysterious statue and many claim to have seen it inexplicably turn around at the hour of midnight.

When asked about the story, a cemetery spokesperson replied, "It's a myth. She's been here fifty or sixty years and she doesn't turn around."

While they deny the story, officials are reluctant to even discuss the angel, although not for supernatural reasons. They are afraid of vandals. People have wandered into the cemetery at night to get a look at the famous statue and have taken home fingers and even one of her arms as souvenirs. No one knows how the story got started about the angel but countless people have made the trek into Calvary to see if she really turns. Many years ago, it was a popular spot for club and fraternity initiations but today, the cemetery hires its own security to insure the angel is not damaged again.

Has the angel ever turned on her pedestal? "Absolutely not!" the staff states without hesitation. "There's absolutely nothing to the story."

Perhaps they're right, but I always wondered how such a story got started in the first place?

BLACK ANGEL OF OAKLAND CEMETERY

Just about anyone familiar with strange ghost tales from cemeteries, or with stories of "haunted" cemetery artwork, has heard a tales of cursed graveyard statues. In the state of Iowa, perhaps the most notorious of these cursed monuments dwells in the haunted Oakland Cemetery in Iowa City.

For those who have grown up in the area, a nighttime visit to the "Black Angel" is almost a rite of passage, a necessary part of growing up and facing your darkest fears. To many, who can often recite dark tales of the "Angel", the story is little more than a local legend. However, the Black Angel does have a very real history... and according to some, there is reason to be afraid of her!

Teresa Feldevert commissioned the bronze statue in 1911 as a monument for both her husband Nicholas and her teenaged son, Eddie. Many consider it to be one of the greatest works of art in the area, having been created by Daniel Chester French, the same sculptor responsible for the gigantic statue of Abraham Lincoln at the memorial in Washington.

Yet, despite the artistry, the gleaming bronze memorial weathered and darkened to a foreboding black color. All attempts to restore the nine-foot tall figure with outstretched wings have failed miserably. The black remains and according to legend, grows a shade blacker every Halloween.

No one knows how the stories of death and curses got started, but perhaps they came about because of the appearance of the statue itself. The eyes of the figure are truly eerie with swirled irises that seem to bulge from the blankness of the rest of the eye. They seem to stare at the visitor from beneath strangely drooping eyelids... and effect that can be unnerving at best. The sheer size of the statue does little to convince the visitor of the angel's celestial goodwill either.

Many years ago, stories began to be told of this bronze creature. It seems that anyone who touches the statue risks the pain of death, except for virgins, who are reportedly immune to her power. It is also said that vandals who have attempted to deface the monument have come down with mysterious, and sometimes fatal, ailments.

A number of people have told personal stories of the angel over the years, most of them recounting apparitions spotted in the cemetery, strange sights and sounds around the monument and stories of those who have tempted fate, seeking out proof of the paranormal, only to vanish without a trace. Of course, most of these stories seem to involve the proverbial "friends of friends" or distant relatives. Some claim that looking directly into the mysterious eyes of the Angel at midnight will result in a fatal curse upon the gazer. Others maintain that the curse is transmitted only if a person actually touches the statue. Still, concrete accounts of anyone being cursed are nonexistent at best.

One of the most popular stories told concerns a group of young men who tested the supposed "evil powers" of the site by urinating on the angel. As the legend holds, they were involved in a four-car accident later that night. Truth or fiction?

One has to wonder if there is any truth to these legends at all? It's doubtful, but who can really say for sure? As nearly every legend has some basis in fact, I can't help but wonder (once again) how this story got started in the first place. Is the Black Angel of Oakland Cemetery really cursed? I don't know, but I don't suggest waiting around the cemetery at midnight to find out!

SOME CHICAGO CEMETERY HAUNTS

There are two very different stories connected to grave monuments in Chicago's historic Graceland Cemetery. While one of them has widely become accepted as a folk legend, the other one finds a surprisingly receptive, and believing, audience.

The first tale concerns the statue that was placed over the resting place of a man named Dexter Graves. He was a hotel owner and businessman who brought an early group of settlers to the Chicago area in 1831. He passed away and was buried but his body was moved to Graceland in 1909. At that time, a statue that was created by the famed sculptor Lorado Taft was placed on his grave. Taft christened the statue "Eternal Silence" but the brooding and menacing figure has become more commonly known as the "Statue of Death".

The figure was once black in color but over the years, the black has mostly worn away, exposing the green, weathered metal beneath. Only one portion of it remains darkened and that is the face, which is hidden in the deepest folds of the figure's robe. It gives the impression that the ominous face is hidden in shadow and the look of the image has given birth to several legends. It is said that anyone who looks into the face of the statue will get a glimpse of his or her own death to come.

In addition, it is said that the statue is impossible to photograph and that no camera will function in its presence. Needless to say though, scores of photos exist of the figure so most people scoff at the threats of doom and death that have long been associated with "Eternal Silence".

Without a doubt, the most famous sculpture (and most enduring ghost) of Graceland is that of Inez Clarke. In 1880, this little girl died at the tender age of only six.

Tradition has it that she was killed during a lightning storm while on a family picnic. Her parents, stunned by the tragic loss, commissioned a life-size statue of the girl to be placed on her grave. It was completed a year later, and like many Chicago area grave sculptures, was placed in a glass box to protect it from the elements. The image remains in nearly perfect condition today. Even in death, Inez still manages to charm cemetery visitors, who discover the little girl perched on a small stool. It is said that the likeness was cast so that Inez was wearing her favorite dress and carrying a tiny parasol. The perfectly formed face was created with just the hint of a smile. It is not uncommon to come to the cemetery and find gifts of flowers and toys at the foot of her grave. The site has become one of the most popular places in the cemetery, for graveyard buffs and curiosity seekers alike.

You see, according to local legend, this site is haunted. Not only are their stories of strange sounds heard nearby, but some claim the statue of Inez actually moves under its own power. The most disconcerting stories may be those of the disembodied weeping that is heard nearby but the most famous are those of the statue itself. It is said that Inez will sometimes vanish from inside of the glass box. This is said to often take place during violent thunderstorms. Many years ago, a night watchman for the Pinkerton agency stated that he was making his rounds one night during a storm and discovered that the box that holds Inez was empty. He left the cemetery that night, never to return. Other guards have also reported it missing, only to find it back in place when they pass by again, or the following morning.

Does the spirit of little Inez still manifest in this part of the cemetery? Recent accounts say that occasional visitors to Graceland will spot a child who sometimes disappears in the vicinity of her monument. Perhaps she is still entertaining herself, just on the other side?

Another "statuary spirit" comes from Rosehill Cemetery and while this burial ground boasts a number of ghosts (see the later chapter on "Graveyards of the Heartland"), perhaps the most romantic and tragic tale involves the grave of Frances Pearce. This striking monument was moved from the old Chicago City Cemetery to Rosehill many years ago and depicts the life-sized images of Frances and her infant daughter. Both of them are reclining, with the little girl in the arms of her mother, atop the stone. The figures are encased inside of one of the already described glass boxes.

Frances was married to a man named Horatio Stone around 1852. The two of them were said to be very much in love and lived a happy life together. Then, in 1854, Frances tragically died at the age of twenty. To make matters worse, her infant daughter followed her to the grave four months later. Horatio was nearly destroyed by these terrible events and he commissioned sculptor Chauncey Ives to create a memorial sculpture to be placed on their graves in the City Cemetery. Later, both the remains and the memorial were moved to Rosehill.

According to local legend, on the anniversary of their deaths, a glowing, white haze fills the interior of the glass box. The stories go on to say that the mother and daughter are still reaching out from beyond the grave for the husband and father they left behind.

BLACK AGGIE OF DRUID RIDGE

When General Felix Angus, the publisher of the Baltimore 'American', died in the 1925, he was buried in Pikesville's Druid Ridge Cemetery, right outside of Baltimore. On his grave was placed a rather strange statue. It was a large, black mourning figure. The statue's creator (sort of), Augustus St. Gaudens, was said to have called her 'Grief" but to legions of Baltimore residents, she was dubbed with a different name, "Black Aggie".

In the daylight hours, the figure was regarded as a beautiful addition to the graveyard art of the cemetery. The sculpture was copied from one of the premier artisans in Maryland at the turn-of-the-century and the statue was highly regarded..... at least until darkness fell and the legends began.

Marian Adams

Augustus St. Gaudens was a premiere American sculptor of the late 1800's. Before his death in 1907, he created some of the most honored works in America, including the figure of Diana that once topped Madison Square Gardens and monuments to American heroes and statesmen like Lincoln and Sherman. One of his greatest pieces of work was a memorial for Marian Adams, the wife of Henry Adams. Marian, called 'Clover" by her friends, had fallen into a dark depression after the death of her father in 1885. In December of that year, she committed suicide by drinking potassium.

Henry Adams plunged into his despair and in search of comfort, traveled to Japan in June 1886 with his friend, artist John La Farge. When he returned from his trip, he decided to replace the simple headstone that he had ordered for his beloved 'Clover" in Washington's Rock Creek Cemetery with a more elaborate memorial. He turned to St. Gaudens and asked him to create something with an "eastern" feel to it, perhaps combining the images of the Buddha with the work of Michelangelo.

The endeavor took over four years, frustrating Adams, but creating what some called 'one of the most powerful and expressive pieces in the history of American art, before or since". It was placed in the cemetery in 1891 and Adams was delighted with both the design and the setting. The statue was never officially named, known as the "Adams Memorial" and later by the more popular name of "Grief". The stories for this nickname vary. Some say that the statue was dubbed this by St. Gaudens himself and others say Mark Twain, who viewed the memorial in 1906, coined the name.

Rumors circulated about the death of Marian Adams and her husband's strange reaction to it. He had discovered her body collapsed in front of the fireplace in their Lafayette Square home in Washington. He never discussed the circumstances of her suicide and when Adams wrote his autobiography, Marian was never mentioned. As time passed, he spent less and less time in their former home and neighbors began to claim that it was haunted. At dusk, they reported the sounds of a woman weeping inside of the dark mansion and even after it was sold, later residents claimed to experience a persistent cold spot in front of the fireplace. They could never explain this, especially when the fireplace was piled high with burning logs. Another story claimed that the apparition of Marian could sometimes be seen sitting in a wooden rocking chair in her old bedroom. It was said that she often appeared in front of several witnesses at one time and a terrible feeling of loneliness would overwhelm each of them. In moments, the ghost would simply fade away. Stories have persisted about the house, even today.

Strangely, Marian's grave monument was something of an enigma itself. Henry Adams refused to ever speak publicly about his wife's death and would never officially name the monument. He also refused to acknowledge its popular nickname. Thanks to Adams' silence and the fame of his esteemed political family (he was the grandson of President John Quincy Adams), many became curious about the monument. Adams furthered this curiosity by refusing to have an inscription placed on the monument and by placing it behind a barrier of trees and shrubs. The challenge of finding it only fueled the public interest, first by word of mouth and later in guidebooks and magazine articles. The grave became a popular site for the curious, especially as the statue was so unnerving to look at. It was so fascinating that it became the subject of an incredible piracy by a sculptor named Eduard L.A. Pausch.

It would be from the original Adams design that the sculptor created his own, unauthorized copy of "Grief" in the early 1900's. The statue would later come to be known as the infamous "Black Aggie".

Within a few months of the statue being placed on Marian Adams' grave, Henry Adams reported that someone had apparently made a partial casting of the piece. He wrote to Edward Robinson in 1907 that "Even now, the head of the figure bears evident traces of some surreptitious casting, which the workmen did not even take the pains to wash off."

The copy would go on to become even more famous than the original!

General Felix Angus purchased the Pausch copy of the sculpture in 1905, perhaps after having admired the original work at the Adams grave. Why he decided to use the copy to grace his family tomb, instead of commissioning an original work of some sort, is unknown... but perhaps something about the Pausch statue compelled him to own it. We will never know for sure.

Felix Angus was born in France in 1839. At the age of only 13, he traveled around the world and at 20, fought in the army of Napoleon III against Austria and later served with General Garibaldi's forces in Italy. In 1860, he came to New York and went to work as a silver chaser and sculptor at Tiffany's. When the Civil War broke out, he enlisted as a private in the Union Army and began a war record so incredible that he was promoted to the rank of Brigadier General by age 26. He saw action in dozens of battles, including Big Bethel, Richmond, the Siege of Port Hudson and the Battle of Gaines' Mills. He was wounded more than 12 times by both bullet and saber. His friend, writer H.L. Mencken later said that Angus "had so much lead in him that he rattled when he walked."

After a severe shoulder injury at Gaines' Mills, then Lieutenant Angus was brought to Baltimore for treatment. There, he met Charles Carroll Fulton, the publisher of the Baltimore "American" newspaper and his daughter, Annie, who nursed Angus back to health. Fulton had met the young officer at the Pratt Street Pier when the medical steamer docked and had taken him to his home for care and rest. When the war was over, Angus returned to Baltimore and asked Annie to marry him. She quickly accepted. After that, Angus continued his remarkable career, working briefly in the internal revenue office, then as Consul to Londonderry, Ireland for the United States Senate. He later retired from this position to take over for his father-in-law at the newspaper. He remained the publisher of the newspaper until his death.

In 1905, Angus began construction of a family monument in Druid Ridge Cemetery. It was during this time that he purchased Black Aggie and then had a monument and pedestal created that would closely match the setting of the Adams Memorial in Washington. The first burial at the site was of the General's mother, who had been brought over from France.

A year later, the widow of the artist Augustus St. Gaudens sent a letter to Henry Adams to inform him of the poor reproduction that had been done of "Grief" and which was now resting in Druid Ridge. There was nothing they could do legally about the theft of the design so St. Gauden's widow traveled to Baltimore to see the site for herself. She discovered a nearly identical statue, seated on a similar stone, but with the name "Angus" inscribed on the base. She also noted that the stone was a nondescript gray color and not the pink granite of the original. The Baltimore site also did not have the bench and the rest of the stonework as the original Washington gravesite had.

After seeing the site, Mrs. St. Gaudens declared that General Angus "must be a good deal of a barbarian to copy a work of art in such a way". Angus quickly responded and claimed to be the innocent victim of unscrupulous art dealers. The artist's widow then requested that he give up the sculpture and file suit against the art dealers. Strangely, Angus did file suit (and won a claim of over $4500) but he refused to give up the copy of the statue.

The General's wife, Annie, died in 1922 and Angus himself died three years later at the age of 86. He was also laid to rest at the feet of "Aggie".... and shortly thereafter, her legend was born.

While the Angus Monument seemed innocent enough in the daylight, those who encountered the statue in the darkness, gave her the nickname of "Black Aggie". To these people, she was a symbol of terror and her legend grew to become an occasional story in the local newspaper and of course, the private conversations of those who believed in a dark side. Where else could you find a statue whose eyes glowed red at the stroke of midnight?

The legend grew and it was said that the spirits of the dead rose from their graves to gather around her on certain nights and that living persons who returned her gaze were struck blind. Pregnant women who passed through her shadow (where strangely, grass never grew) would suffer miscarriages.

A local college fraternity decided to include Black Aggie in their initiation rites. Not really believing the stories, the candidates for membership were ordered to spend the night in the cold embrace of Black Aggie. Those who remember the statue recall her large, powerful arms. The stories claimed that the local fraternity initiates had to sit on Aggie's lap and one tale purports that "she once came to life and crushed a hapless freshman in her powerful grasp."

Other fraternity boys were equally as unlucky.... One night, at the stroke of midnight, the cemetery watchman heard a scream in the darkness. When he reached the Angus grave, he found a young man lying dead at the foot of the statue.... he had died of fright, or so the story goes. Just another legend that grew over the years into a ghost story? Maybe, and then again, maybe not.

One morning in 1962, a watchman discovered that one of the statue's arms had been cut off during the night. The missing arm was later found in the trunk of a sheet metal worker's car, along with a saw. He told the judge that Black Aggie had cut off her own arm in a fit of grief and had given it to him. Apparently, the judge didn't believe him and the man went to jail.

However, a number of people did believe the man's strange story and almost every night, huge groups of people gathered in Druid Ridge Cemetery. The public attention gained by the news story brought the curiosity-seekers to the grave and the strange tales kept them coming back.

Were the stories told about Aggie merely "urban legends" and eerie tales told about a spooky piece of graveyard art? Some thought so... while others weren't so sure. One man that I was able to interview (who we'll call "Frank") grew up in the New Jersey area and became intrigued with the stories of Black Aggie, especially after a strange event that took place in the early 1950's. Was what happened just a coincidence... or something more? I'll let you be the judge!

One night, Frank and two of his friends came down to Baltimore from Atlantic City for a visit. They wanted to see some young women they had met previously, while the girls were in New Jersey on vacation. The group decided to go sightseeing and one of the stops they made that night was to see the legendary statue of Black Aggie. The young women took them to the cemetery and told them a story or two about the monument.

Frank and his friends walked over for a closer look, curious to see (as the girls told them) if anyone had placed coins in Aggie's hands for good luck, as was the local tradition. They didn't find any coins, but Frank's friend, "Freddy", thought it would be funny to snuff out his cigarette in Aggie's hand instead.

"We told him not to," Frank later recalled, "but Freddy just laughed. He didn't believe in any of that stuff..... about ten years later, Freddy was found in a dump in South Carolina. He had been shot in the back of the head, mafia-style. They never found out who did it."

Frank paused for a moment and appeared thoughtful. "'It's been many years now, but I will never forget the feeling that I had standing in front of Aggie that night... as if she knew the future and could see what lay ahead for us."

Such lurid tales brought many listeners and the Angus grave site began to be trampled by teenagers and curiosity-seekers. Although Pikesville (where Druid Ridge is located) was fairly remote at the time, the site was visited, and vandalized, by hundreds or perhaps thousands of people over several decades. In addition to the statue's arm being stolen, hundreds of names and messages were scrawled on the statue, the granite base and the wall behind it. Today, these have been blasted away, although some evidence of the damage sadly remains.

Cemetery groundskeepers did everything they could to discourage visitors, including planting thorny shrubs around it, but they failed to keep people away. There is no indication as to why the cemetery was not better patrolled at night, but perhaps they just couldn't afford it. For every trespasser arrested, dozens of others managed to reach the site. A fence surrounds the grave of the Angus family today, but back then, the cemetery was wide open, especially at night.

Eventually, the number of nighttime visitors and the destruction they caused became too much for the cemetery to handle. By the 1960's, it had gotten so bad that the descendants of Felix Angus elected to donate Black Aggie to the Maryland Institute of Art Museum. However, this move never took place and the statue remained at her resting place for one more year, until 1967. On March 18, the Angus family donated Aggie to the Smithsonian Institution for display.

For many years, this donation would prove to be quite an enigma for researchers who attempted to track down the whereabouts of Black Aggie. You see, according to the Smithsonian, they didn't have her. Despite some people recalling that Aggie was displayed in the National Gallery for a brief period, officials at the Smithsonian claimed they had never displayed her at all. Conspiracy theorists "smelled a rat" and believed that perhaps she was simply placed in storage, rather than put on display... because of her cursed past. "Maybe, just maybe," wrote a columnist for the Baltimore Sun, "they're not taking any chances."

The real answer would not be as strange. Somewhere along the line, the staff at the Smithsonian gave Aggie away, which explains why she does not appear in their records. They had no interest in displaying her and instead, gave her to the National Museum of American Art, where she was then put into storage and never displayed. For years, she would remain in a dusty storeroom, shrouded in cobwebs, until recently... when Black Aggie would "rise from the dead"!

In 1996, a young Baltimore area writer named Shara Terjung did a story on Black Aggie for a small newspaper. After having been long fascinated with the legends, she became determined to track down the present location of the statue. Finally, shortly after Halloween, she got a call from a contact at the General Service Administration who was able to discover where the elusive Aggie had ended up. The statue can still be seen today at the Federal Courts building in Washington, in the rear courtyard of the Dolly Madison house.

The mysterious statue had finally been found!

Black Aggie may be gone from Druid Ridge Cemetery, but she's certainly not forgotten. "We still have people coming to Druid Ridge, asking for Black Aggie all the time," said one of the cemetery spokesmen in an interview. "I don't think there's a week that goes by when we don't get a call about it."

The Angus grave site is well cared for today and shows little sign of the desecration of the past. Grass grows now in the place where for many years it could not. The only lingering evidence of Black Aggie is a chipped area on the granite pedestal and a faint shadow where she once rested. At least that's the only lingering presence that can be seen... some say there is more. Who knows? Whether the Angus grave site was ever haunted or not, Black Aggie has left an indelible mark on not only Druid Ridge Cemetery... but the annals of the supernatural in America as well.

· CHAPTER TWO ·
THE DARK SIDE OF
DEATH

In the early pages of this book, we discussed man's fear of death. One has to wonder if perhaps the fear of what may be waiting for us on the other side may also extend to our fear of ghosts? Our fear of death has its roots in the not so distant past. In centuries gone by, life was short and death came far too soon. A mother during the Victorian era might give birth to six children in order that three might survive to adulthood. People simply didn't live very long in those days, creating a fear of death that was both primal and deep-seated.

Today, things have changed. We live much longer and death has become remote and sanitized. In these modern times, few adults under forty have even seen a corpse. When death finally comes for us, it does so in the clinical setting of a hospital. We are protected and shielded from our dark dreams of death.... or are we?

In spite of all of these changes, death is just as mysterious now as it was two hundred years ago. Our cause of death may differ, but the result is still the same. What happens when we die? Is there a life beyond this mortal one?

And thus, our fear of ghosts is born.

What rational person wishes to return from the grave to wander the earth for eternity? Who would wish to spend their postmortem days and nights aimlessly pacing the corridors of the house where they once lived, doomed to loneliness, isolation and despair? Most importantly, what creature would desire to be trapped for all time among the crypts, monuments and tombs of a forgotten graveyard?

Earlier in this volume, I asked a question... do haunted graveyards really exist? And if so, what causes the spirits to linger in them? The ghosts who haunt these spots seem to stay behind because of events that take place after their deaths. An indignity carried out on our body after we die is a fear that has remained with us since the days of the "body snatchers". Society endows on a lifeless corpse the capacity for feeling hurt and the expectation of respect. All forms of the defilement of the dead, especially thefts and the desecration of corpses, are regarded as not only distasteful but almost unholy.

And perhaps society is right about that, for the majority of graveyard ghost tales stem from terrible events that occur within the bounds of the cemetery, long after the hapless victims have died. Cemeteries gain a reputation for being haunted for reasons that include the desecration of corpses, grave robbery, unmarked graves, natural disasters that disturb resting places and more. Could such events literally create the ghosts of these haunted cemeteries?

In the coming pages, we will take a closer look at what I call "The Dark Side of Death". This darker side not only includes the reasons why some cemeteries might become haunted, like premature burial, grave robbery, desecration of corpses and more, but also the unexplained and the mysterious side of death as well.

I offer a word of warning though... some of these tales are not for the faint of heart or for the weak of stomach. Read on if you dare!

- BURIED ALIVE -

To be buried alive is, beyond question, the most terrific of these extremes which has ever fallen to the lot of mere mortality... the boundaries which divide Life from Death, are at best shadowy and vague. Who shall say when one ends and the other begins?

So wrote author Edgar Allan Poe in his macabre short story, "The Premature Burial". In his tale, Poe refers to being buried alive as a "certain theme" that is "too entirely horrible for the purposes of legitimate fiction". The narrator in Poe's story had reason to be afraid of such an end because he suffered from catalepsy, a neurological condition that could produce episodes of extreme paralysis, mimicking, and being mistaken for, death. Many believed that Poe himself suffered from this horrid disease, but this was not the case. His terror of being buried alive came from the dark recesses of his imagination, but he was not alone in this fear. It was a very common phobia during the 1800's and one that was justified given the state of medical technology at that time.

The fear of being buried alive is perhaps as old as the fear of death itself. Being taken from this world at the moment of death is bad enough, but the prospect of being mistakenly identified as dead and then waiting in suffocating horror... well, it's too much for most of us to think about.

The obsession with premature burial reached its peak during the Victorian era but anecdotes of those unfortunate enough to be buried alive stretch back to for centuries. One early instance was written about in 1308. A grammarian named Johannes Duns Scotus was mistakenly thought to be dead and was interred in his tomb. Some time later, the vault was reopened and Scotus was found outside of his coffin. His hands were torn and covered in crusted blood from his futile attempts to open the tomb from the inside.

Anxiety of premature burial still exists today, but thanks to advances in the medical world, it remains more of a private fear that one of public hysteria, as seen in years past. The terror has it roots in 1742, when a distinguished French doctor named Jacques Benigne Winslow wrote *The Uncertainty of the Signs of Death*. The book was based on the fact that doctors of the time were most likely misjudging the ailments of their patients and pronouncing them dead too early. Dr. Winslow was said to be well qualified to write such a book as he claimed to have been placed in a coffin alive on two different occasions.

Needless to say, writings from a well-known doctor on the subject of premature burial got people talking and published accounts by authors like Edgar Allan Poe made matters all the more intriguing. Poe even wrote an article on what was believed to be a true account of a woman being entombed alive. It reportedly happened to the wife of an eminent official in the Baltimore area. She was seized by an unknown illness, and to all outward appearances, was dead. She was placed in the family vault and was left undisturbed for three years. At the end of that time, the tomb was opened for an interment and as the door was pulled open, the skeleton of the woman in her burial clothing tumbled out! Apparently, she had revived soon after her funeral and had succeeded in knocking her coffin from the ledge where it rested. It broke open and she was able to escape. She was not able to get through the door of the tomb however and she died there, her screams unheard by those passing outside.

While the medical profession was quick to disregard the claims of "rampant" premature burials, it was hard to ignore the accounts and evidence that came in response to public interest. One physician, Franz Hartmann, published a book called *Premature Burial* in 1895. He collected over 750 cases of people being buried alive and earned the almost universal condemnation of the book by other doctors. How could they not disagree? The public mania over premature burials highlighted the fact that doctors were merely human and sometimes made mistakes... perhaps even mistakes that had people waking up from a trance and finding themselves entombed in a coffin.

This famous painting by artist Anton Wiertz was a grisly depiction inspired by the hasty disposal of cholera victims in the 1840's.

The stories and alleged incidents of premature burial fueled the public's imagination and created both scandalous and spine-tingling reading. In 1849, a severe cholera epidemic killed 199 people. An old woman, who was in charge of the cholera wards, stated that as soon as patients died, they were placed into wooden coffins and the lids screwed down. They were then moved outside into a small shed so that they would be out of the way.

"Sometimes", she coldly told authors William Tebb and Edward Vollum, "they'd come to afterwards and we did hear them kicking in their coffins, but we never unscrewed them, because we knew they had to die".

A particularly gruesome case was recounted in the *Undertaker's Journal and Funeral Directors' Review* for July 1889. A portion of the article recalled a New York case from 1854 in which a baker placed the coffin of his deceased daughter in a temporary vault in order for the girl's older sister to come to New York from St. Louis for the funeral. This was possible, testified the undertaker who performed the services, because the death occurred in the winter and the outdoor temperature prevented severe decomposition.

When the rest of the family arrived, the vault was opened for the funeral. When the lid of the coffin was removed, they discovered that the girl had apparently been buried alive. Her grave clothes had been torn to shreds and according to the report, several of her fingers had literally been bitten off. She had supposedly eaten them in a vain attempt to prolong her life.

Another account, from Eddowe's Journal of August 1844, tells of a child who was accidentally buried alive. While the sexton was filling in the grave, he was startled to hear the boy calling for help. He quickly uncovered the coffin and the boy was rescued. He later made a full recovery and while this tale had a happy ending, the account ended with a somber postscript. "Not long ago, in making a grave in the same cemetery, a coffin was broken into, and it was found that the occupant had revived after burial, and had gnawed the flesh of both wrists before life was finally extinguished."

In the 1979 book *Buried Alive*, author Dr. Peron-Autret and his colleague Dr. Louis Claude-Vincent interviewed more than sixty gravediggers who had been working in Paris cemeteries for many years. He asked them if they had ever seen evidence of corpses buried alive and to the author's surprise, all of them had. The most commonly reported bits of evidence were bodies with bite marks that had been gnawed from the hands and forearms. None of the coffins had ever been broken into but nearly all of them had internal marks of scraping and scratching on the lids. One gravedigger even described fingernails that had become embedded in the wood.

While it is possible that some of those who were entombed alive did resort to self-cannibalism to survive, or perhaps bit chunks out of their flesh in a state of terror, it is more usual to find physical damage inflicted on the casket and body caused by desperate efforts to escape. In his book *The Lazarus Syndrome*, author Rodney Davies tells of a London cemetery that was damaged by a German bomb during World War II and the resulting discoveries.

The explosion damaged a large part of the cemetery and unearthed many caskets and bodies. The gravediggers that were summoned to replace the corpses in the ground noticed that many of the cadavers exhibited signs of having been buried alive. Not only was skin torn away from the hands and the knees, but fingernails were split, broken and ripped away and some still had fabric from the inside of the coffin clinging to them. Some of the bodies also had broken fingers and toes as well.

The grim discoveries were kept from the public but one of the gravediggers leaked the story to a local policeman named William Repton and his daughter passed the story along to Davies. Repton was so unnerved by the story that he made his wife and daughter promise that they would have him cremated at the time of his death, rather than buried.

Today, it hard for us to guess just how fearful the Victorians needed to be about being buried alive. Certainly, there were many tales and stories of those who discovered bodies in a state that appeared as if they had been trying to escape from the grave. There were also plenty of "near-miss" experiences, told by those who fell into a stupor and were almost buried alive. In all honesty though, most of the fears probably came from the popular press. Such tales of death and gruesomeness played right into the public demand for ghosts and frightening stories. How much more frightening is a macabre event that can actually occur to you?

In addition, the Victorian era also gave birth to the popularity of the "vampire" tale, which involved an undead creature that rose from the grave. Stories of premature burial may have even spawned the original lore of the vampire, a subject that we will discuss later in this chapter.

Regardless though, premature burials did take place, but the question remained as to how they actually occurred? As we already mentioned, medical technology was not exactly at its best in previous centuries. Tests for medical conditions and even the pronouncement of a person being dead were crude at best. It is commonly known today that we do not die all at once, but rather in bits and pieces. For example, our hair and our fingernails often continue to grow after death takes place. This is accepted today, but in years past, it was thought to be one of the supernatural signs of the living dead.

It was also accepted that true corpses feel no pain. This was often a fact that was used to decide if a person was dead or not. In the 1800's, a Dr. Josat invented a pair of sharp forceps that were used to viciously pinch the nipples of someone thought to be dead. Another idea was to thrust long needles under the finger and toe nails. (I would sincerely hope to be already dead if forced to undergo either of these tests!

Doctors also used temperature to determine if a person was dead. Unfortunately, touching a cold corpse is not always accurate, as deeply comatose patients are also known for being quite cold. In the late 1800's, "necrometers" were used to check body temperatures and were calibrated to indicate if the patient was "alive", "probably dead" or "dead". Needless to say, they were not all that accurate and mistakes were sometimes made.

It has also long been a tradition to check for a person's breath in determining whether or not they are dead. The "Mafia Mirror Test" was often used by Chicago gangsters and involved placing a mirror under the nose of the possibly deceased to see if the glass fogged up. It had actually been used for many years and had never been very reliable.

So, if we accept the fact that people could often be mistaken for being dead, what sort of ailments most commonly caused this to occur?

Catalepsy, as mentioned earlier, was probably the most common sickness to mimic death during the Victorian period. It has been characterized by the immobility of the muscles and was easily mistaken for death. During a trance state, a victim's limbs have a wax-like flexibility that causes them to be shaped into odd positions, where they can remain indefinitely. Catalepsy often occurred during moments of hysteria and was a common side effect to schizophrenia before drug treatments came into use.

Comas were often mistaken for death in the days of more primitive medical treatments. They tend to create a very deep, sleep-like state and it often takes a lengthy period for the victim to recover. The fate of the comatose patient in those days often depended on the patience and the vigilance of doctors and relatives and the legal time limits placed on the interval between death and burial.

Many of those who awoke from trances just in time to escape the grave were able to give accounts of having been fully aware of what was going on around them. In every case though, they were unable to react. Miss Eleanor Markham wrote of her own experiences in *Banner of Light* in 1894 and said, "I was conscious all the time you were making preparations to bury me and the horror of my situation was altogether beyond description. I could hear everything that was going on, even a whisper outside the door, and although I exerted all my will power, and made a supreme physical effort to cry out, I was powerless."

As you can imagine, such horrific tales fed the public frenzy over premature burial. The Victorians soon began a search for ways to prevent such atrocities from taking place. In days past, the surest way to avoid being buried alive was to obtain the services of a doctor who could be trusted enough to actually view and examine the corpse. Many instances of premature burial occurred because of misdiagnosis by relatives or because of absentee doctors who, acting in perfect accordance with the law, were not required to actually see a body to pronounce the person dead. A certificate of death only needed to state that the doctor had been told they were dead. The obvious answer to this problem was for the relatives to be in no doubt about whether you were dead or not and if there was some question, for them to have explicit instructions about what to do to eliminate that lingering doubt.

The mystery writer Wilkie Collins always carried a letter with him detailing the elaborate precautions that his family should take in order to prevent his premature burial. Other people added to their wills that no one in the family would benefit until it was absolutely sure they were a corpse. They even went as far as to write friends into the will who would be given a substantial amount of money to sever their heads from their body or to pierce their veins.

For example, a woman named Francis Power Cobbe had a last request that was designed to prevent her reawakening in the grave. She wrote that a doctor should "perform on my body the operation of completely and thoroughly severing the arteries of my neck and windpipe, nearly severing my head altogether, so as to make any revival in the grave absolutely impossible".

The *Undertaker and Funeral Director's Journal* in 1889 told of a family in Virginia that had developed a curious custom and one it had kept for more than a century. Over one hundred years before, a member of the family had been exhumed and was found to have been accidentally buried alive. From that time on, each member of the family who died was stabbed in the heart with a knife by the head of the household. They apparently ended the custom around 1850 when a young woman in the house apparently died. The knife was plunged into her heart and she suddenly gave a terrible scream and died, awakened from the trance that she had been in. The incident broke her father's heart and he committed suicide a short time later.

Lady Burton, the wife of the famous British explorer Sir Richard Burton, stated that she thought it infinitely preferable to be killed outright by the embalmer's needle than to regain consciousness below the ground. Apparently, she was not alone in these feelings.

But again, what was to be done for the deceased to insure they were dead?

Those who wrote on the subject agreed that putrefaction, or the decaying of the body, was the surest sign of irreversible death. Unfortunately, there were also a lot of disadvantages to keeping one's loved one around until they had time to rot. So, for a price, "waiting mortuaries" began to appear so that families would have a place to keep the bodies until they started to decay.

The mortuaries became popular after several cholera epidemics in the late 1860's. Cholera had a habit (as the reader will recall from earlier in the chapter) of inducing a trance-like state that imitated death. A short time after death was presumed, the bodies were taken to the nearest mortuary, Here, they were washed and dressed and placed in a zinc tub that was filled with antiseptic fluid. The tub was then surrounded with flowers, for both aesthetic and sensory reasons, and the family could come for final photographs with the deceased. The bodies would remain exposed for up to seventy-two hours, or less if signs of decay appeared earlier.

Interestingly, an intricate system of cords and pulleys was attached to the corpse so that if the fingers moved at all, an alarm bell would ring and attendants would be summoned. Staff members remained on duty twenty-four hours a day and made frequent inspections of the bodies. They rarely had time to get bored either, for such was the sensitivity of the bell system that false alarms were common, usually caused by air drafts or the post-mortem movement of muscles.

Such mortuaries fell into disuse with the improvement of the medical community.

There is no doubt that the worst possible experience of premature burial would be awakening while trapped inside of a coffin, below six feet of earth. No matter how loudly you screamed or clawed at the lid of the coffin, there was little chance for escape... or was there?

In 1896, Count Karnice-Karnicki, chamberlain to the Tsar of Russia, invented an ingenious device to prevent premature burial. The count imagined the nightmare faced by anyone who might be buried underground. How could such a person summon help? The apparatus that he constructed was a tube that passed vertically from the lid of the coffin and then ended in an airtight box above the level of the ground. Resting on the chest of the deceased was a glass sphere that was attached to a spring running the entire length of the tube. It connected to a mechanism inside of the box. The slightest movement of the chest would move the sphere in a way that the spring would cause the lid of the box above to fly open and admit air and light. The spring also activated a flag, a light and a loud bell to attract the attention of anyone who might be in the cemetery.

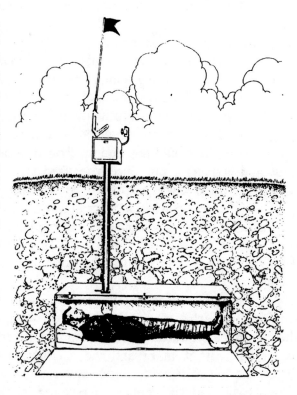

This device could be rented for a small amount of money and after a length of time went by, and there was no chance for revival, the tube could be pulled up and used in another coffin.

There were other devices invented too that allowed anyone who awoke in the grave to ring bells, sound alarms and wave flags. There is no record of what the success rate for these devices might have been but I can imagine that the inventions gave many Victorians no small amount of comfort.

Others looked for a more direct solution to notify their families that they were alive. One man, John Wilmer, was actually buried in the back garden of his home. A switch that was placed in his hand, at the time of his burial, was connected to an alarm in his house. If he awakened from any sort of trance, he could immediately summon help. For some reason though, apparently fearing a technical failure, he asked his relatives to be sure that they carried out an annual inspection of the wiring!

The reader is bound to laugh at such a suggestion, wondering just how long Wilmer planned to remain alive in his grave! However, that laughter is bound to turn into a shudder after they read the strange account that follows.

Martin Sheets was a wealthy businessman who lived in Terra Haute, Indiana in the early 1900's. One of his greatest fears was that of a premature burial. He often dreamt of being awake, but unable to move, at the moment the doctor pronounced him dead and then regaining consciousness while trapped in a coffin below the ground. Sheets decided to fight his fears by investing some of his resources in the prevention of his being buried alive.

First of all, he had a casket custom-designed with latches fitted on the inside. In this way, should he be placed inside prematurely, he would be able to open the coffin and escape. He also began construction on a mausoleum so that when he died, or was thought to have died, he would not be imprisoned under six feet of dirt. The mausoleum was well built and attractive but Sheets realized that even if he did manage to escape from his casket, he would still be trapped inside of a stone prison.

He came up with another clever idea. He installed a telephone inside of the tomb with a direct line to the main office of the cemetery. In this way, he could summon help by simply lifting the receiver. The line was fitted with an automatic indicator light so that even if no words were spoken, the light would come on in the office and help would soon be on the way.

Death came for Martin Sheets in 1910 and he was entombed in the mausoleum. I would imagine that for several days afterward, cemetery staff workers kept a close eye on the telephone indicator light in the office. After more time passed though, it was probably forgotten. Years went by and the telephone system in the area changed. Eventually, the direct line to the cemetery office was removed but thanks to very specific instructions in Sheets' will, and the money to pay for it, the telephone in the mausoleum remained connected and active.

A number of years later, Sheets' widow also passed away. She was discovered one day lying on her bed with the telephone clutched in her hand. In fact, she held the receiver so tightly that it had to be pried from her fingers. It was soon learned that she had experienced a severe stroke and family members assumed that she had been trying to call an ambulance when she finally died. A service was held and after a quiet memorial service, she was taken to the family mausoleum, where she would be interred next to her husband.

When cemetery workers entered the mausoleum, they received the shock of their lives. Nothing there was disturbed, they saw, except for one, very chilling item. Martin Sheets' telephone, locked away for all of these years, was hanging from the wall.... its receiver inexplicably off the hook!

Ghostly tales connected to persons who have been buried alive appear frequently in the annals of the supernatural and many of them are connected to the greater lore of a given location. For instance, one of the most terrifying tales of a Greenwood Cemetery in Central Illinois involves the spirited fates of a number of prisoners of war that were accidentally buried alive on the edge of the graveyard. This area is now considered one of the most haunted sites in the cemetery and we'll take a closer look at the entire haunted graveyard in a later chapter.

Author Rodney Davies also told of a ghostly man who was believed to have been buried alive. An encounter with this apparition took place on the Saturday before Easter 1978. A cleaning woman was in her local church with several members of her family. They were sweeping and tidying things up before the service the next day. She later reported that she suddenly became very cold and glanced up to see an old man walking around the sanctuary. He was peering about, as if he had lost something.

She described him as wearing old-fashioned clothing. His suit was dark brown with a pale stripe in it and he carried a pocket watch on a chain. "He looked quite normal," she said, "walking all around the altar and through the choir stalls, then out through the door to the back rooms of the church."

After he disappeared, she went over and asked the flower delivery woman who the man was. "There's no one else here," the other woman replied.

A few moments later, the man appeared again and this time, he walked toward the cleaning woman, her husband and her children. He reached out and touched her hand. She described his skin as being "colder than ice." She also noticed some other things about him. His fingers were bleeding and very dirty, with black soil under his nails. His shoes were worn through at the toes.

The woman's husband managed to speak up. "Where have you come from?", he asked the specter.

"You could say that I have kicked and clawed my way out of the grave," the spirit replied and then he turned and walked away. The family followed him to the door but he quickly disappeared.

The lady continued working at the church for the next five years but she never again saw this strange ghost. She had no idea who he might have been but suspected that he may have been the ghost of a man who was buried alive.

THE "SLEEPING" MEDIUM

Another unusual story comes from the little New England town of Damariscotta, Maine and concerns a woman named Mary Howe... a woman that many people believe was buried alive!

Mary's family had originally come to Maine after the War of 1812. Her father, Colonel Joel Howe came up from Massachusetts and settled into the sleepy little village. He brought with him his wife and his five daughters and four sons and they opened up Howe's

Tavern, a popular local spot and stagecoach stop that attracted a lot of business to town.

Besides being hard working, the family also became known for being a bit on the eccentric side. Edwin Howe was known locally for being an "oddball" inventor and had come up with what he called a "perpetual motion machine" and a mold for minting his own half-dollars. In later years, when the tavern was renovated, the new owners discovered a number of Edwin's perplexing and mysterious contraptions. Unfortunately, few of them had much practical use.

Edwin's sister, Mary, was also known for being a bit strange. One day, she decided that she possessed the ability to fly. Reportedly, she climbed to the top of the stairs, spread her arms and then fell down the steps, managing to get pretty banged up and breaking an ankle. Not long after this, Mary, the rest of the Howe family and many of the townspeople, became interested in Spiritualism. The family soon began trying their hands at contacting the dead but of all the children, Mary seemed to have a real gift at spirit communication. She was able to go into trances and see and speak with ghosts in a way that no one else could.

When word of this got out, many friends and neighbors came around to see her. In time, thanks to the many travelers who passed through Howe's Tavern, word of Mary's seances spread beyond Damariscotta. Soon, people were coming from all over New England to see her performances.

Mary differed from other mediums in that when she went into a trance for her seances, she would often remain in a coma-like state long after it was over. It was said that she once stayed in a trance for several days and that she did not even breathe. Edwin Howe even stated that she gave no sign of a heartbeat. However, he did keep warm stones stacked around her body so that she would stay warm. Days after going into a trance, Mary would emerge from it and appear to be completely fine.

Mary seemed to have little difficulty in communicating with the spirits and was known for avoiding generalities and for giving detailed information to the sitters who came to the seances. A man named Harold W. Castner once wrote in a *Yankee* magazine article about the time his grandmother attended one of Mary's seances. While she and several others waited in the room, Mary went into her trance. Although no one else in the room knew it, one of the sitters had a relative who was visiting New York City. Hoping to possibly catch Mary off guard, she asked when this person would be returning to Damariscotta. Mary moaned several times before she managed to speak. "Yes, I see him. But wait! I see lights... many lights all around him. He will not return.. when those lights come on, he will die!!"

No one had any idea what she was talking about, but a few days later, the bizarre prediction came true. The sitter received word that her relative had died of a heart attack in New York... at the exact time that the lights were turned on at the newly completed

Brooklyn Bridge!

In the summer of 1882, Mary slipped in a trance during a routine seance. At first, it seemed no different from the others, until more than a week went by and found her still asleep. Friends and family members began to worry and officials began to wonder if she might be dead. Edwin Howe played the situation for all that it was worth. He escorted the many hundreds of visitors through the house and gave detailed descriptions of what was happening (or rather, what wasn't happening) to Mary. The situation soon began to bother the local authorities and especially the members of the clergy.

Finally, they called in the local doctor, Dr. Robert Dixon, to examine Mary and see if she was still alive. Dr. Dixon, a family friend, faced the difficult task of examining the young girl. He admitted that she didn't look dead. Her body as warm and her limbs were pliable and although she had been lying there for a few weeks, there was no trace of rigor mortis. He even noted that there was no smell of decay.

Still, as a medical man, Dr. Dixon could not ignore the fact that Mary wasn't breathing. He could also find no heartbeat. As much as he hated to say it, it was obvious that Mary had died. He issued an order to the constable and told him that it was necessary to seize Mary's body from the family and bury it.

In spite of the protests of Edwin and many other local people, the constable, the undertaker and several ministers came, prepared the body and carried it away. The undertaker set a funeral date but the day came and went, for no one would dig a grave for Mary. She was supposed to be buried in Hillside Cemetery, directly across the street from the tavern, but owner Benjamin Metcalf refused to give them a plot. Everyone hoped that if they delayed long enough, Mary would wake up and be saved from a premature grave.

Officials were determined to see her buried however so they transported Mary's body to Glidden Cemetery in nearby Newcastle. They found a plot for her there but still could find no one to dig the grave. Eventually, the constable, the undertaker and one of the preachers had to dig the grave themselves.

The stories say that onlookers forced the men to open the coffin one last time before they lowered it into the hole. It was said that Mary was still warm and that her face had a lifelike color. Despite all of that, she still refused to breathe. The lid of the casket was closed and Mary was committed to the earth.

Although more than a century has passed, it remains a mystery as to whether or not Mary Howe was buried alive. Unfortunately, many believe that she was.

Mary's grave was never marked in Glidden Cemetery, in order to keep Edwin from coming there and digging her up, but that hasn't kept the stories from being told about the graveyard. For years, people avoided coming here at night. They heard stories from those who dared to wander about the grounds... stories of cries, moans and sobs coming from below the earth. Others swear they have seen strange lights and misty figures wandering about. Is it the ghost of Mary Howe? Or perhaps it is the spirit of Edwin, still searching for the place where his sister was buried prematurely?

GRAVE ROBBERY & DESECRATION

Beyond the fear of death itself, man has great concern over what becomes of his body after his spirit has departed from it. The fear of indignities being perpetrated on the body was a deciding factor for many years in cremations and the construction of private crypts and mausoleums. Unfortunately, there are many ways that a body, or grave, can be desecrated but in this section, we will take a look at the defilements carried out by the hands of man himself!

Grave robbery is perhaps one of the most gruesome crimes to ever exist. In the late 1700's and early 1800's, the chances of being dug up and removed from one's coffin were much greater than your chances for being buried alive. The early history of grave robbery was created more out of necessity than desire. In those days, medical schools were faced with dire problems. A surgeon was only as good as his knowledge of anatomy and yet it was illegal in those days to dissect a corpse. Because of this, the schools were unable to legally procure an adequate supply of dead bodies for the teaching of medical students. Thanks to this, the schools had to depend on the services of loathsome men called "body snatchers", or more eloquently "resurrectionists", who would seek out fresh corpses in the local cemeteries. They would then sell the bodies to doctors and scientists for medical experimentation and teaching. There were said to be thousands of graves visited by mourning family members from which the deceased had vanished long before!

Despite what many believe, body snatching was largely a British phenomenon, although it did happen in America too. Unfortunately though, most of the body snatching done in the United States has been for more gruesome reasons than for medical practice, as we will explore a little later in the chapter.

Most of the grave robberies committed in America were not for the bodies in the graves, but for the valuables the deceased had been buried with. It was not uncommon in the 1800's and early 1900's for caskets to be found broken open in the local cemetery and the rings and jewelry of the corpse to have disappeared.

The standard operating procedures for such men would be to attend burials and wakes, looking for loot that would be placed in the casket with the body. The scouting trips also led to payments made to gravediggers and cemetery workers, who would pretend to close the graves after the services. A few shovels of dirt would be thrown down into the grave while the mourners were still present, just for good measure. Later, in the dead of night, the thieves would return to the graveyard and remove the valuables from the coffins. In addition to jewelry and personal belongings, other valuable prizes including gold-rimmed spectacles and the gold crowns from the teeth of the departed. These small amounts of gold were often melted down and sold on the black market.

Undoubtedly worse than the removal of valuables from the grave is the violation of the corpse itself. As mentioned, in America, the practice of "body snatching" has had little to do with medical experiments. The practice here is of a much more horrifying and sickening sort. Necrophilia, the most reviled of all sexual perversions, is pleasure derived from sexual intercourse with a corpse. It represents posthumous indignity of the most twisted sort.

Necrophilia is thought to be fairly rare but it has been recognized since ancient times. It was often thought that the death of a loved one could lead to the practice.

Body Snatchers at Work in a Contemporary Engraving.

Legend says that King Herod continued to have sex with his wife Marianne for seven years after he killed her. In a case that was prosecuted in the 1760's, Sir John Pryce embalmed his first wife when she died and kept her in bed with him, even after he married a second time. When his second wife died, she too was embalmed and placed in the same bed. His third wife, however, wanted no part of his gruesome hobbies.

Historically, Necrophilia was a frequent theme in the writings of the Marquis de Sade. In 1886, a criminal named Henri Blot was arrested for raping a number of disinterred corpses. A gravedigger who was also arrested for this offense, justified his perversion by saying that he could find no live woman to yield to his desires, so he saw no harm in giving his affections to dead woman instead.

In 1931, a bizarre case took place in Key West, Florida. A man named Carl van Cassel fell in love with a beautiful young woman named Maria Elena Oyoz, who was dying from tuberculosis. Although she would have nothing to do with him when he was alive, he exhumed her body when she died and first placed it in a mausoleum. Later, he took the body home, dressed it in a wedding gown, and took to sleeping with it. This continued for seven years before he was discovered. A court hearing was held, but it was clear to the judge that the law would not cover this bizarre set of circumstances. As he was not to be convicted, van Cassel even had the nerve to ask for Elena's body back! The judge ordered it buried in a secret location and van Cassel disappeared a short time later.

Looking back at these cases, history has mistakenly identified these types of individuals as harmless eccentrics. However, in many cases of Necrophilia, there is a much darker and much more dangerous pathology at work. Although we have only identified serial criminals in more recent times, they have always been with us. Many even speculate that the legends of monsters, werewolves and vampires came about because of serial killers, necrophiles and mass murderers. It was impossible, in those days, for the populace to comprehend the brutal and twisted acts that man was capable of. For this reason, they created the monsters of myth and folklore to explain it all away.

This may be especially true when it comes to Necrophilia. It has been called the most monstrous of all perversions, so we should not be surprised to learn that it is common among the monstrous of our killers and criminals. Many infamous psychopaths, from Edmund Kemper to Ted Bundy, occasionally raped the bodies of their freshly slain victims. We have to realize though that this type of outrage has been identified by criminal psychologists like John Douglas as being more of a malevolent desire to dominate and violate than a passion for dead things. Such passion is much rarer, but it does occur.

Jeffrey Dahmer was well known for his collection of corpses and body parts but the most famous American necrophile was undoubtedly the Wisconsin madman known as Ed Gein. He was totally uninterested in living women and found his sex partners in local cemeteries, which he plundered for more than a dozen years. While he was not as dangerous as a hunting serial killer, he was far from harmless. When the nearby cemetery ran low on females, he went looking for a likely prospect and killed her. Gein was also a collector of macabre souvenirs and his depraved urges spawned books and films like *The Texas Chainsaw Massacre* and *Silence of the Lambs*.

While there have been several hauntings linked to grave robbery, one case may have even been linked to Necrophilia as well. It was certainly not recognized as such in the region of Utah in the 1800's, but today, the story of Jean Baptiste has some pretty strange sexual undertones to it. There is little doubt that in the modern school of thought, this unusual gravedigger was helping himself to more than just the corpse's clothing.

THE GHOST OF THE GREAT SALT LAKE

The story of Jean Baptiste revolves around Utah's Great Salt Lake. It covers more than 2300 square miles in the northern region of Utah and is one of the world's saltiest bodies of water. It is also a very shallow lake for its size, plunging to depths of only 27 feet in its deepest parts. While these may be the facts behind the lake... there is also a legend. It is a story of a Salt Lake City gravedigger that was exiled to an island on the lake for his ghoulish crimes. He disappeared on that island without a trace but many feel that his ghost still walks today.

John Baptiste was one of the first gravediggers ever employed in Salt Lake City in the late 1800's. He lived in a two-room house with a lean-to at the corner of K Street and Temple and he was believed to be well-off and lived comfortably. He was also known to be a hard worker and punctual, always carrying out his appointed duties at the city cemetery. He was a quiet fellow though and had few friends, so most people never paid much attention to him as he went about his work.

About three years after Baptiste came to work for the city, a man died in Salt Lake City and was, of course, buried by the gravedigger in the local cemetery. A short time later, the man's brother came to Utah from the east. He was not familiar with the Mormon religion as his brother had been and wished to have his sibling returned to the east to be buried in the family plot. His wish was granted and the grave was uncovered. The casket was pried open and the corpse inside was discovered to be nude and lying in the coffin facedown, as though it had been dumped there.

Needless to say, the brother was outraged and city officials began an immediate investigation. The investigation focused on John Baptiste and several men were assigned to keep him and the cemetery under surveillance. Soon after another burial, Baptiste was seen pushing a wheelbarrow from a nearby storage shed to a freshly opened grave. Authorities stopped him and found a pile of clothing hidden in the bushes. The corpse had been removed from the grave, his clothing removed, and was now being moved from the storage shed in the wheelbarrow.

Baptiste was arrested and his home was searched. His house was filled with clothing! He had used some of it for drapes and furniture covers and in the cellar, a large vat was placed for boiling the clothing of the dead.

The news spread and local citizens descended on the cemetery to check on their deceased loved ones. Authorities believed that he had stolen clothing from more than 350 corpses! All of the clothing from Baptiste's home was taken to City Hall for identification by relatives. They also went to local second-hand stores, where they learned the gravedigger had sold large amounts of jewelry for cash.

And what became of Baptiste? He was tried and convicted of grave robbery, was branded with a hot iron and exiled to an island in the Great Salt Lake, northwest of the city. There has been some dispute as to where he was sent, either to barren Fremont Island or the larger Antelope Island. Regardless, he was put ashore there, never to return to Salt Lake City again. But this was not the end....

A few weeks later, lawmen returned to the island to check on the prisoner, only to discover that he had vanished. A search discovered the remains of a fire and a small shelter, but no Baptiste. Some believe that he may have taken his own life and others that he built a raft and escaped, but no matter, he was never heard from again. Or was he?

It has been said that Baptiste still haunts the shores and beaches of the lake today. The stories claim that he has been seen walking along the water's edge, clutching in his hands a bundle of wet, rotted clothing.

THE HAUNTED PRESIDENT

Perhaps the most famous haunting connected to a grave robbery in American history involves the ghost stories associated with the tomb of Abraham Lincoln in Springfield, Illinois. In this case, we don't have just the grave robbery to explain why Lincoln's spirit might be restless either. As you will soon see, the posthumous wanderings of his corpse, and an ongoing mystery, may be more than enough to explain this haunting. You see, Lincoln's monument and tomb in Springfield's Oak Ridge Cemetery has long been a place of mystery, intrigue, speculation and bizarre history.... and from the very beginning, it was believed to be haunted by the ghost of the President himself.

Following his assassination in April 1865, the President's body was returned to Springfield and to a grave in a remote, wooded cemetery called Oak Ridge. The cemetery had been started around 1860 and it mostly consisted of woods and unbroken forest. In fact, not until after Lincoln was buried there was much done in the way of improvement, adding roads, iron gates and a caretaker's residence.

Lincoln was taken to the receiving vault of the cemetery and placed there with his sons, Willie, who had died during the presidency and Eddie, Lincoln's son who had died many years before. A short time later, a temporary vault was built for Lincoln and in seven months, on December 21, he was placed inside. Six of Lincoln's friends wanted to be sure the body was safe, so a plumber's assistant named Leon P. Hopkins made an opening in the lead box for them to peer inside. All was well and Lincoln and his sons were allowed a temporary rest.

The new construction on a permanent tomb would last for more than five years and it was during this time that strange things began to be reported in the vicinity of Lincoln's resting place. A few days after the body was placed in the receiving vault, Springfield residents and curiosity seekers began to tell of sighting a spectral image of Lincoln himself wandering about near the crypt. The legends say that he was taking walks to investigate the broken ground where his tomb would someday stand. And the stories didn't end there either.... after the bodies were moved to the monument tomb, strange sobbing noises and sounds like footsteps were often heard at the site.

On September 19, 1871, the caskets of Lincoln and his sons were removed from the hillside crypt and taken to the catacomb. The tomb was not quite finished yet, but the completed portion was a suitable place for them to be moved to. The plumber, Leon P. Hopkins, opened the coffin once more and the same six friends peered again at the president's face. The dead president was laid to rest again, for another three years, while the workmen toiled away outside.

On October 9, 1874, Lincoln was moved again. This time, his body was placed inside of a marble sarcophagus, which had been placed in the center of the semi-circular catacomb. A few days later, the monument was finally dedicated. Money had been raised for the groups of statues that were situated outside and the citizens of Springfield seemed content with the final resting place of their beloved Abraham Lincoln.

But then a new threat arose from a direction that no one could have ever predicted... In 1876, a band of thieves broken into the tomb and almost made off with the president's remains. They had planned to hold the body for ransom and only failed because one of the men in their ranks was a spy for the Secret Service.

It did not take long before the story of the Lincoln grave robbery became a hotly denied rumor, or at best, a fading legend. The custodians of the site simply decided that it was something they did not wish to talk about. Of course, as the story began to be denied, the people who had some recollection of the tale created their own truth in myths and conspiracies. Hundreds of people came to see the Lincoln burial site and many of them were not afraid to ask about the stories that were being spread about the tomb. From 1876 to 1878, custodian John C. Power gave rather evasive answers to anyone who prodded him for details about the grave robbery. He was terrified of one question in particular and it seemed to be the one most often asked... was he sure that Lincoln's body had been returned safely to the sarcophagus after the grave robbers took it out?

Power was terrified of that question for one reason.... because at that time, Lincoln's grave was completely empty!

On the morning of November 1876, when John T. Stuart of the Lincoln National Monument Association, learned what had occurred in the tomb with the would-be robbers, he rushed out to the site. He was not able to rest after the incident, fearing that the grave robbers, who had not been caught at that time, would return and finish their ghoulish handiwork. So, he made a decision. He notified the custodian and told him that they must take the body from the crypt and hide it elsewhere in the building. Together, they decided

the best place to store it would be in the cavern of passages which lay between the Memorial Hall and the catacomb.

That afternoon, Adam Johnson, a Springfield marble-worker, took some of his men and they lifted Lincoln's casket from the sarcophagus. They covered it over with a blanket and then cemented the lid back into place. Later that night, Johnson, Power and three members of the Memorial Association stole out to the monument and carried the 500-pound coffin around the base of the obelisk, through Memorial Hall and into the dark labyrinth. They placed the coffin near some boards that had been left behind in the construction. The following day, Johnson built a new outer coffin while Power set to work digging a grave below the dirt floor. It was slow work, because it had to be done between visitors to the site, and he also had a problem with water seeping into the hole. Finally, he gave up and simply covered the coffin with the leftover boards and wood.

For the next two years, Lincoln lay beneath a pile of wood in the labyrinth, while visitors from all over the world wept and mourned over the sarcophagus at the other end of the monument. More and more of these visitors asked questions about the theft... questions full of suspicion, as if they knew something they really had no way of knowing.

In the summer and fall of 1877, the legend took another turn. Workmen arrived at the monument to erect the naval and infantry groups of statuary on the corners of the upper deck. Their work would take them into the labyrinth, where Power feared they would discover the coffin. The scandal would be incredible, so Power made a quick decision. He called the workmen together and swearing them to secrecy, showed them the coffin. They promised to keep the secret, but within days everyone in Springfield seemed to know that Lincoln's body was not where it was supposed to be. Soon, the story was spreading all over the country.

(Left) A Caricature of President Lincoln from an 1864 Harper's Weekly called "Long Abraham Lincoln a Little Longer". It made an eerie prediction as the president only had a few more months to live.

Power was now in a panic. The body had to be more securely hidden and to do this, he needed more help. He contacted two of his friends, Major Gustavas Dana and General Jasper Reece and explained the situation. These men brought three others to meet with Power, Edward Johnson, Joseph Lindley and James McNeill, all of Springfield.

On the night of November 18, the six men began digging a grave for Lincoln at the far end of the labyrinth. Cramped and cold, and stifled by stale air, they gave up around midnight with the coffin just barely covered and traces of their activity very evident. Power promised to finish the work the next day. These six men, sobered by the responsibility that faced them, decided to form a brotherhood to guard the secret of the tomb. They brought in three younger men, Noble Wiggins, Horace Chapin and Clinton Conkling, to help in the task. They called themselves the Lincoln Guard of Honor and had badges made for their lapels.

After the funeral of Mary Lincoln, John T. Stuart told the Guard that Robert Lincoln wanted to have his mother's body hidden away with his father's. So, late on the night of July 21, the men slipped into the monument and moved Mary's double-leaded casket, burying it in the labyrinth next to Lincoln's.

Visitors to the tomb increased as the years went by, all of them paying their respects to the two empty crypts. Finally, in 1886, the Lincoln National Monument Association decided that it was time to provide a new tomb for Lincoln in the catacomb. A new and stronger crypt of brick and mortar was designed and made ready.

The press was kept outside as the Guard, and others who shared the secret of the tomb, brought the Lincoln caskets out of the labyrinth. Eighteen persons who had known Lincoln in life filed past the casket, looking into a square hole that had been cut into the lead coffin.

Strangely, Lincoln had changed very little. His face was darker after 22 years but they were still the same sad features these people had always known. The last man to identify the corpse was Leon P. Hopkins, the same man who had closed the casket years before. He soldered the square back over the hole, thinking that he would be the last person to ever look upon the face of Abraham Lincoln.

The Guard of Honor lifted the casket and placed it next to Mary's smaller one. The two of them were taken into the catacomb and lowered into the new brick and mortar vault. Here, they would sleep for all time.....

"All time" lasted for about 13 more years. In 1899, Illinois legislators decided the monument was to be torn down and a new one built from the foundations. It seemed that the present structure was settling unevenly, cracking around the "eternal" vault of the president.

There was once again the question of what to do with the bodies of the Lincoln family. The Guard of Honor (who was still around) came up with a clever plan. During the

15 months needed for construction, the Lincoln's would be secretly buried in a multiple grave a few feet away from the foundations of the tomb. As the old structure was torn down, tons of stone and dirt would be heaped onto the grave site both to disguise and protect it. When the new monument was finished, the grave would be uncovered again.

When the new building was completed, the bodies were exhumed once again. In the top section of the grave were the coffins belonging to the Lincoln sons and to a grandson, also named Abraham. The former president and Mary were buried on the bottom level and so safely hidden that one side of the temporary vault had to be battered away to reach them.

Lincoln's coffin was the last to be moved and it was close to sunset when a steam engine finally hoisted it up out of the ground. The protective outer box was removed and six construction workers lifted the coffin onto their shoulders and took it into the catacomb. The other members of the family had been placed in their crypts and Lincoln's was placed into a white, marble sarcophagus.

The group dispersed after switching on the new electric burglar alarm. This device connected the monument to the caretaker's house, which was a few hundred feet away. As up-to-date as this device was, it still did not satisfy the fears of Robert Lincoln, who was sure that his father's body would be snatched again if they were not careful. He stayed in constant contact with the Guard of Honor, who were still working to insure the safety of the Lincoln's remains, and made a trip to Springfield every month or so after the new monument was completed. Something just wasn't right.... even though the alarm worked perfectly, he could not give up the idea that the robbery might be repeated.

He journeyed to Springfield and brought with him his own set of security plans. He met with officials and gave them explicit directions on what he wanted done. The construction company was to break a hole in the tile floor of the monument and place his father's casket at a depth of 10 feet. The coffin would then be encased in a cage of steel bars and the hole would be filled with concrete, making the president's final resting place into a solid block of stone.

On September 26, 1901, a group assembled to make the final arrangements for Lincoln's last burial. A discussion quickly turned into a heated debate. The question that concerned them was whether or not Lincoln's coffin should be opened and the body viewed one last time? Most felt this would be a wise precaution, especially in light of the continuing stories about Lincoln not being in the tomb. The men of the Honor Guard were all for laying the tales to rest at last, but Robert was decidedly against opening the casket again, feeling that there was no need to further invade his father's privacy.

In the end, practicality won out and Leon P. Hopkins was sent for to chisel out an opening in the lead coffin. The casket was placed on two sawhorses in the still unfinished Memorial Hall. The room was described as hot and poorly lighted, as newspapers had been pasted over the windows to keep out the stares of the curious.

What actually took place in that room is unknown except from the reports of the select few who were present. Most likely, they were the same people who had been present several years before when the body had been placed in the brick and mortar vault.

A piece of the coffin was cut out and lifted away. According to diaries, a "strong and reeking odor" filled the room, but the group pressed close to the opening anyway. The face of the president was covered with a fine powder made from white chalk. It had been applied in 1865 before the last burial service. It seemed that Lincoln's face had turned inexplicably black in Pennsylvania and after that, a constant covering of chalk was kept on his face.

Lincoln's features were said to be completely recognizable. The casket's headrest had fallen away and his head was thrown back slightly, revealing his still perfectly trimmed beard. His small black tie and dark hair were still as they were in life, although his eyebrows had vanished. The broadcloth suit that he had worn to his second inauguration was covered with small patches of yellow mold and the American flag that was clutched in his lifeless hands was now in tatters.

There was no question, according to those present, that this was Abraham Lincoln and that he was placed in the underground vault. The casket was sealed back up again by Leon Hopkins, making his claim of years ago to be true.... he really was the last person to look upon the face of Lincoln.

The casket was then lowered down into the cage of steel and two tons of cement was poured over it, forever encasing the president's body in stone.

You would think that would be the end of it, but as with all lingering mysteries, a few questions still remain. The strangest are perhaps these: does the body of Abraham Lincoln really lie beneath the concrete in the catacomb? Or was the last visit from Robert Lincoln part of some elaborate ruse to throw off any further attempts to steal the president's body? And did, as some rumors have suggested, Robert arrange with the Guard of Honor to have his father's body hidden in a different location entirely?

Most historians would agree that Lincoln's body is safely encased in the concrete of the crypt, but let's look at this with a conspiratorial eye for a moment. Whose word do we have for the fact that Lincoln's body is where it is said to be? We only have the statement of Lincoln's son, Robert, his friends and of course, the Guard of Honor.... but weren't these the same individuals who left visitors to the monument to grieve before an empty sarcophagus while the president was actually hidden in the labyrinth, beneath a few inches of dirt?

And what of the stories that claim that Lincoln's ghost still walks the tomb?

Many have reported that he, or some other spirit here, does not rest in peace. Many tourists, staff members and historians have had some unsettling impressions here that aren't easily laughed away. Usually these encounters have been reported as the sound of ceaseless pacing, tapping footsteps on the tile floors, whispers and quiet voices, and the sounds of someone crying or weeping in the corridors.

Do the events of the past merely echo here in this lonely tomb? Or does the phantom of Abraham Lincoln still linger behind, wondering where his body might now be buried?

While it may not necessarily be what we think of when the word "desecration" comes to mind, many believe that graves that are left purposely, or accidentally unmarked, can cause cemeteries to become haunted as well. The annals of the supernatural are filled with stories of ghosts who walk because their graves have been left unmarked and many of those tales will be featured in later chapters.

However, there is one case, from Rosehill Cemetery in Chicago that may perfectly illustrate our point. Rosehill Cemetery was started in 1859 and remains one of the most beautiful burial grounds in the city. It serves as the final resting place for more than 1500 notable residents of the city.

As mentioned, ghostly lore is filled with tales of the deceased returning from the grave to protest the manner in which they were laid to rest and Rosehill boasts at least one legend of this type. In October 1995, a groundskeeper at the cemetery reported that he had seen a woman wandering about in the graveyard at night. She had been standing next to a tree, not far from the wall that separates the cemetery from Peterson Avenue. The staff member stopped his truck and got out. The cemetery was closed for the night and he was going to tell the woman that she had to leave and offer to escort her to the gate. When he approached her, he realized that the woman, who was dressing in some sort of flowing white garment, was actually floating above the ground! Before his eyes, she turned into a mist and slowly vanished. Not surprisingly, the groundskeeper wasted no time in rushing to the cemetery office to report the weird incident.

Strangely, a woman from Des Plaines, Illinois called the cemetery office the following day and requested that a marker be placed on the grave of her aunt, Carrie Kalbas, who had died in 1933. The grave site had previously been unmarked but the night before, the woman claimed that her aunt had appeared to her in a dream. She asked her niece to be sure that her burial place was marked because she wanted to be remembered. The aunt's grave was located in an old family plot and staff members went out to the site to verify the location and to see what type of monument was needed. They were amazed to find that the grave was located in the exact spot where the apparition had been reported the night before! The grave stone was ordered and the ghost was never seen again.

Of all of the reasons why cemeteries become haunted, the desecration of graves remains probably the highest cause on the list. There are many graveyards that have been disturbed (in one way or another) and currently boast ghosts and hauntings. There are also many different ways that a cemetery can become disturbed. In some cases, nature plays a hand in the desecration as natural disasters take place that may unearth bodies or destroy grave sites.

In most cases though, it is the hand of man that does the most damage. The expansion of cities and homes can often be the culprit as new building sites are laid out without much thought as to what may have been present on the location before. Construction crews often uncover some gruesome surprises in the course of a day's work.

In other cases, the work of vandals has been cited or even perhaps the rumored "cultists" who practice their dark rituals in abandoned cemeteries. Such deeds are said to attract a negative energy to the location. Both of these have been said to play a part in the haunting of Bachelor's Grove Cemetery, one of the most haunted spots in the Chicago area and a place that we will examine more closely in a later chapter.

The question remains though as to how or why the disturbance of the graves causes the cemetery to be considered haunted. Is it because of natural or supernatural reasons? Ghost lore tells us that the spirits remain behind when their remains are disturbed and are unable to find rest. This may explain why desecrated cemeteries are so often believed to be haunted. But what if there was a natural explanation for the activity? Suppose the disturbance of graves or physical remains releases an energy that might account for the bizarre happenings reported in cemeteries. Could this energy have seemed to our ancestors to mimic a "haunting"? Science tells us that all matter is energy and energy cannot be destroyed. Could this "energy" explain the phenomena that is reported?

Regardless, there is little doubt that disturbed burial grounds exist and strangely, not all of the sites have to be official cemeteries in order to become haunted. For instance, take into consideration the graves of the settlers who were killed during the Fort Dearborn Massacre in 1812. While never officially buried in a cemetery, the disturbance of their resting places created a historic Chicago mystery.

GHOSTS OF FORT DEARBORN

In the early 1800's, Fort Dearborn was located at the site of what would someday be Chicago. In those days, this was a small frontier settlement that was staffed by soldiers and a few hardy settlers.

The first threat came to the fort with the War of 1812, a conflict that aroused unrest with the local Indian tribes, namely the Potawatomi and the Wynadot. The effects of the war brought many of the Indian tribes into alliance with the British for they saw the Americans as invaders into their lands. After the British captured the American garrison at Mackinac, Fort Dearborn was in great danger. Orders came stating that the fort's commander, Captain Nathan Heald, should abandon the fort and leave the contents to the local Indians.

Unfortunately, Heald delayed in carrying out the orders and soon, the American troops had nowhere to go. The unrest among the Indians brought a large contingent of them to the fort and they gathered in an almost siege-like state. The soldiers began to express concern over the growing numbers of Indians outside and Heald realized that he was going to have to bargain with them if the occupants of Fort Dearborn were going to safely reach Fort Wayne. On August 12, Heald began several days of bargaining that eventually led to an agreement for the Indians to provide safe conduct for the soldiers and settlers to Fort Wayne in Indiana.

Part of the agreement was that Heald would leave the stores and ammunition in the fort for the Indians, but his officers disagreed. Alarmed, they questioned the wisdom of handing out guns and ammunition that could easily be turned against them. Heald reluctantly agreed with them and the extra weapons and ammunition were broken apart and dumped into an abandoned well. In addition, the stores of whiskey were dumped into the river. Needless to say, the Indians outside observed this and they too began making plans that differed from those agreed upon with Captain Heald.

On August 14, a visitor arrived at the fort in the person of Captain William Wells. He and 30 Miami warriors had managed to slip past the throng outside and they appeared at the front gates of the fort. Wells was a frontier legend among early soldiers and settlers in the Illinois territory. He was also the uncle of Captain Heald's wife and after hearing of the evacuation of Fort Dearborn, and knowing the hostile fervor of the local tribes, headed straight to the fort to assist them in their escape. Unfortunately, he had arrived too late.

Throughout the night of August 14, wagons were loaded for travel and reserve ammunition was distributed, amounting to about 25 rounds per man. Early the next morning, the procession of soldiers, civilians, women and children left the fort. The infantry soldiers led the way, followed by a caravan of wagons and mounted men. A portion of the Miami who had accompanied Wells guarded the rear of the column.

The column of soldiers and settlers were escorted by nearly 500 Potawatomi Indians. As they marched southward and into a low range of sand hills that separated the beaches of Lake Michigan from the prairie, the Potawatomi moved silently to the right, placing an elevation of sand between they and the white men. The act was carried out with such subtlety that no once noticed it as the column trudged along the shoreline. A little further down the beach, the sand ridge ended and the two groups would come together again.

The column traveled to an area where 16th Street and Indiana Avenue are now located. There was a sudden milling about of the scouts at the front of the line and suddenly a shout came back from Captain Wells that the Indians were attacking! A line of

Potawatomi appeared over the edge of the ridge and fired down at the column. Totally surprised, the officers nevertheless managed to rally the men into a battle line, but it was of little use. So many of them fell from immediate wounds that the line collapsed. The Indians overwhelmed them with sheer numbers, flanking the line and snatching the wagons and horses.

What followed was butchery.... officers were slain with tomahawks.. the fort's surgeon was cut down by gunfire and then literally chopped into pieces ... Mrs. Heald was wounded by gunfire but was spared when she was captured by a sympathetic chief, who spared her life... the wife of one soldier fought so bravely and savagely that she was hacked into pieces before she fell... In the end, cut down to less than half their original number, the garrison surrendered under the promise of safe conduct. In all, 148 members of the column were killed, 86 of them adults and 12 of them children. One of the dead was Captain Wells, who was captured and his heart cut out. A Chicago street now bears the name of this brave frontiersman.

In the battle, Captain Heald was wounded twice, while his wife was wounded seven times. They were later released and a St. Joseph Indian named Chaudonaire took them to Mackinac, where they were turned over to the British commander there. He sent them to Detroit and they were exchanged with the American authorities.

The other survivors from the massacre were taken as prisoners and some of them died soon after. Others were sold to the British as slaves, who quickly freed them, appalled by the carnage they had experienced. The victorious Indians burned Fort Dearborn itself to the ground and the bodies of the massacre victims were left where they had fallen, scattered to decay on the sand dunes of Lake Michigan. When replacement troops arrived at the site of Fort Dearborn a year later, they were greeted with not only the burned-out shell of the fort, but also the grinning skeletons of their predecessors and the luckless settlers. The bodies were given proper burials and the fort was rebuilt in 1816, only to be abandoned again in 1836, when the city would be able to fend for itself.

Not surprisingly, the horrific massacre spawned its share of ghostly tales. For many years, the site of the fort itself was said to be haunted by those who were killed nearby. The now vanished fort was located at the south end of the Michigan Avenue Bridge.

The actual site of the massacre was quiet for many years, long after Chicago grew into a sizable city. According to author Dale Kaczmarek, in his book *Windy City Ghosts*, construction in the earthy 1980's unearthed a number of human bones. At first thought to be the victims of a cholera epidemic in the 1840's, the remains were later dated more closely to the early 1800's. Thanks to their location, they were believed to be the bones of victims from the massacre. They were reburied elsewhere but within a few weeks, people began to report the semi-transparent figures of people dressed in pioneer clothing and military uniforms. They were seen wandering in a field just north of 16th and while many seemed to run about haphazardly, others appeared to move in slow motion. Many of them reportedly looked very frightened or were screaming in silence.

Perhaps these poor victims do not rest in peace after all.....

More common are the cemeteries that have been "removed" and then have been built over. When it comes to historical graveyards, all of the graves are seldom found, which can lead to problems later on. This is especially true of two small cemeteries in Decatur, Illinois.

THE COMMON BURIAL GROUNDS

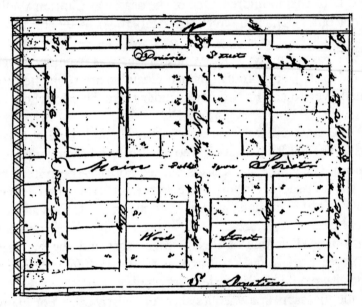

Decatur is a town that is rather notorious for building over the sites of former cemeteries and such poor planning goes back even to the earliest days of the city. The city happens to rest on land where a number of American Indian burial sites are located. Centuries ago, the land around Decatur belonged to tribes within the large Illinwek Confederation. During this time, a number of these tribes settled in the area, although none of them lived within the boundaries of the future city limits.

An old Plat Map of the original site of Decatur. What is not shown are the burial grounds beneath the planned streets and buildings.

When the first settlers arrived, they would find this land abandoned by the Native Americans. They had used it for their burial grounds.

Besides the Indian burial sites, sketchy records exist today to say that there were once a number of private and family cemeteries scattered throughout old Decatur. Most of these sites have been forgotten over the years. Early burial records in the city were largely nonexistent and many of the forgotten graves were marked with primitive wooden planks and they deteriorated in a few short years. It is not really surprising that many of these tiny graveyards faded from memory within a generation or two, but what of the secrets left behind by Decatur's first "official" cemetery?

Actually, there were two cemeteries located at this site and were located so close together that they have since been listed under the name of the larger of the two, the Common Burial Grounds. The other graveyard, King's Cemetery, was located nearby and accounts state that it was hard to tell where one ended and the other began. The two cemeteries were located on the far west side of the early Decatur settlement and today the corner of Oakland Avenue and West Main Street marks that area. The two cemeteries comprised several acres of ground and probably extended as far east as Haworth Street.

The exact size of the Common Burial Grounds is unknown but it was a part of the Amos Robinson farm. The Robinson family had settled in Decatur just a few years prior to 1836, when Amos Robinson died. He was buried in an orchard on his property, which later became part of the burial grounds.

King's Cemetery was platted in 1865 and was owned by John E. King. The cemetery ran alongside Haworth Street and extended down Wood to Oakland. The cemetery also lay on the edge of the old Robinson farm and as mentioned before, published accounts of that time stated that they were so close together that they were usually mistaken for one.

No one knows for sure when the first burials took place here but it was probably in the early 1830's. The cemeteries were used for many years but were finally closed down because of overcrowding in 1885. The land was sold off to the city to use as building plots for many of the homes and buildings that still stand in that area today. Once the sale went through, workmen were called in to remove the bodies to Greenwood Cemetery, a larger cemetery that was located on the city's south side.

However, these luckless workmen faced a problem. No one had any idea just how many people had been buried in the two cemeteries over the years, thanks to unmarked graves, poor records and lost grave markers and stones. The city pushed the move ahead and the workmen were advised to do the best they could with what information they had to work with. Construction was started a few months later and the old cemeteries were all but forgotten. But they wouldn't stay that way for long.....

In 1895, while work crews were building an extension onto West Main Street, they discovered dozens of lost skeletons, the remains of caskets and buried tombstones. This was the first grisly find, but it would not be the last. For years after, new construction brought to light skulls, bones and pieces of wooden coffins. There were no clues as to just how many bodies had been left behind and these gruesome discoveries have continued for years, even up until today.

In 1935, a building on West Wood Street had its basement lowered and a broken wooden box that contained a complete skeleton was found beneath the dirt. Late that same year, a man working in his backyard found four skulls and three long bones in the spot where he planned to put a vegetable patch. This convinced him to find another location. The discovery of bones throughout the neighborhood became such a sensation that young boys organized "digging parties" and more remains surfaced each week. A 1938 newspaper report covered the furor over the lost cemeteries and even stated that Amos Robinson himself was still buried under a driveway on West Main Street.

In recent years, even Decatur's landmark restaurant the Blue Mill has not been safe from rumors of strange discoveries. According to anonymous staff members, a number of skeletons were found beneath the basement floor a few years ago. The story has not been substantiated, but these same employees also believe the bones are tied into other weird happenings in the place. A number of ghostly encounters have supposedly taken place in the kitchen area and many of them are afraid to go down into the basement alone.

And this is not the only place within the bounds of the former graveyards where reports of the restless dead occasionally come. Many of the people who work and live here believe that spirits, whose rest was disturbed more than a century ago, still roam this area today. They may be right!

One family that was plagued by a disturbing ghost contacted a friend who claimed to have psychic abilities to identify the problem behind the knocking and pounding sounds in the house. I was actually able to speak to one of the residents of the house years after this incident. Charles Sanders (not his real name) was a small child at the time of the haunting but is an adult who lives in the Chicago area today. He told me that the family had been awakened at all hours of the day and night by knocking and rapping on the walls and what they all believed to be footsteps pacing back and forth in one hallway.

"My mother had this friend who was supposed to be psychic," Sanders explained to me, more than 40 years after the events. "We called her and she came over to have a seance. She thought that if she could get in touch with this ghost, or whatever, she could make everything stop."

The family sat down around the table and the friend, who Sanders called "Aunt Sandra", lit a candle and began speaking to the ghost. It wasn't long before some strange things began to occur.

"We could still hear all of these knocking sounds," Sanders recalled, "but then all of the dishes in the cabinets started rattling. My sister was pretty scared at this point, and so was I. Aunt Sandra then took out a piece of paper and a pencil and started writing down whatever she was hearing from the ghost."

According to the information the psychic gained through her "automatic writing", the ghost was that of a person who had been died long ago. His grave was now located beneath the front porch of the house and he wanted someone to help him. A short time later, Charles' father climbed beneath the porch with a shovel and began digging. It wasn't long before he discovered a number of scattered bones. They turned them over to the authorities and with the help of their pastor, arranged for a proper burial for them. The ghost troubled them no longer.

Charles Sanders has never forgotten the incident. "I laugh now when I hear people say there are no such things as ghosts," he told me in our interview. "I can tell them differently!"

Another man that I spoke with lived on West Wood Street as a boy. He told me about an experience that he had many years ago. He was playing outside one afternoon and caught a glimpse of a man standing in the far corner of the lot. His features were blurry and his clothing was hard to make out.

"He seemed to be looking at me," the man remembered, "although it was hard to tell because it was early in the evening and the yard was very shaded by the trees."

He said that the phantom figure only stood there for a few moments before he noticed something very strange about him. "The man was visible only to the knees... below that, he just sorta faded away," the man explained to me. "I have never forgotten that, even after 20 years."

An additional house, on West Main Street, is haunted by the ghost of a pale young girl who endlessly walks back and forth through the house. She seems oblivious to the people who live there now, as if she is from another time, but has also been seen skipping, running and playing with a small red ball. The occupants have also heard the sounds of knocks and whispers in the house on occasion. One has to wonder if she might be another of the specters from Decatur's two most famous "lost" cemeteries?

THE BLACK HOPE HORROR

One of the most strange, but often overlooked, cases of cemetery disturbance took place in the town of Crosby, Texas in the early 1980's. That was at about the same time that the film *Poltergeist* was playing in movie theaters across the country. In the movie, spirits and strange activity besiege a family because their home was inadvertantly built over the top of a cemetery. In Crosby, these same events were taking place, except this was no movie... these events were happening for real!

The macabre story really began back in 1981 when Ben and Jean Williams moved into their brand new home on Poppets Way. It was located in the Newport subdivision of Crosby, an upscale housing addition. Within a few years, the Williams' and seven out of eight of the families who lived close to them would move away from the area. All of them did so at great expense, including the loss of their mortgages.

Shortly after the Ben and Jean moved into the house, they began to notice something odd about the place. Mostly it was the oppressive feeling that seemed to loom over the structure, but soon it was other things too. It all started naturally enough, but when combined, each of the events formed a more terrifying picture. Hundreds of ants began invading the house, followed by snakes that acted uncharacteristically hostile. Plants died for no reason and pets began acting very strangely.

Perhaps most odd were the sinkholes that began to appear in the yard. Located out near an oak tree that bore some peculiar markings, the depressions slowly widened and collapsed. Even when dirt was added to them, they refused to fill. No one noticed at the time how eerily the holes resembled open graves.

Then other, more mysterious and frightening, events began to occur. The toilets in the house suddenly began flushing on the own. Lights turned on and off without explanation and the garage door somehow began opening and closing itself. Ben and Jean separately began to hear footsteps pacing back and forth through the house. Both of them assumed that it was the other, but when they went to check, the found no one there. Tapping and knocking sounds were sometimes heard by not only the Williams', but by neighbors and visitors to the house too. Finally, a number of people began to report seeing shadowy shapes and what could be apparitions in the yard.

Was the house haunted? If so, how could it be? The house had only been completed a short time before the family moved into it? What Ben and Jean and the other families in the neighborhood didn't know was just what had been located on the property before the subdivision was built. They would soon find out!

In 1983, Sam Haney, a neighbor who lived near to the Williams house, contracted for a swimming pool to be built in his back yard. During the digging, two bodies were unearthed by workers. They later turned out to be the remains of a black man and woman. Unfortunately, this was only the beginning... according to local estimates there were dozens of bodies buried underneath the entire neighborhood!

Originally, the entire subdivision had been located on land that belonged to the McKinney family. Although long gone by this time, the McKinneys had been wealthy landowners and farmers and had maintained a large plantation and a number of slaves. One corner of the property had been given over to the slaves, and was later used by their descendants, as a graveyard. A number of those descendants, along with a large local African-American community, now lived in the nearby town of Baird Station. The older people there had used the burial ground for many years and had called it Black Hope Cemetery. Some of the elderly folks had buried relatives there and easily recalled the location... it was directly beneath the houses on Poppets Way!

After this frightening disclosure, Ben Williams went to see a man named Will Freeman, an older black man, who claimed to have carried out some of the burials. He said that the burials were often haphazard but that they always tried to bury on the higher ground and avoid the rocks and the boggy low spots. The Haneys and the Williams' later discovered their homes were located on this "higher ground". Freeman also told them that no one could really afford tombstones in those days and on one occasion when he had buried two of his sisters, he had chosen an oak tree as a marker. He had marked an arrow on the tree, along with some other carvings that he couldn't recall. Ben and Jean realized this tree was located in their yard!

By this time, Sam Haney was involved in a lawsuit against the Purcell Corporation, the developers of the land. The lawsuit was expensive and not going well, so the Williams' lawyer advised them to sell the house and get out. However, if they did try to sell it, they would have to disclose the fact that it had been built on top of the Black Hope Cemetery. They decided to wait and see what happened with the Haney suit, which would not come to trial until 1987, but they did try unsuccessfully to sell the house. Their attorney also tried pressuring the title and realty companies, ensnaring the property in mountains of red tape and legal hassles. What it boiled down to was that the house was impossible to sell... and it was impossible to prove the graveyard existed. The only way to prove it was to dig and to dig for the bodies was illegal.

Meanwhile, the strange events in the house continued. The unexplainable sounds and incidents still occurred and the strange shapes were still seen both inside and outside of the house. The entire family was plagued by nightmares and several of the family pets mysteriously died.

Finally, Jean could stand it no more and she took a shovel from the garage and went out into the yard. She found the tree that had been marked so many years ago by Will Freeman and she started digging. Jean was only able to dig down a short distance before a terrible piercing pain stabbed through her back. She was forced to stop. Later that afternoon, her daughter, Tina, suddenly died. She had been in remission from cancer for some time but her health was fine. Tina's death was completely unexpected and remained unexplained.

Their nerves shattered, the Williams family fled the house and moved to Hamilton, Montana, where they owned a vacation home. They were convinced that if they stayed in the house on Poppets Way, the entire family would be destroyed. In the end, they lost their entire $18,000 down payment, seven years worth of mortgage payments and ruined their credit rating. In spite of this, they were glad to be out.

In May 1987, the Haney family lost their lawsuit against the Purcell Corporation. The jury that heard the case first awarded them $142,000 in damages but the judge nullified the verdict and left them with nothing. Purcell executives had testified that they knew nothing of a graveyard in the area and the judge ruled that Purcell had not been intentionally negligent... despite the fact that rumors had placed the graveyard on the site for years before the development began.

As far as I know, the case was never settled and nothing was ever done to rectify the desecration of the Black Hope Cemetery.

EL CAMPO SANTO CEMETERY

El Campo Santo Cemetery is located in Old Town San Diego, California, just two blocks away from the legendary Whaley House, rumored by some to be one of the most haunted houses in America. As far as ghosts go though, there are few places in the area that can rival this small and secluded graveyard.

Old Town San Diego in 1877.
(courtesy Rob & Anne Wlodarski)

While it is restored today, this tiny cemetery has seen more than its share of desecration over the years. The tiny enclave is located between two commercial buildings and behind a low, adobe wall. The bare grounds are filled with white wooden crosses and a number of stone monuments in honor of the city's early Hispanic and Anglo settlers.

Until July 1998, there was also a scattering of white crosses that were painted on the sidewalk and on the roadway outside of the cemetery itself. These painted marks had been meant to symbolize the presence of other graves. They were burial places that had been violated by the pavement that had been so recklessly placed there years before. Many feel that this disregard may be the reason the cemetery is so haunted today.

Founded in 1849, this Catholic burial ground once held 477 bodies. According to author John Lamb in his book *San Diego Specters*, the graveyard began to fall into decline when the fortunes of San Diego's Old Town district began to decline and the population departed for what was the more prosperous New Town. Soon, weeds began to grow and overtake the grounds and the sun and the weather destroyed the simple wooden grave markers. Before long, it was impossible to tell just who was buried where and at what point the graveyard ended and the open land began. The first real desecration to the cemetery came in 1889, just two years after the last burial took place here, when a street car company constructed one of their lines through a portion of the cemetery.

Over the next few decades, a problem was realized and those who saw a threat to the cemetery banded together and built a low wall to protect a portion of the burial ground.

It did little good though. In 1942, a dirt lane called San Diego Avenue was covered with pavement. This roadway passed along the front of El Campo Santo and a number of graves vanished beneath the new pavement. When questioned, local officials claimed that workers were unaware of the boundaries of the cemetery and hadn't deliberately desecrated it. This was unlikely and descendants of the original settlers repeatedly complained and petitioned the city government to acknowledge what had happened. Finally in 1993, technicians using ground-piercing radar discovered at least 18 graves below the street. They were then marked with white crosses, until July 1998, when a new coating of asphalt was applied to the street. The markings were obliterated and not replaced and strangely, ever since that time, there has been an increase in mysterious car alarms activations along this stretch of roadway.

There has also been an increase in the sightings of apparitions as well.

El Campo Santo has been considered haunted for many years. It is a small and gloomy place and definitely has an atmosphere where one might imagine a bevy of spirits would dwell. Not surprisingly, for over 50 years, residents of the area and visitors have claimed to see phantoms appearing among the scattered white markers and passing along the sidewalk outside the cemetery gates. There are many reports of strange activity in nearby buildings and as mentioned, car alarms shriek without any explanation... other than that they are parked above forgotten graves.

Author John Lamb, who conducts ghost tours of Old Town San Diego, finds this a frequently active spot during the outings. There have been many occasions when visitors on the tours have spotted ghostly figures and have heard unexplained sounds at the cemetery. On one night in June 1998, he was leading a group through El Campo Santo when one guest, a young woman, suddenly stopped walking and immediately ran out of the cemetery. Curious, he joined her out on the sidewalk a short time later and asked her what had happened. She explained that she had been walking along and listening to Lamb when the air around her suddenly turned icy. She stated that it was like walking into a freezer, then changed her mind. It was not like walking into something.... "No, it was like walking into *someone*," she told him. "You don't need to tell me another ghost story about this place. I *know* it's haunted."

So, does the El Campo Santo Cemetery remain haunted? John Lamb certainly thinks so. He advises that no search for ghosts in Old Town would be complete without a visit to this forlorn place but advises that "you might want to pay attention to where you park your car. After all, you wouldn't want to disturb the former residents."

Without a doubt, the strangest form of disturbance comes from what some have called "ritual desecration". In this type of situation, cemeteries become haunted because of cult-type rituals and black magic that is practiced within the bounds of the graveyard.

Many believe that this type of activity actually draws negative spirits or energy to the location. Others disagree and say that the cult groups are attracted to these places, or "power spots" *after* they become haunted in order to tap into the power that is present.

Regardless, it is common to hear of desecrated cemeteries where rituals are supposed to be taking place. In most of these cases, the so-called "satanists" are merely confused and lonely teenagers looking for a thrill or pretending to be "witches". However, can the practice actually draw negative energy to the place? Can those who believe this makes a cemetery become haunted actually be right?

One of the most famous haunted graveyards, where cult activity has been accepted as fact rather than fable, is Bachelor's Grove Cemetery near Chicago. We will be taking a closer look at this site in a later chapter and truthfully, while most likely haunted, this cemetery does not really fit into our present category. There is no doubt that horrible vandalism and desecration has taken place here, as well as cult activity. I do not believe though that the occult rituals are what caused the cemetery to become haunted in the first place. Unfortunately, the same may not be able to be said for another Illinois cemetery, located several hours downstate.

PECK CEMETERY

Peck Cemetery is located in the northeastern part of Macon County, near the towns of Oakley and Cerro Gordo. The cemetery is an isolated place, enclosed by a rusted iron fence, and it is hidden from the road by thick woods. It is surrounded by heavy forest and trees loom over the grounds. In addition, the graveyard is accessible only by way of a rutted dirt road and through a metal gate, which is usually kept locked. Trespassers are not welcome here.

The reason for this is because since the 1970's, Peck Cemetery has been a popular place for teenagers to go and have parties and attempt to scare themselves silly. If this were the end of it, that would not be a problem. Unfortunately, a small minority of these teenagers has also felt the need to vandalize the cemetery. The burial ground is now in deplorable condition as the majority of the stones have been toppled and broken, have been turned over and even have been sprayed with bright paint. There are very few of the monuments now standing upright and many of these lean dangerously to the side, thanks to digging that has been done around their bases. The vandals who did this, and who have so badly violated the cemetery, originally came here because they heard the place was haunted. The problem is that it may have been other vandals, who came here first, who actually caused it to become that way!

As mentioned already, vandalism is not the only thing that is believed to attract negative spirits either. It has long been said that occult groups in the area have practiced black magic in Peck Cemetery. Some researchers believe this can attract negative spirits as well and most occultists will readily admit that they seek out sites like this one, where great energy is present, to perform their rituals. They believe they can tap into the atmosphere of the place, especially when the place is thought to be charged with what some would call "bad vibes". Regardless of whether you believe in this type of thing, the rumor of occult practices has certainly given the graveyard the reputation for being one of the most sinister places in Central Illinois.

But is it really? We have already discussed the fact that most alleged "satanists" are little more than disturbed teenagers. I also believe that most "devil worshipping cults" are simply the fevered imaginings of fundamentalist religious groups trying to scare the general public. However, I will say that I think that "evil" does exist. There are also those people out there, practitioners of the "black arts" if you will, who are capable of channeling that evil. This type of thing if nothing to fool with, although many do, and I have it by very good authority that many have done so at Peck Cemetery. While the stories may have grown a little larger than life over the years, some pretty strange and bizarre things have taken place here.

But satanic cultists aside, stories have been told for more than 20 years that suggest something malevolent may walk the night in Peck Cemetery. There are many tales that have been told here and witnesses and late night visitors to the cemetery have come forward to claim a number of strange happenings and to recall many frightening events. Such stories include apparitions in the graveyard, inexplicable cries, whispers and voices, hooded figures, eerie lights, and even the sound of a woman's scream that seems to come from nowhere!

One young man talked to me in 1995 about an unexplained experience from a summer night about eight years prior to our discussion. He and his former girlfriend decided to brave the stories of the place and find the cemetery. They spent an hour or so here without incident and soon, the sun went down. A short time later, as darkness began to fall, they saw a blue ball of light that flickered out from between the damaged stones. It weaved back and forth and up and down, hovering in odd circles and moving with no real pattern to its path. They watched it dance through the cemetery and the dark woods for a few minutes and then it disappeared. "We had no idea what it was," he told me later. "It wasn't really scary, just weird. I have never seen anything like it since."

Another person I spoke with, Amanda Carter (not her real name), told me of a weird encounter she and several of her girlfriends had at Peck Cemetery. In 1998, this experience had taken place about ten years before. The young women had come to the graveyard very late one night and had driven up the dirt road and around the corner to the left, where the cemetery gates are located. It was very dark and all of them were nervous and excited about the trip. However, Amanda promises me that this in no way influenced what they all saw. They parked the car outside of the cemetery and everyone got out. As it had been with my friends and I a few years before, the girls decided to test their courage by walking across the cemetery and back. This was a common practice for high school students from all around the Decatur area. In a giggling cluster, they began walking out among the graves.

"And that's when we saw him," Amanda told me.

The young women were just entering the grounds when they saw a man standing near one of the large, fallen tombstones. After they got over their initial shock and surprise, they were curious as to how he had gotten there. They hadn't seen any other cars nearby and hadn't seen anyone go past them into the cemetery. One of Amanda's friends started to speak to him and then the just wasn't there anymore. He had simply vanished.

"I know I saw him and the others did too," Amanda assured me. "He looked very solid and not like a ghost or anything. He had dark hair and was wearing a coat. I just assumed that he had come there like we did, but all of the sudden he was just gone. And so were we! We ran back to the car and I have never been out to that place since!"

I have spoken to other people too, who have also had experiences at Peck Cemetery they cannot explain. My only explanation for the things that go on here is the one that I have already offered.... that this place is haunted! Believe me when I tell you that it does not take a psychic to know that something is wrong in this place. You can literally feel it when you leave the old road and pass through the gates. There is a coldness and a feeling of oppression here that nature cannot explain.

It is not a good place... and it hasn't been one for a long time now.

MYSTERY OF THE INCORRUPTIBLES

While just slightly outside the darkest elements of death, the mysterious stories of "incorruptible" bodies have puzzled man for centuries. Some would say that they fall into the realm of the mummy, for which different types exist. The first type is the body that is naturally desiccated, by burial in desert sand or under conditions that produce a mummified form. There are also mummies that have been artificially produced by embalming or by mummification processes like those of ancient Egypt. Some would also cite a third group of mummies, consisting mostly of saints, whose bodies have somehow resisted decay by other than ordinary means. These types of corpses are referred to as "Incorruptibles".

To the devoutly religious, these corpses serve as proof of the deceased person's piety and virtue because they do not decay. Also, unlike natural and artificially created mummies, whose hard and dry bodies show signs of shrinkage and rigidity, Incorruptibles stay supple and flexible, even over the course of centuries. They are often described as looking as though they are sleeping rather than dead.

Of course, debunkers disagree about the miraculous intervention of God in these cases and merely believe the bodies were accidentally preserved by some sort of unusual circumstance. Worse yet, there has been evidence that some of the bodies have been subjected to clandestine embalming once they started to decay. This would keep the faithful from doubting in the "miracle". They also cite instances when wax masks and cosmetics have been applied to the bodies in further effort to hide their putrefaction .

While it would serve these skeptics well if all of the Incorruptibles could be so easily exposed, there are a few that continue to defy explanation. One such case is that of St. Teresa Margaret of the Sacred Heart, who was born Anna Maria Redi in 1747. Born in Italy, she entered a Carmelite convent as a teenager and was credited with a number of miraculous cures during her lifetime. She died herself in 1770 from a gangrenous condition that kept her in constant pain for eighteen months. At the time of her death, reports say that her blackened and diseased skin somehow took on a faint rose-colored hue. Two days later, her face became even more beautiful and she appeared to be "quietly sleeping". Her lips were red and her flesh was soft and pliable. In short, the corpse refused to decay and became Incorruptible.

More than two weeks later, she was examined by an archbishop, numerous minor priests and clerics and three doctors. All of them testified that her condition had not changed and that there were still no signs of decay and in fact, the body gave off a "most delightful odor". Thirteen years passed after her burial and at that time, the body was exhumed in order to move it to a drier location. An examination at that time found the corpse to be perfectly incorrupt. In 1805, she was again disturbed and was described as having a healthy skin tone, although dry, and vibrant blond hair that had gone unchanged since her death. In 1934, she was canonized and became St. Theresa. Today, her body, now dry and dark, can still be seen in the chapel of the monastery of Santa Teresa dei Bruni in Florence, Italy.

Obviously, strange tales surround all of the Incorruptibles, but we have to search pretty hard to find any ghost stories. In all of my research, I have only been able to discover once such tale... but I don't think you will be disappointed by it.

THE ITALIAN BRIDE

In Hillside, Illinois, just outside of Chicago, is Mount Carmel Cemetery. In addition to being the final resting place of Al Capone, Dion O'Banion and other great Chicago mobsters, the cemetery is also the burial place of a woman named Julia Buccola Petta. While her name may not spring to mind as a part of Chicago history, for those intrigued by the supernatural, she is better known as the "Italian Bride".

Julia's grave is marked today by the life-sized statue of the unfortunate woman in her wedding dress, a stone reproduction of the wedding photo that is mounted on the front of her monument. The statue marks the location where Julia's apparition is said to appear. Not surprisingly, the ghost is clad in a glowing, white bridal gown.

Julia died in childbirth in 1921, at only twenty years of age. Shortly after she was buried, her mother, Filomena Buccola, began to experience strange and terrifying dreams every night. In these nightmares, she envisioned Julia telling her that she was still alive and needed her help. For the next six years, the dreams plagued Filomena and she began trying, without success, to have her daughter's grave opened and her body exhumed. She was unable to explain why she needed to do this, she only knew that she should. Finally, through sheer persistence, her request was granted and a sympathetic judge passed down an order for Julia's exhumation.

When the casket was opened, Julia's body was found not to have decayed at all. In fact, it was said that her flesh was still as soft as it had been when she was alive. A photograph was taken at the time of the exhumation and shows Julia's "incorruptible" body in the casket. Her mother, and other admirers, placed the photo on the front of her grave monument, which was constructed after her reburial. The photograph shows a body that appears to be fresh, with no discoloration of the skin, even after six years. The rotted and decayed appearance of the coffin in the photo however, bears witness to the fact that it had been underground for some time. Julia appears to be merely sleeping.

What mysterious secret rests at the grave of Julia Petta? How could her body have stayed in perfect condition after lying in the grave for six years? No one knows, but not surprisingly, reports have circulated for years claiming that a woman in a bridal gown haunts this portion of the cemetery.

Some of the stories come from students at Proviso West High School, which is located just east of the cemetery on Wolf Road. They have reported a girl walking in the cemetery at night and they are not alone. A carload of people traveling down Harrison Street was startled to see a woman passing through the tombstones one night. Thinking that it was simply a Halloween prank, they stopped the car for a closer look. They did not become unnerved until they realized that, even though it was pouring down rain, the girl was perfectly dry. They didn't choose to investigate any closer and immediately drove away!

· VAMPIRES IN AMERICA ·

RECENT ETHNOLOGICAL RESEARCH HAS DISCLOSED SOMETHING VERY EXTRAORDINARY IN RHODE ISLAND. IT APPEARS THAT THE ANCIENT VAMPIRE SUPERSTITION STILL SURVIVES IN THAT STATE, AND WITHIN THE LAST FEW YEARS MANY PEOPLE HAVE BEEN DIGGING UP THE DEAD BODIES OF RELATIVES FOR THE PURPOSE OF BURNING THEIR HEARTS.

- FROM THE NEW YORK WORLD, FEBRUARY 2, 1896 -

There is perhaps no supernatural creature, outside of ghosts, as closely connected to the graveyard as the vampire is. Although long considered to be nothing more than a myth, the vampire is a still a strangely attractive and enticing being to the modern reader. We think of them as being nothing more than the fanciful creation of folklore and literature, but what if we are wrong? What if vampires are real... and what if they once stalked the fields and towns of historic America?

Impossible, you say? You might be surprised at what you find lurking around the dark corners of New England!

Few can really say what the traditional vampire is. Some believe that he is an evil spirit that wears the body of the newly dead, while others believe that he is a corpse, re-animated by his original soul. What everyone can agree on is what this creature must have to survive and that is blood. This vital bodily ingredient must be taken from the veins of a living person so that the vampire can survive.

In nearly every case, a vampire that is exhumed from his grave, or resting place, is always found to be ruddy of complexion, well-nourished and apparently in good health. This is in spite of the fact that he had been dead for some time. His appearance is always marked by long, curving fingernails (having grown long in the grave) and blood smeared about the mouth. According to European legends, the only way to destroy one of these living corpses is to drive a stake through its heart. After that, the body should be burned. The American legends suggest a different method of disposal. According to old reports, the heart of the vampire must be cut out of the chest and then burned. Often, a potion must be mixed from the ashes and must be given to the vampire's victims. In this way, they do not die and become vampires themselves.

The legends of vampires have their roots in traditional fears. In days past, it was not uncommon for people to be fearful about the dead returning from their grave, especially in cases of suicides or of unfortunates being buried without the last rites. Occasional deviants who practiced necrophilia or corpse-stealing often provided apparent "proof" that some of the dead could leave the graveyard. An empty coffin was not seen as evidence of theft, but evidence of vampires instead.

Terrible and what seemed to be mysterious outbreaks of disease and plagues were sometimes thought to be caused by supernatural means. In America, an outbreak of the "white death" or tuberculosis was believed to actually be a string of vampire-related deaths. Another ailment thought to have created the vampire legend was a rare disorder called *porphyria*. This is a skin pigment disorder in which the body produces an excess of red blood cells. The result is an unbearable itching, redness and bleeding cracks in the skin that appear after a brief exposure to sunlight. Sufferers naturally avoided coming out in the daylight and appeared only at night. The disease was not diagnosed until the 19th century and many afflicted individuals were regarded with superstitious fear.

Probably the most common source of vampire legends came from premature burials. People suffering from catalepsy and other ailments sometimes found themselves buried alive and when later exhumed, the distorted state of the corpses led many to believe the dead had been coming and going from their coffins for some time. In the 1700's, it was not uncommon for bodies to be dug up to see if they had become vampires, especially when it involved the death of a suicide, a murder victim or someone who had died during a spate of unexplained deaths. If a body was discovered to be in any way out of the ordinary, it was burned to prevent it leaving the grave again.

As mentioned previously, brutal and horrific crimes and murders were also sometimes blamed on monsters and vampires. Many had a hard time believing that a human being could be capable of bloody and terrifying crime, so it was explained away as the work of a supernatural creature. So-called "human vampires" existed as well. In 1924, a German named Fritz Haarman earned the nickname the "Hanover Vampire" after he murdered 24 young men and boys. A savage throat wound had dispatched almost every one of them. In a somewhat similar case, a British man named John George Haigh was hanged in 1949 for the murder of nine people. He had killed them in order to drink their blood and then had disposed of the bodies in a vat of acid. His bizarre thirst earned him the moniker of the "Vampire of London".

Obviously, these depraved individuals were not the supernatural vampires of legend. While these creatures had allegedly been around for centuries, they became a part of popular culture in 1897 with the publication of Bram Stoker's book, *Dracula*. This was certainly not the first fictional story written about vampires, but it made the greatest impression on history. It also set the standard for the elegant, European vampire, a standard that is still very prevalent today. This image of the vampire taught us to hate the creature's evil nature but to be seduced by his powerful and charismatic charm.

In America, our colonial ancestors were well aware of vampires, but they certainly did not see them as graceful "creatures of the night". The vampire was a death-bringer and something to be feared. An unsuspecting community that fell under the spell of one of these monsters could very well be destroyed. You see, in historic America, vampires were not mythical creatures from books and folklore, they were unquestionably real!

THE WOODSTOCK VAMPIRE

In October of 1890, a story appeared in the *Boston Transcript* newspaper about some events that allegedly took place in Woodstock, Vermont in the 1830's. The article recalled a series of events that were said to have occurred years before, a short time after a local man named Corwin passed away. He was supposed to have died of consumption and there was reason to doubt this... at first anyway. Regardless, he was buried in Cushing Cemetery, where he was laid to rest for all eternity.

Author Bram Stoker

Not long after the funeral, Corwin's younger brother also began wasting away. His symptoms were remarkably like his brothers and today, we would assume that he had the same disease. It wasn't long in those days though before someone suggested a more mysterious culprit behind his illness. Rumor had it that the dead Corwin was returning from the grave as a vampire. Many believed that he was feeding off his younger brother's blood, causing his health to slowly fail.

There was only one way to find out for sure and a group of men from town disinterred Corwin's body. To their horror, they soon discovered they were indeed dealing with a supernatural being. The town's doctor, and head of the Vermont Medical College, Dr. Joseph Gallup, examined the body and observed that the "vampire's heart contained its victim's blood". They removed it from the Corwin's chest and destroyed it by heating up an iron pot and cooking the organ until it was in ashes. Most of the town turned out for this macabre event, which ended with the men placing the iron pot into a deep hole in the center of the town square. A stone slab was then placed over it and the area was purified by sprinkling bull's blood over it.

Finally, they forced the ailing, but still living, Corwin brother to drink a horrible concoction that was mixed from blood and the ashes of his dead brother. It was believed this mixture would cure the man of vampirism and stop his body from wasting away. Whether or not it actually worked is anyone's guess, but this was the last report of vampires to ever come from Woodstock.

But it was not the last weird event to be connected to this story. Author Joseph Citro, the master of Vermont and New England lore, states that a few years later, several men tried to discover the resting place of the Woodstock vampire. They began digging under the town common and after uncovering several feet, they heard a great roaring noise and the "smell of sulphur began to fill the cavity". Alarmed, they refilled the hole and quickly left.

Citro believes that this indicates the entire story may have been a Halloween tale of some sort, but does admit that Dr. Gallup and the other townspeople were actually real. He goes on to add though that, although people have tried, no one has been able to find the iron pot of ashes beneath the Woodstock town green.

THE DEMON VAMPIRE

Another reported vampire in Vermont, this time in the town of Manchester, caused a great public uproar in 1793. Locals stated that a "Demon Vampire" was at work in the small town.

The story began in 1789 with the marriage of Captain Isaac Burton to a beautiful young woman named Rachel Harris. Shortly after the wedding, Rachel's health began to fail. Her illness was quickly diagnosed as consumption, a common enough disease at that time. She continued to weaken until February 1790, when she died.

From there, our story turns to vampires.

It is not hard to imagine how consumption may have given birth to the legends of vampires in New England. Consumption, or what we now call tuberculosis, was the plague of the 1800's. Death tolls from the illness were staggering as it was highly contagious and would pass easily through entire families. It was generally fatal and often referred to as the

"White Death". The name came from the fact that the affected person's skin became very pale, thin and almost ghost-like. There was also a reddening of the face, fainting spells and a general weakening of the body. It was easy to see, in more superstitious times, how this could have been mistaken for the draining of the lifeblood by a vampire. It was thought that when someone died from consumption, they might come back from the dead and try to feed off their living relatives, who by this time, had probably come down with the disease themselves. In order to stop them from coming back, family members would go to the grave and try to "kill" the deceased again.

You might think that one look at the decaying corpse would dispel any rumors of vampires, but you would be wrong! In fact, when the coffin was opened, the recently dead consumptive would be found to be bloated in death, even though the disease had made them wasted and thin when alive. Their fingernails and hair would have grown and worst of all, their mouths would be filled with naturally regurgitated blood. The evidence of vampirism was blatantly obvious! Or so it was thought.

Now, we return to the story of Rachel Harris.

Nearly a year after her death, Captain Burton decided to marry again. His new bride was Hulda Powel, another attractive local girl who was described as fit and healthy. But our health didn't last either. A short time later, Hulda also began to develop the symptoms of the "White Death". Her vitality faded away, she became unnaturally pale and she developed a harsh, bloody cough. By February 1793, she was very ill and it was feared she would soon die.

That was when the rumors started about vampires. Perhaps the creature had been responsible for Rachel's death and now was feeding off Hulda too. Or what if the vampire was actually Rachel herself? Perhaps she had been transformed into one of the undead and was now jealously preying on her husband's new wife!

A group of men from town and some of Captain Burton's relatives went to the graveyard and dug up Rachel's coffin. Expecting to find a vital and terrifying corpse, they discovered a badly decayed body instead. Rachel couldn't be the vampire, but they were taking no chances. They removed what was left of her heart and liver and burned them in the blacksmith's forge. The burning would kill the vampire and hopefully, would save the life of Hulda Burton.

Unfortunately, it didn't work. Hulda died on September 6, 1793, although no trace of the "Demon Vampire" was ever found.

VAMPIRES IN CONNECTICUT

The Henry Ray family of Jewett City, Connecticut were poor farmers with five children to feed in the winter of 1845. Henry and his wife Lucy had raised their children to religiously have faith in God, so it must have been especially hard that year when their second oldest son, Lemuel, began wasting away. He grew sicker and sicker as the cold weather months wore on and finally, in March he died and was laid to rest in the local cemetery.

The Rays continued to struggle with their farm over the course of the next four years. Then, in 1849, the unthinkable happened when Henry Ray began to experience the first symptoms of consumption. Soon, he too was dead.

Two more years passed and in 1851, Elisha, Lucy's oldest son, also took sick. He came down with a terrible, wracking cough and within weeks, followed his father and brother to the grave. Many believed that the Ray family was dying out far too quickly, even by the standards of the times.

The next tragedy came almost a decade later in 1854, but the signs of death were all too familiar. The last of the two sons, Henry Nelson Ray, also began to get sick. He began suffering from fainting spells and grew weaker with each day that passed. That May, friends and remaining members of the family realized that they had to take desperate measures if they were going to save Henry's life. With so many deaths in the family, the Rays realized that Henry's wasting illness must be caused by his dead brother, Lemuel. He had been the first to die and now was apparently coming back to carry off his family members. He had apparently become a vampire and had drained his father and brother to survive.

The Rays contacted a few of their friends and set off for the Jewett City Cemetery. They unearthed the coffins of their brothers, Lemuel and Elisha, but for some reason, left the body of their father alone. They broke open the caskets and burned the corpses there in the graveyard. According to the legend, the family suffered no more mysterious deaths.

Almost a century and a half later, in 1990, the specter of the vampire reared its head in Connecticut again. One afternoon, two children were playing at a newly developed construction site when they made a gruesome discovery. They had been taking turns sliding into a recently dug gravel pit and apparently they somehow disturbed a private burying ground from decades past. The tangle of bones fell out of the hill and tumbled to the bottom of the pit.

The boys ran off to tell their parents and soon, police investigators were on the scene. Several officials were summoned to the site of what was feared to be the dumping spot for a killer. They quickly learned otherwise, thanks to the work of Dr. Nicholas Bellantoni, the state archaeologist from the University of Connecticut.

This was not the burying ground of a killer... but of vampires instead!

The researchers made a number of disturbing discoveries but one grave in particular attracted the most attention. One coffin, marked "JB" was found within a fieldstone crypt, but strangely, bones from the coffin were found on the outside of the crypt rather than the inside. In addition, they found the crypt and casket that had been broken into at some point in the past. The corpse inside of it had been mutilated. The rib cage had been split open and long leg bones rested where the chest should have been. The skull was positioned on top in the configuration of the skull and crossbones. Who would do such a thing?

What the officials soon discovered was that the boys had found an old unmarked cemetery. It had belonged to a family named Walton. They had lived in the area in the late 1700's and had died out around 1840. Their bones, all 29 sets of remains, were packed up and shipped to the National Museum of Health and Medicine in Washington, where they came under the care and study of Dr. Paul Sledzik.

After examining the bones, Dr. Sledzik was able to learn quite a bit from "JB", whose body was the only one in the graveyard that had been disturbed. Whoever the man had been, he had died some time in his mid-50's and had perished from consumption. Evidently, he had been the one held responsible when others in the family, and surrounding area, also began to get sick and die. His remains had been disturbed more than ten years after he had died.

The question remained as to who would have done such a thing to his bones? A vampire hunter would have, and apparently did. One can't help but wonder if this act still failed to end the rash of deaths in the neighborhood... or was JB a vampire after all?

VAMPIRES IN RHODE ISLAND

As you can see, historic America was steeped in the lore of vampires. If a death seemed mysterious or could not be explained, it was often blamed on the living dead. Of all of the states where vampires were most prevalent, Rhode Island boasts more cases than any other. Why is that? No one really knows for sure but author Christopher Rondina believes that perhaps the resistance to change and the lack of education in the farming communities of the past provided ample fuel for the festering of old world fears. Besides that, he adds, one can simply detect a *darker* spirit in the Ocean State.

From 1796 to 1892, there were more than a dozen cases of reported vampires in Rhode Island. In this section, we'll take a look at one piece of this chilling bit of Americana and then explore the most famous American vampire case of all, Mercy Brown.

Over the years, this case has caused a lot of confusion among historians and collectors of vampire lore. It was always referred to as the "Stukeley Case", but it's likely this was wrong. No one really seemed sure when the event actually took place either, or even what the names were of those involved. It remained a mystery until Rhode Island folklorist Michael Bell was able to determine that the family involved was "Stutley and Honor Tillinghast" of Exeter. He also learned that the events in question occurred in 1799.

This vampire tale has traditionally always started with a dream. Stutley Tillinghast was a well-off farmer from Exeter. He was liked and admired in the community and in the local church and was thought of as a good provider and excellent father. He and his wife had raised fourteen children and all of them, against the odds in those days, had survived into adulthood.

Then one night, the farmer awoke after an unsettling and disturbing dream. The nightmare was especially vivid and had left him in a cold sweat. He dreamed that he was walking between the rows of his apple orchard. On one side, the trees were very healthy, their limbs weighted down by an abundance of fruit. On the other side of the orchard, the trees had withered and died. The branches had dropped their leaves and wasted and rotted apples lay scattered about on the ground. Tillinghast awoke with a terrible feeling of dread. He was sure the dream was some sort of portent of things to come... but of what?

A short time later Sarah, the couple's oldest daughter, grew sick. No one thought much of the farmer's strange dream and in fact, it was forgotten completely as Sarah began to get sicker. Not long after she first fell ill, she died and was buried in a small family cemetery that was located nearby.

Then, a second daughter began wasting away and she too died. Strangely, before she died, she began to complain repeatedly that her dead sister, Sarah, was coming to her in the night. She came as a ghostly figure, entering the room through the window. Sarah would then come to the side of the bed and push down on the girl's chest, making it difficult for her to breathe.

In the days and weeks that followed, more of the Tillinghast children weakened and died. By the time the fifth child perished, the old farmer suddenly remembered the strange dream that he had experienced about the apple orchard. In this vision, exactly half of the orchard had withered and died. He finally realized what the dream had been trying to tell him. In despair, he realized that seven of his children were going to die. He didn't try to ponder the supernatural meanings behind the dream however. At this point, he was trying to puzzle out the meaning behind his children's complaints about nighttime visits from Sarah. Before each of them died, they claimed the girl came into their room at night. What could this mean?

Shortly after the sixth Tillinghast child died, the seventh sibling also began to complain of strange feelings of fatigue and of seeing Sarah in their room at night. When this child died, Honor Tillinghast also began to weaken. She too began to say that Sarah was coming to her in the darkness.

After talking it over with some of his neighbors, Tillinghast began to believe that Sarah was responsible for the string of deaths in his family. Knowing the only way to stop the deaths was to take action, the men went out to the cemetery and opened the graves of all of the dead children. All of the corpses were rotting and decayed, except for one. Sarah's body was in perfect condition. The story says that her hair and nails had grown, her flesh was soft and supple, and upon investigation, fresh blood was pumping through her body.

Immediately, Sarah's body was cut open and her heart was torn from her chest. The men built a small fire and they burned it there on the cemetery grounds. Just for safe measure, they also cut the hearts from the other corpses and burned those as well. Shortly after, Honor Tillinghast began to regain her strength and amazingly, she recovered from the illness.

Stutley Tillinghast's eerie vision had come true.... he and his wife had lost half of their "orchard" from an unexplainable scourge.

MERCY BROWN

The spirit of a vampire still lingers in Exeter, Rhode Island.

Whether or not this spirit literally remains here or not may be an unanswered question but regardless, if you ask anyone in the region of the most famous vampire in American history, you are sure to hear about Mercy Brown. Her story is told and re-told and of Rhode Island's many vampire tales, hers is the best known and perhaps even the most tragic.

The story of Mercy Brown may end in the Chestnut Hill Cemetery in 1892, but it actually started a number of years before that in 1883. The story is a somewhat familiar one but was heartbreaking to the members of the George Brown family, who first succumbed to the "White Death" in the winter of that year.

George Brown was a hard-working farmer who prospered in the Exeter area. He and his wife, Mary, had raised six children and lived a comfortable but simple life. In late 1883, the first in a series of terrible events occurred on the Brown farm. Late that year, Mary Brown began to show signs of consumption. The sturdy, once healthy woman began to suffer from fainting spells and periods of weakness. Most of all, she was gripped with a harsh cough that kept her awake through the night. The disease began to ravage her body and on December 8, she slipped into unconsciousness and did not awaken.

The following spring, Mary Olive, George's oldest daughter, also came down with the dreaded illness. She began to complain of terrible dreams and of a great pressure that was crushing her chest at night, making it impossible for her to breathe. Mary Olive grew paler and weaker with each passing day and on June 6, 1884, she followed her mother to the grave.

Several years of peace followed the death of Mary Olive and during this time, Edwin Brown, George and Mary's only son, got married and bought his own farm in nearby West Wickford. Here, he hoped to make a life for himself and his new bride while he worked in a store to support his family and save money for the future. All was going well until about 1891, when Edwin began to notice the symptoms of the disease that had killed his sister and mother. He resigned from his job and following advice from friends, moved west to Colorado Springs. Here, he hoped that mineral waters and a drier climate might restore his health.

While Edwin was out west, things got worse for the family in Exeter. In January 1892, he received word that his sister Mercy had become sick and had died. He also began to realize that his health was not improving either. He came to the decision that he should return home and spend the remainder of his days with his family, friends and loved ones.

By the time he reached Rhode Island, he found his father in a dreadful and worried state. He had become convinced that the family was being preyed upon by a vampire. After much debate, it was decided that they should exhume the bodies of the other family members and see which one of them it was. How they convinced Edwin to go along with this is unknown, but a group of men went out to the cemetery during the early morning hours of March 18,1892.

It is likely that this exhumation would have remained a secret, if not for the fact that the men sought official sanction for it from the local doctor. They approached the district medical examiner, Dr. Harold Metcalf, and asked him to come to the graveyard to examine the bodies. He discouraged them but eventually agreed to go along, realizing that he could not persuade them from what they believed was their duty. By the time that he arrived at the cemetery, the bodies of Mary Brown and her daughter, Mary Olive, had already been unearthed. Dr. Metcalf took a look at them and found them in a state of advanced decay. They were "just what might be expected from a similar examination of almost any person after the same length of time", he stated with certainty.

Mercy's body had not yet been buried. As she had died in the winter, the ground was too hard for a burial. Her body had rested for the past two months inside of a small crypt on the cemetery grounds. The coffin was placed on a small cart inside of the tomb. Once the casket was opened, Dr. Metcalf looked inside and began a quick autopsy of the corpse. What he noted, mainly decay and the marks of consumption on the lungs, did not convince him that she was a vampire. He finished the examination and quickly left.

The other men remained behind. To them, Mercy seemed relatively intact, or at least more so than she should be after two months in the grave. In addition, they were also sure that her body had moved. She had been laid to rest on her back and somehow, the corpse was now resting on her side. Could she have left the casket?

They were nearly sure that Mercy was a vampire and what happened next convinced them entirely. One of the men opened up her heart with his knife and was startled to see fresh blood come pouring out of the organ. It was quickly removed from her chest and burned in the cemetery. As it was engulfed in the flames, ashes were gathered with which to make a tonic that would hopefully cure Edwin of the disease.

Edwin consumed the macabre mixture, but it did no good and he died soon afterwards. On May 2, he too was buried in the cemetery. While tragic, all was not lost. He became the last of the Brown family to die from the mysterious "White Death". The exhumation had ended the vampire's control over the family once and for all.

Even though these events took place more than a century ago, Mercy Brown has not faded from the memory of those in Exeter. Famous Rhode Island author H.P. Lovecraft even included a thinly disguised Mercy Brown in his vampire tale *The Shunned House*. In addition, the story has appeared many times in documentaries and books about the supernatural.

Gone, but not forgotten... Mercy Brown lives on as America's most celebrated vampire.

CHAPTER THREE
THE LORE OF THE GRAVEYARD

It has been said that graveyards often rival haunted houses for popularity when it comes to ghost stories and eerie legends. Some of the most famous stories of all time revolve around cemeteries and many of them have nothing to do with ghosts at all. Often they are concerned with the burial of living persons, grave robberies and deaths from fright. Others, which came about later and are often referred to as "teenagers in the car" stories, involve cemeteries, but more for the setting than for incidents taking place in the graveyard itself.

I should say before we continue on with this chapter that few of the stories contained in it purport to be true. These tales are included here to enlighten the reader about the most common ghostly stories told concerning burial grounds. Stories such as these are often told by people, who believe them to be true, which makes them legends or oral folklore.

However, I cannot help but wonder how many of these stories got started in the first place. Could any of them have a basis in truth? What if an incident like one of these actually happened somewhere and then was told and re-told to the point that it lost many of the elements of truth? As the story spread, it was embraced by people all over the country and became a part of their local lore. It has long been believed that people provide an explanation for something that they cannot understand. This is usually done by creating mythology that made sense at the time.

For instance, there are many tales of "spook lights" across the country. These mysterious balls of light appear and disappear at will and are sometimes seen by hundreds of people. What are they? No one really knows for sure. They probably have a natural explanation but according to the local stories in nearly every location, the lights always have a supernatural source. In the majority of the cases, the lights are the ghostly manifestation of a person who, for one reason or another, lost his head. They are usually the lanterns of railroad workers, farmers and frontiersmen who were beheaded and now wander the area where they were killed in a lonely search for their missing head.

These stories were created to explain the "spook lights" that appear, but how did the explanation get started? Was there really a railroad brakeman who lost his head in an accident? And did a strange light begin to appear along the railroad tracks where the accident took place? Perhaps someone heard of such a story and then invented a similar legend to explain the weird light that was being seen in his or her own neighborhood.

My point is this, never disregard a graveyard legend just because it seems too good to be true. In all likelihood, it is probably just a legend, but what if it isn't? Who knows if there may be a very small kernel of truth hidden inside of the folk tales that sends shivers down your spine?

BURIED ALIVE

There are many tales of graveyard revivals after people have been buried alive. As we learned in the last chapter, such tales were not just fable, but often fact. One Southern Illinois legend tells of a middle-aged woman who took ill and died. After a wake was held for her, she was buried in the local cemetery.

That same night, two grave robbers came to the cemetery and noticed the fresh grave. They soon set to work uncovering the coffin, hoping to make off with any valuables the deceased had been buried with. When the lid of the coffin was raised, they were thrilled to see a ruby ring and another plain gold ring were on the fingers of the corpse. However, they were soon disappointed as they tried to remove them and found them impossible to budge. They had little choice, if they wanted to steal the rings, but to cut off the woman's fingers.

As the knife cut into the woman's flesh, both robbers were startled to see her hand twitch and move. Suddenly, the dead woman sat up straight in the coffin and let out a blood-curdling scream! The grave robbers also let out screams of their own and they ran from the cemetery.

As for the woman, she climbed up out of her grave and made her way back home. She explained that she had been alive the entire time and had even been aware of the doctor pronouncing her dead. However, she had been unable to move or speak and could not prevent being buried. When she awakened, thanks to the dubious efforts of the grave robbers, she made her way back home. She was shaken, the story goes, but alive.

Another similar story involved a young medical student who was forced to look for an experimental cadaver wherever he could find it. The place turned out to be the local cemetery and he went there one night in search of a fresh grave. After looking about the graveyard, he discovered a recent burial and he went to work. When he uncovered the coffin, he opened it up and found himself face-to-face with a woman who was not only alive, but also totally insane!

The next day, the bodies of the woman and the student were found in the cemetery. Both of them were dead. It was obvious that a terrific struggle had taken place and that the mad woman had managed to overpower the hapless student. Her hands were found still clutched about his neck.

The authorities came to the conclusion that the woman had been buried alive and had lost her sanity when she had awakened and realized what had happened. The student was apparently in the wrong place at the wrong time!

THE BOYFRIEND'S DEATH & "THE HOOK"

Two classic legends are often set in the vicinity of the graveyard. In fact, when I was growing up, I heard these two stories (which, of course, I was assured by the teller actually happened) in conjunction with a local graveyard and the "lover's lane" that ran nearby. Since that time, I have learned that people all over the country tell these stories and in every case, set the stories around a creepy area that is located in the immediate vicinity.

Both stories are popular additions to the lore of Bachelor's Grove Cemetery near Chicago, which already has the reputation of being one of the most legitimately haunted sites in the region. The inclusion of these legends is not really surprising and local storytellers even taken them one step further. In both cases, the ghosts of the victim and the killer are both said to still be haunting the area!

Don't be surprised if you immediately recognize these stories. And don't be surprised if you have already heard of them occurring at a cemetery near you!

The story of the "Boyfriend's Death" seems to have its roots "many years ago", according to every version, although folklorist Jan Harold Brunvand has been able to trace the story to Iowa around 1964 or so. From there, the story continued to spread and soon, every community (or so it seemed) had a version of it. The story that you will read here is the version that was told to me in the early 1980's and it is placed in a rural setting. There was just something about an old country road at night that seemed to give the tale an extra thrill as it was repeated around the campfire.

One night, two high school students are out on a date and decide to do a little parking in the country. They drive out along the rural roads for awhile, searching for the perfect spot and then unbelievably, they run out of gas. As the young man coasts the car to a stop at the side of the road, his date notices that they are now parked very close to an old cemetery. It is an old and creepy place, filled with large trees that overhang the narrow road, making it seem even darker out than it really is.

The boyfriend apologizes and then volunteers to walk back to the nearest farmhouse that he can find and buy some gas. He is sure that his girlfriend will be perfectly fine out here in the country, but he insists that she wait in the car with the doors locked. Make sure, he cautions her, not to open the door for anyone else. He quickly retrieves a gas can from the trunk and begins walking. Soon, his figure disappears into the darkness.

An hour or so passes and the girlfriend fidgets in boredom in the car, idly changing radio stations until she begins to fear that she is going to wear down the car's battery. Finally, she gets her coat from the backseat and using it as a blanket, stretches out to take a little nap.

She has no idea how long she has been asleep when she is awakened by a sound from outside. She listens closely and realizes that it is coming from the roof of the car. It is a scratching noise, going back and forth. At first afraid, she then laughs to herself as she remembers that they are parked beneath a stand of trees. There is apparently a tree branch hanging down low enough that it scratches the roof of the car. Still drowsy, she ignores the scratching and drifts back off to sleep.

The next time the girl is awakened, it is caused by a sharp rapping on the window glass. Confused and disoriented, she sits up and is blinded by the sunshine that is now streaming into the car. It is morning and it dawns on her that her boyfriend has never returned. The girl turns her head to see who is knocking on the window and sees a police officer standing outside of the car. She then sees that there are several police cars and an ambulance parked along the edge of the road.

The girl unlocks the door and the officer quickly opens it. He takes her hand and gently helps her out of the car. She asks him what is going on? What's happening? Where is her boyfriend? The policeman doesn't answer her questions but merely leads her away from the stranded automobile. He urges her to come with him and then adds that she should not, no matter what, turn around and look behind her.

Of course, those simple words are a guarantee that she will look back and when she does, she begins to scream. There, hanging upside down and above the roof of the car is the mutilated body of her boyfriend. His clothing is in tatters and he has been flayed alive and is drenched in blood. The girl suddenly realizes what the scratching sound had been in the middle of the night... for under her boyfriend's fingernails is paint from the top of the car!

Pretty scary, huh? Well, it seemed pretty scary when I was a teenager and weekends were often spent navigating gloomy country roads. This cautionary tale (probably started by someone's parents) never really explained what had killed the boyfriend. The idea that "something" from the cemetery did the job was always just something that was implied.

With that in mind, we were left to think that something supernatural was the culprit in that version of the tale. This was not the case in the next story though, where a very human serial killer is reportedly on the loose!

Once again, this is the version of "The Hook" story that circulated widely where I grew up. The following story was also "true" and happened "many years ago" along a wooded lover's lane that was located behind an old cemetery.

A pair of young lovers goes out for the evening and decides to do a little parking at the local lover's lane. The dark, wooded road is especially inviting on this night, as their car is the only one parked at this popular spot. For once, they have the whole place to themselves. Things begin progressing nicely to the soft sounds of music on the radio and time slips away.

Suddenly, the music is interrupted by the strident voice of the announcer, cutting into the middle of a song with an urgent news bulletin. According to police reports, he explains, a brutal killer has escaped from the hospital for the criminally insane and is loose in the area. He is very dangerous and police are warning everyone to be on the look out for him. He can be identified by the fact that he walks with a limp... and that is left hand has been replaced with a sharp steel hook! Citizens are warned to lock their doors and windows and to stay away from dark secluded areas.

Even though the young man is convinced that everything is all right, his date feels otherwise and suggests that they should leave. The boyfriend tries to convince her otherwise to the point that she becomes angry and demands that he take her home right away. Frustrated, he starts the car and roars out of the gravel lane, throwing dirt, rocks and dust behind the wheels of the car. He angrily drives straight to the girl's house and parks on the street out front.

By this time though, he is calmed down somewhat and he apologizes to her for the way that he acted. She smiles in acceptance and invites him to come inside for a little while. The boyfriend then climbs out of the car and goes around to his date's door to open it for her. Just as he reaches for the door handle though, his face turns white and he clumsily falls to the curb, coming close to fainting.

Startles, his girlfriend opens to door to see what is wrong and as she does, she hears the clink of metal. Turning around, she sees that dangling from the door handle is a gleaming steel hook!

Once again, another chilling and cautionary tale of what can happen to you if you take your date out on some dark country road at night. While still pretty scary, this story has some obvious flaws. The most glaring is the unlikelihood that the police and hospital officials would allow this bloodthirsty killer to keep a deadly weapon like a steel hook attached to his prosthetic. The other problem with the story, at least in my area growing up, was the absence of a "hospital for the criminally insane" being located nearby. As you can imagine though, this didn't stop the story from being told for years.

THE GRAVEYARD WAGER

Another popular tale is so old that it was first recorded back in the Middle Ages in Europe. Since that time, it has spread into almost every culture and is still told today. The story is so well known that in 1961, it was adapted for an episode of the television series the *Twilight Zone*, with Lee Marvin in the role of the man who dies of fright.

There are a number of different variations of the story, but here are a couple of the best known ones.

There was a group of college girls who were at a party one evening and as it was in late October, talk turned to stories of ghosts and hauntings in the area. One story involved an old cemetery that was located just across the road from the sorority house where the party was taking place. One of the girls scoffed at the stories and not believing in ghosts, said that she would not be afraid to go into the graveyard at night by herself. Several of the young women warned her about the foolishness of such a stunt, but she insisted that she wasn't scared.

Finally, not really convinced of the girl's bravery, one of the others dared her to go. She even went as far as to say that this girl had to go to a certain grave in the cemetery and mark it in some way to prove that she had been there. This particular grave was rumored to be haunted and was the subject of discussion earlier in the evening. The others would wait for her at the sorority house until she returned.

At midnight, the girl climbed over the fence and set off into the cemetery. She stumbled along in the darkness until she found the grave that she was supposed to mark. She had brought along a wooden stake from a croquet set that was in the basement of the sorority house. She would leave it planted in the ground to show that she had really been there. Smiling in satisfaction, she couldn't get over how easy it had been. She knelt down and then taking the stake in both hands, she drove it down into the ground.

The other women waited for an hour for their friend to return, at first anxiously watching the clock. After a little more time passed, they began to realize that she must have been playing a trick on them and one by one, they gave up their watch and went to bed.

The next morning, two of the girls decided to go out to the cemetery and see if the girl really had placed the stake on the "haunted" grave. As they walked across the street, they noticed a flurry of activity inside of the cemetery. There were several cars parked there, alongside the caretaker's truck, and their flashing lights identified them as police cars. Fearing the worst, the girls ran out into the cemetery toward where the men were gathered. When they arrived there, they made a terrifying discovery!

Sprawled across a grave was the body of their friend. When she had knelt down to plunge the wooden stake into the ground, she had accidentally driven it through the hem of her dress as well. When she tried to leave, she found that something seemed to be holding on to her. The doctors later determined that she had died of fright.

Whether or not anyone can actually "die of fright" is a question that I have long pondered, but regardless, it always makes a fitting end to the story. Another version of the "Graveyard Wager" was featured in my own book, *Haunted New Orleans*. In this case, the tale centered on the tomb of the Voodoo Queen, Marie Laveau, in the city's St. Louis Cemetery No. 1. Some people claim that this legend actually has its American origins in this atmospheric graveyard.

This version of the tales states that three young men spent a night drinking and carousing in the French Quarter. Their talk soon turned to death, voodoo and Marie Laveau. Before long, one of the men was enticed into a wager. His friends bet him $30 that he would not climb the cemetery wall and drive a spike into the wall of Marie's resting place. He accepted the wager and a short time later, entered the cemetery.

His friends waited for him to return but soon, minutes turned into hours. Dawn came and with it, the opening of the cemetery gates. The worried young men hurried to the tomb and there, they found their friend... lying dead on the ground!

In his drunken state, he had hammered the spike through his coat and into the stone wall of the crypt. As he started to leave, what he believed was an unseen force (actually the misguided nail) held him in place. Panic and fear overwhelmed him and he literally died of fright. But was it really just confusion which fueled his horror, or did he see something on that dark night which so terrified him that his heart couldn't stand it? Those who allege that the cemetery is haunted are certain that it is the latter.

OTHER GRAVEYARD LEGENDS

Not all graveyard legends and folktales are frightening. Some of them, like these two examples from the Ozarks, are more entertaining than they are chilling. Perhaps some storytellers understand that death is inevitable. As it has often been said... why take life too seriously? You never get out of it alive!

One late night, two boys went out stealing apples from a neighbor's trees. They simply waited until the farmer was out milking his cows and then slipped into his orchard and filled a bag with fruit. Since there were two boys and only one sack, they had to divide up the stolen loot. As it was growing dark out, they decided that the local graveyard would be a good place where they would not be disturbed. They climbed over a stone wall and sat down on the ground to split up the apples.

"You take this one, and I'll take that one", one boy said to another and they began counting.

Shortly after they set to work, a big, strapping local boy came walking down the road. He was whistling to himself as he walked past the cemetery, picking up the pace as little as the graveyard shadows loomed closer. Suddenly, the whistling died on his lips as he heard voices coming from the graveyard. They were very clear and sounded just like "you take this one, and I'll take that one."

The poor country boy, never having been accused of being smart, was scared half to death. He took off running and never slowed down until his reached his house. He burst in through the front door and hollered for his father. "I heard them!", he shouted. "It was the Lord and the Devil out in the graveyard dividing up the souls!"

The boy's father looked up at him in disbelief. The old man was crippled up with rheumatism and was sitting in a cane rocker in the front room. He had hardly moved in more than ten years. He first asked the boy if he had been drinking.

"No," the boy insisted, "I did hear them. They was dividing up the souls, going 'you take this one, and I'll take that one'. I really did hear them!"

"All right, son," the old man groaned, "but I am going to have to hear this one for myself. You know I ain't stirred a step in years, so you're going to have to carry me down to the graveyard."

The massive young man picked up the skinny old fellow and put him up on his shoulders. They left the house and headed back down the road to the graveyard. As they got closer, the boy slowed down and they began creeping up to the cemetery wall. The boys were still there, dividing up the apples, and by now they were down to the last two.

Just as the boy and his old father got to the stone wall and leaned close to listen, one of the apple thieves said to the other one, "There's only these two left. You take that big fat one and I'll take the shriveled-up old one".

At that, the boy jumped back and threw his daddy off his shoulders and started running toward home! And his old father, who had hardly walked in ten years, ended up beating his son back to the house!

Many years ago, shortly after the turn of the last century, there was an old backwoods preacher who was leaving his church late one night. Services had long since ended but he had waited around, reading his Bible, and waiting for the fire in the stove to die out. Finally, he was ready to leave and he stepped out in the cold, dark night. A fierce wind was blowing, right through to his bones, and he pulled the collar of his coat up close around his throat.

He locked the door of the church behind him and started walking down the rock road to the farmhouse where he was staying the night. As he walked along, he looked about him to the darkened woods and fields. Halloween had fallen on a Sunday this year and while the preacher was not a superstitious man, he did shudder a little and he picked up his pace a little faster.

The preacher had to cross over a hill and down through two hollows to get to the house and on the top of one of the hills was a graveyard. As he walked down into the first shadowy hollow, he heard a strange noise on the road behind him. He stopped and turned to look, but saw nothing, so he continued on. A minute or so later, climbing up the hill toward the cemetery, he thought he heard the sound again. He stopped and stood still, listening closely to the sounds of the night. He couldn't hear the noise of hooves, nor of trace chains jangling, so he knew that it was not a wagon. He didn't hear the puttering of an engine either, so he knew that it wasn't a new-fangled automobile either. So, he walked on.

Just as he reached the edge of the clearing where the graveyard was, he heard the sound again. It was a low, rumbling sound like something heavy was creeping along the rock road. Whatever it was, it seemed to be following him, crunching the gravel underneath its feet as it came. The preacher backed up a few steps and was just getting ready to run when the mysterious creature came into the light of the clearing. At that moment, he saw that it was an automobile... but its lanterns were not lit and it was not making any sound at all. The car pulled up alongside of him and then stopped.

The preacher was both surprised and pleased. He believed that perhaps some deacon from the church was on his way home and had stopped to offer him a ride. He stepped up to the car, opened the door and then climbed inside. When he leaned over to thank the driver for the lift, he discovered that the car was empty! He was the only person inside of it!

Just then, the car began moving again. Very slowly, it began moving along past the cemetery, making no sound other than the crunch of the rock under its wheels. In front of the iron gates to the graveyard, the car suddenly stopped. The preacher, now shaking in fear, jumped out. He had gotten enough of the "haunted" car!

The preacher hurried away from it and ducked behind the cemetery gate. He was then startled again by a harsh sound that came from behind a large gravestone. It was heavy and sounded like growling. Although he was frightened, the preacher peered around the edge of the stone. On the other side of it stood a deacon from his church. The man was all hunched over with his hands on his knees. He was panting and blowing like a horse that had just run a big race.

"Brother Dan!" cried the preacher and he pointed toward the strange automobile on the other side of the gate. "Don't go near that car! There's something wrong about it!"

"I know," Brother Dan managed to wheeze, "I've been pushing that damned thing for almost a mile!"

THE PHANTOM HITCHHIKER

Undoubtedly, the greatest piece of cemetery lore is that of the "phantom" or "vanishing" hitchhiker. There is not a region of the country that does not boast at least one tale about a pale young girl who gets a ride with a stranger, only to vanish from the car before they reach their destination. Many, but not all, of these stories seem to also revolve around cemeteries and in some versions of the story, a graveyard plays a very prominent role.

Folklorist Jan Harold Brunvand calls the "Vanishing Hitchhiker"- the classic automobile legend but also goes on to show how the story got its start long before the invention of the car. In fact, there were stories of "vanishing hitchhikers" being told as far back as the late 1800's, when men would tell stories of ghostly women who appeared on the back of their horses. These spectral riders always disappeared when they reached their destination and would often prove to be the deceased daughters of local farmers. Not much has changed in the stories that are still told today, outside of the preferred method of transportation.

In this section, we'll take a look at not only several variations of the story, but also some different stories from around the country.

One evening, a man was driving along through the country and spotted a young woman hitchhiking along the road. He stopped and picked her up and she climbed into the backseat. As she did, she explained that she lived in a house about five miles further up the road. She didn't really speak after that, but simply sat and stared out the window. When the man saw the house, he turned to the girl to tell her that they arrived, but she was gone!

Stunned, he decided to go knock on the door of the house and tell the people what had happened. They told him that they had once had a daughter who looked much like the girl he described, but she had disappeared some years ago. She had last been seen hitchhiking on the same road where he claimed to have picked her up... and today would have been her birthday.

There are literally dozens of variations of this same basic theme but my favorite version is one that is often told about a stretch of Route 40 in Maryland.

In this story, two Baltimore City College students are on their way to a dance one night. They picked up an attractive blonde girl who was standing on a corner in a cocktail dress and took her along with them. Everyone at the party found her to be very charming and after the dance was over, the boys offered to drive her home as the night had turned quite chilly. She accepted and because it was so cold out, one of the young men gave her his coat to wear.

The boys asked for her address and she gave it to them and they all left together. A short time later, they pulled into the driveway of the house where the girl said that she lived and the driver turned to tell her that they had arrived. To his astonishment, she was gone! The backseat of the car was empty, although the door had never opened... the blond had simply vanished.

Not knowing what else to do, the boys went up to the door and knocked. An elderly woman answered the door and they explained to her what had happened. Right away, she seemed to know exactly what they were taking about. The young girl they had taken to the dance was her daughter... but she had died ten years before in an auto accident.

The horrified boys didn't believe her, even though the name of the girl they had taken to the dance and the woman's daughter were the same. In order to convince them, the old woman even told them where to find the grave of the dead girl in the local cemetery. The young men quickly drove there and following the directions they had been given, found the stone with the girl's name on it. Folded neatly over the top of the marker was the coat that the girl had borrowed to ward off the night chill!

Another, slightly different version of the story comes from Berkeley, California in the 1930's.

A man was driving along Hearst Avenue one rainy evening and as he approached a corner, he saw a young girl, a student with books under her arm, standing there waiting for a streetcar. Since they had already stopped running for the night, he offered her a ride. She told him that she lived out on Euclid and so he set off in that direction.

The driver was engrossed in conversation with her and as they crossed an intersection, failed to notice a car that was coming directly toward them down a steep hill. Luckily, the girl leaned over and pulled up the emergency brake, effectively bringing the car to a sudden halt. The other automobile swerved just in time and kept on going.

The driver was shaken and turned to thank for girl for thinking so fast. To his surprise, she was gone! Since it was near her home though, he assumed that she had gotten out of the car after the near miss and had walked home. However, he did notice that she had forgotten one of her books on the seat of the car.

The next day, he went to return the book and found her father, an English professor, was at home. He listened to the man's story and explained that the girl was his daughter but that she had been killed in an auto accident at that same corner a few years before. Sadly, he took the book from the young man and sent him on his way. That same afternoon, the professor went down to the library with the book and searched the shelves for its location. He discovered that the place where it was supposed to be was vacant... as though someone had just taken it off the shelf!

Highway 365 in Arkansas, just south of Little Rock, is home to a number of "Vanishing Hitchhiker" stories. Many witnesses claim over the years to have picked up a young woman, usually wearing a white dress. She mysteriously vanishes from their cars while they are taking her home.

One story that took place near Woodson, Arkansas had a driver giving a lift to a young woman one rainy night and driving her to a house in Redfield. He got out of the car and walked around to her side of the vehicle to open the door...only to find the girl had disappeared. Bewildered, he went up to the house and was told by the man who answered the door that his daughter had been killed on that night four years ago. On each anniversary of her death, she found an unwitting driver to bring her home.

Another similar story involved a man who gave a lift to a young girl that he picked up on a bridge one night. She asked to be taken to a house, again in Woodson, and when they arrived, she asked the driver to go knock on the door because the house looked dark. A woman answered the door and he told her that he had brought her daughter home. The horrified woman stated that her daughter had died one year before on that very night. The driver went back to the car and found it empty....except for a coat. The woman from the house stated that the coat had belonged to the dead girl.

Another tale involves a bridge near Batesville and a driver who picked up a girl there on a night in 1973. The girl was bruised and battered, with a cut above her eye, and she told the driver she had been in an accident. He gave her a ride home and when he turned to speak to her, she had vanished from his car. He went to the door of the house and the man who answered claimed to be the girl's father. He said that his daughter had died one month before in an accident at the bridge near Batesville. He said that other people had also brought her home before. The story goes that drivers are still bringing the girl home today.

There is also said to be the ghost of a beautiful young girl who has been appearing near Greensboro, North Carolina since around 1923. She stands next to the US Highway 70 underpass in a white evening gown and waves frantically for someone to stop and pick her up. Those travelers who do so are introduced to a young woman who says her name is "Lydia". She always asks them to take her to an address in High Point. She tells them that she has spent the evening at a dance in Raleigh and is anxious to get home, having run into car trouble on the way.

Just as the drivers approach the house, the girl always vanishes from their car. The door never opens and she never gets out. She is simply there one minute and then gone the next! The stories say that those drivers who go on to inquire at the house are always told that Lydia died in a car wreck many years ago as she was coming home from a dance in Raleigh. The accident happened near where the US Highway 70 underpass is now located. It is also said that a portrait on the piano in the house is always identified as being that of the mysterious passenger in the car.

Not all of the hitchhikers, who have allegedly vanished, have been picked up alongside the highway either. One story, which comes from Los Angeles around 1940, involves a girl who was picked up in a downtown "beer joint".

One night, a man and his buddy were drinking in a downtown Los Angeles tavern and they met a young girl there. She asked if they wouldn't mind giving her a lift home as she lived in the Belvedere Gardens neighborhood. This was the same area where the man lived.

The two fellows agreed and they went outside to the car. The girl climbed into the back seat and one of the men was kind enough to lend her his overcoat. It was a very chilly evening, especially for southern California.

They drove along until they passed Evergreen Cemetery. At that point, the girl asked if they might stop for a moment and let her out. The driver pulled to the side of the road and they watched as she climbed out of the backseat. They waited several minutes and when she didn't come back, they thought she had stolen the overcoat. Aggravated, the two men drove home but went out the next morning to the address that she had given them.

When they arrived there, an old man came to the door and after hearing the story said that the girl had been his daughter. She had been murdered a few years before and was buried in Evergreen Cemetery. The two men went to the grave site the girl's father had told them about and there, they found the "stolen" overcoat draped over a tombstone.

Two stories from Chicago also tell of a different sort of "Vanishing Hitchhiker". In these two anecdotes, the anomalies turn out to be "prophesying passengers". Each of them gives ominous warnings to the drivers that pick them up, although in each case, the warnings prove to be wrong.

A Chicago cab driver once told a strange and unsettling fare that he had in December 1941. He was cruising the downtown streets one night and he pulled over to pick up a nun who was dressed in the traditional garb of a Catholic order. She gave him the address that she wished to be taken to and they drove off. The radio was on and the announcer was discussing the events that had taken place at Pearl Harbor a short time before and the preparations that the United States was making for war.

The nun suddenly spoke up from the back seat. "It won't last more than four months", she said and then didn't speak again for the rest of the ride.

When the cabbie pulled up to the address, he got out to open the door for the lady. He was surprised to discover that she wasn't there! Afraid that the little old lady had forgotten to pay her fare, the driver climbed the steps of the address she had given him and discovered that it was a convent. He knocked on the door and was brought to the Mother Superior. He then explained his predicament to her.

"What did she look like?" he was asked. She told him that none of the sisters had been downtown that day.

As the driver began to describe her, he happened to look up at a portrait that was hanging on the wall behind the Mother Superior's desk. "That's her," he said, obviously thinking that he was going to get his fare after all... but he couldn't have been more wrong.

The Mother Superior smiled and quietly said, "But she has been dead for ten years."

During Chicago's Century of Progress Exposition in 1933, a group of people in an automobile told of a strange encounter. They were traveling along Lake Shore

Drive when a woman with a suitcase, standing by the roadside, hailed them. They invited her to ride along with them and she climbed in. They later say that they never really got a good look at her because it was dark outside.

As they drive along, they get into a conversation about the Exposition and she oddly tells them that the "fair is going to slide off into Lake Michigan in September". She then gives them her address in Chicago and invites them to call on her anytime. When they turn around to speak to her, after this doom-filled warning, she had disappeared!

Unnerved, they decide to go to the address the woman gave them and when they do, a man answers the door. They tell him why they have come and he merely nods his head. "Yes, that was my wife", he tells them. "She died four years ago."

So, what do we make of these strange passengers and their mystifying disappearances? Are they all, as some would have us believe, nothing more than folklore? Are they simply stories that have been made up and have been spread across the country over a long period of time? Perhaps this is the case, or perhaps not. At the beginning of this chapter, I asked the reader to keep an open mind. I urged you to look for the truth at the heart of every legend and peel away the outer layers of fiction and see if there remained anything at the center.

As you can imagine. in most of these stories, there is little of relevance that does remain. The stories all occur to "friends of friends" or happened "many years ago" in an unnamed place to unknown people. Could any of these stories be true? It's unlikely, but not all of the stories are the same. In fact, some of them are not only filled with details, but actually list names, dates and locations. What do we make of these tales?

I will leave that up to the reader to decide. In the remainder of this book though, you will undoubtedly encounter other variations of the "vanishing hitchhiker", including one that I consider to be the greatest ghost story of all time! Each one of these stories will lead you to wonder if they are true, or the product of someone's overactive imagination.

Just remember.... don't be too quick to decide!

· CHAPTER FOUR ·
GRAVE MYSTERIES
A COLLECTION OF HAUNTED
GRAVEYARDS FROM NEW ENGLAND &
THE ATLANTIC SEABOARD

Fear about the uncertainty of the afterlife is deeply rooted in human nature and nowhere is this terror better illustrated than in the grave markers of America's original colonies. Immortalizing the spirits of the dead, they graphically portray the horror of the grave in the form of winged death, skulls and crossbones.

The ghosts who walk here, as have already been seen in earlier chapters, are grim and forbidding, much like the Puritans who settled this area centuries ago. The hauntings are steeped in legend and lore and the cemeteries and burial grounds boast a unique sort of spirit, unlike those found in other parts of the country. If you doubt this, look to our earlier tales of the "Sleeping Medium", the Vampires of Vermont and Rhode Island and others.

Another unusual haunting could only be found in New England. It was first uncovered by author Arthur Myers and involves a church in eastern Massachusetts that did not wish to disclose its name. Apparently, the church had a burial chamber in the basement with about forty tombs in it. Each of the tombs held a number of bodies and numbered as many as 800-1000 individual graves. Many of them dated back as far as the late 1700's. He first heard about the church through some psychics who had been hired to investigate the place by a construction company. The contractors had been doing some renovations at the building and the workers had begun to get very uncomfortable while working in the lower levels of the site. Several of the men were even talking about quitting, or being transferred to another job. To make matters worse, the priests at the church were afraid of the area too and didn't want to spend any time at all in the burial chamber.

According to the psychics, the spirits were unhappy about the fact that the burial chamber was also being used for storage by the church. They felt their graves were not being treated with the proper respect and they were unhappy about it. Once the problem was taken care of, both the ghosts and the human element in the church were much more comfortable.

The Graveyards of New England hold many Dark Tales

THE LEGEND OF EPHRIAM GRAY

Author Joseph Citro, who has more than his share of strange tales, once passed along a curious New England story concerning a man named Ephriam Gray and his empty grave. Gray was a reclusive man that lived in the area of Malden, Massachusetts. He was a bit of a mystery to the local townsfolk, as he appeared to have no employment and no visible means of support, although he was never without money. He lived in a large, dark house near the center of town and his only companion was a male servant that he employed. He had no wife and as far as anyone knew, was never seen in the company of women.

Gray kept to himself. His servant did all of the shopping and other chores about town and Gray rarely left the house. It was said that he was seldom even seen, except as a figure in the windows of his home at night. One thing that locals often did comment about was the strong chemical smell that reportedly came from his house. The noxious odors were so powerful that people literally became sick after inhaling them. What could Gray be doing in that gloomy mansion? No one knew and he remained an enigma for many years.

And he became an even greater one after he died!

One day in 1850, Ephraim Gray's servant appeared that the Malden police station and informed authorities that his master had died. Apparently, he passed away from natural causes, dying peacefully in his sleep the night before.

Whispers about Gray's last will and testament spread rapidly. As he had no relatives, he left all of his money and belongings to his faithful servant. The only condition to this was that the servant was to make sure that nothing happened to Gray's body prior to his being buried. He asked for no autopsy or embalming, which greatly concerned the local funeral director. Gray's servant was quick to explain his employer's concern. Gray was a chemist and had been hard at work on a formula that he believed would guarantee eternal life. His genius had been so great that if he had lived longer, he most likely would have been successful. Instead, the formula had only been partially completed but Gray was convinced that it would maintain his corpse, perfectly preserved, for centuries. If in fact it did work, then Gray's servant would inherit a new formula for embalming chemicals that would make him even richer than he already had become. With that in mind, he was determined to make sure that Gray's wishes were carried out.

Ephraim Gray was laid to rest in Malden Cemetery but unfortunately, a short time later, his servant also passed away. He was never able to market his employer's formula and Gray's eccentric and extraordinary claims were forgotten.

Twenty years later, a student physician at the Harvard Medical School heard a strange and intriguing story from a friend of his who had grown up in Malden. There was a weird tale that made the rounds about a bizarre inventor and a preservation formula. Interested, he convinced a small group of curious doctors to travel from Cambridge to Malden. They waited until nightfall and then went out to the cemetery. Even in the darkness, they were able to find Gray's tomb. They forced the door open and slipped inside.

By the light of a lantern, they opened the casket and looked on Gray's corpse. He looked very much alive and displayed no signs of decay, even after two decades. Surprised and perhaps even more curious, they nevertheless re-sealed the tomb and returned to Cambridge. The entire affair had to be kept secret but the young doctor from Malden did make some discreet inquiries among his friends and relatives. Apparently, Ephraim Gray's remarkable formula had been lost and his servant had died before revealing any of its secrets.

The perfect preservation of Gray's corpse was certainly strange, but many years later, the story would get even stranger! In the early 1900's, the Malden Cemetery was relocated in order to make way for a new road construction project. The work went very smoothly, until they reached the tomb of Ephraim Gray.

When the door was broken open, Gray's body was found to be missing!

A major investigation was launched but after many weeks of questions and examinations, the case remained unsolved. The authorities could find no explanation as to how the crypt had been opened and the body removed without someone knowing about it. The seal that the medical students had used to close the tomb was unbroken. So where was the corpse of Ephraim Gray?

Had the same medical students, intrigued by the possibilities of the strange preservation formula stolen the body? Or could, as it appeared, Gray have simply revived after twenty years in "hibernation" and walked out of his own tomb?

No one had any idea and the question still remains unanswered today. Surely it would have been impossible for Ephraim Gray to awake from the dead and leave his tomb after two decades.... wouldn't it?

THE REHOBOTH HORROR

The small town of Rehoboth, Massachusetts is a quaint and historic place, located on Route 44, about forty miles southwest of Boston. It is a perfect example of a stereotypical New England town and so not surprisingly, it does boast its share of haunted places.

One such spot is the Village Cemetery, which dates back to the Seventeenth Century and was a favorite locale of author H.P. Lovecraft. The place is quite ancient, yet has only gained a reputation for being haunted over the past few years.

The cemetery's resident specter has been dubbed "Old Ephraim" and he has become a leading spooky attraction in the village since the first sighting of him back in 1994.

The apparition was first seen on January 17 by a couple that was visiting the cemetery. They were standing near a relative's grave in the center of the graveyard and happened to notice a man that they had not seen earlier. In fact, they were convinced that he had not been there at all just moments before. They described him as an elderly man, wearing old-fashioned, possibly eighteenth-century clothing. They also said that he had a "hooked nose and a sneering facial expression" and he was kneeling on the ground in the southwest rear corner of the cemetery. He seemed to be praying, they said, and alternating back and forth between laughing and sobbing. In less than a minute, the figure vanished.

The second reported sighting came in August of 1995 and the witnesses were Lisa and Karen Mackey, two sisters and long-time residents of Rehoboth. The two girls had no idea that the same figure had been spotted before and yet their sighting was eerily identical.

On August 20, the two women visited the cemetery to pay their respects at their mother's grave, who had been buried there since 1966. The cemetery was completely empty of other people when they arrived and they stayed about twenty minutes. Just as they were getting ready to leave, they heard a strange sound, also coming from the southwest rear corner of the burial ground. The noise was that of a human whistling and calling in a suggestive manner, like the rude sounds sometimes directed at women. Surprised, Lisa and Karen looked up and saw a strange-looking elderly man. He was staring at them and making peculiar gestures with his hands.

They went on to describe the figure just the way that the original witnesses had done, right down to the old-fashioned clothing. They also added that the man did not appear to "natural" and that he moved in a way that was "floating slow motion". His eyes were also said to be black and hollow, as if he had no eyes at all. He was visible for no more than thirty seconds and then he disappeared.

The sisters quickly left the cemetery and, despite the fact that their mother is buried there, have not returned to the graveyard again.

The last (reported) sighting of "Old Ephraim" occurred in April 1996 and he was seen by a schoolteacher from nearby Taunton. She was especially shaken by the sighting, perhaps because she was in the cemetery alone that day, taking a walk for relaxation. In this case, she too saw the same man kneeling and sobbing in the southwest rear corner of the graveyard. When she saw him, she did not at first notice anything out of the ordinary. In fact, she thought that he was simply an old man, perhaps mourning for the loss of his wife. Concerned, she began to approach him and planned to try and offer him some comfort.

When she came to within a few yards of him, the man suddenly sprang to his feet "with a type of liquid movement" and began laughing maniacally. He then turned to the teacher and called her an obscene name. Stunned, she turned away and began to walk very quickly toward her car, which was parked on the far side of the cemetery. The old man, she reported, started to follow her, laughing and yelling out a woman's name that did not belong to the witness. "Catherine, Catherine!", he cried as he stumbled after her.

Now, filled with terror, the teacher began to run toward her car. When she reached it, she turned around and saw that the old man had inexplicably reappeared in the corner of the cemetery where she had first seen him. He had somehow covered the distance in a matter of seconds. She quickly climbed into the car, started it and drove away. As she did, she now saw the man was leaning over and beating the figure of a young woman who was lying on the ground. In seconds, both figures vanished! Could this spectral woman have been the "Catherine" the old man had been calling for?

No one knows, just as no one has any idea who this mysterious and horrifying old man might be. Charles Turek Robinson, the author who interviewed the witnesses, believes that the haunting involves "some terrible human drama conflict that is re-enacting itself over and over again in the cemetery." And perhaps he is right....

THE "VILLAGE OF VOICES"

There is a haunted cemetery located in a small village in New England, but it's not a village that you will find on any map. You see, even today, in places that are as populated as Connecticut, it is still possible for towns to become "lost". One such town, called Bara-Hack, is in a place that is so remote and mysterious that only the strange stories told about the place keep it from being lost altogether.

The lost village of Bara-Hack is located deep in the northeastern woods of Connecticut, close to Abington Four Corners and in the Pomfret township. It can only be found by following a seldom-used trail that runs alongside Mashomoquet Brook. If you ask most people in the region, they will have never heard of Bara-Hack but ask them about the "Village of Voices" and you are much more likely to get a positive response. You see, unlike Dudleytown, Connecticut's more infamous lost village, there is nothing demonic about Bara-Hack, but the things that are said to happen here remain just as unexplained.

Two Welsh families settled the isolated village around 1780 and the name of the place, Bara-Hack, is actually Welsh for "breaking bread". Legend has it that one of the first settlers was Obadiah Higginbotham, a deserter from the British army. He was accompanied by his friend, Jonathan Randall, and his family and both men came to the Connecticut wilderness from Rhode Island.

The Randall family brought slaves with them to the new settlement and according to the stories, the slaves were the first to notice that the village was becoming haunted. As the first of the populace began to die, the slaves claimed that their ghosts returned to the local cemetery. They reportedly saw them reclining in the branches of the graveyard trees at dusk. These were the first ghost stories of Bara-Hack, but they would not be the last ones.

Obadiah Higginbotham started a small factory called Higginbotham Linen Wheels and the mill made spinning wheels and looms until the time of the Civil War. The factory failed after the war and the residents began to slowly drift away from the area. By 1890, the last date recorded on a stone in the graveyard, the village was completely abandoned.

However, travelers and passersby still came through the area and almost immediately after the town died, people began to report strange things were going on in the remains of Bara-Hack. It was not ghosts that they saw though; it was the ghosts that they heard. According to stories and reports, those who came to the ruins of Bara-Hack, and the local graveyard, could still hear a town that was alive with noise! Although nothing would be visible, they could hear the talk of men and women, the laughter of children, wagon wheels passing on the gravel road, farm animals and more. The stories continued and now, more than a century after the town was abandoned, the sounds are still being heard!

A little more than thirty years after it vanished, naturalist Odell Shephard documented the village's anomalies. Although not a writer on the supernatural, Bara-Hack was mentioned in his 1927 book, *The Harvest of a Quiet Eye*. He wrote:

> "Here had been there houses, represented today by a few gaping cellar holes out of which tall trees were growing; but here is the Village of Voices. For the place is peopled still... Although there is not human habitation for a long distance round about and no one goes there except for the few who go to listen, yet there is always a hum and stir of human life... They hear the laughter of children at play, ... the voices of mothers who have long been dust calling their children into homes that are now mere holes in the earth. They hear vague snatches of song.... and the rumble of heavy wagons along an obliterated road. It is as though sounds were able in this place to get round that incomprehensible corner, to pierce that mysterious soundproof wall that we call Time."

Over the years, many people have visited Bara-Hack, although it remains a fairly unknown place in New England lore. Few people have ever written about it and even fewer have ever investigated the claims made by generations of curiosity-seekers. Perhaps the most extensive investigations were carried out by college students in 1971 and 1972. The group was led by then student Paul F. Eno, who wrote about their adventures in *Fate* magazine in 1985 and in his book *Faces in the Window* (1998). The group was escorted to the site by Harry Chase, a local man who had a long interest in the history of the area and in the mysteries of the vanished village. Chase had documented his own explorations of the town with photographs that dated back to 1948. The blurs and misty shapes that appeared in some of the photos have been deemed "unsettling" to say the least.

According to Eno, the groups of students documented many bits of puzzling phenomena. Although the village site was isolated, well over a mile from the nearest house, the students often heard the barking of dogs, cattle lowing and even human voices coming from the dense woods. They also reported the frequent sound of children's laughter coming from the Bara-Hack graveyard.

It was hear that the group had their most unnerving encounters. Eno wrote that for more than seven minutes his group "watched a bearded face suspended in the air over the cemetery's western wall, while in an elm tree over the northern wall we clearly saw a baby-like figure reclining on a branch."

One member of the group claimed that his hat was pulled off and was tossed up into a tree here. In addition, another member, who was a middle-aged man that had come along as an advisor on cameras and equipment and quite definitely a skeptic, was physically restrained by an unseen force. He could move, he said, but not in the direction of the cemetery. He could not explain what had happened to him, other than to say that he felt as though he had been "possessed".

Finally, just as Eno's group was departing, they claimed to hear the sounds of a rumbling wagon and a teamster shouting commands to his animals. The sounds began at the cemetery and then moved away, fading off into the dense and mysterious forest.

THE COURTEOUS GHOST

One of the most historic sites in Saddle River, New Jersey is Ringwood Manor, a majestic mansion that was in 1807. For years there have been numerous stories told about the ghost who haunts this place, a mixed race man who was the descendant of runaway slaves. This restless spirit was named Jackson White in life and his ghost somehow ended up at Ringwood Manor in death. His distinctive footsteps have been heard roaming the house, especially in the upstairs hallway and in the corridors of the lower floors.

While Jackson White is certainly an enigmatic ghost, the most famous specter attached to the location is undoubtedly that of Robert Erskine, who built the first house on this property in 1762. Although he may not haunt the manor house, Erskine is never far from the site of his beloved home. His ghost is usually encountered at the Ringwood Manor Cemetery, which is accessible by a dirt road from the grounds of the estate. Here, Erskine has been seen for well over a century, always appearing near his tomb.

Robert Erskine was a General in the Continental Army and was invaluable to George Washington during the War for Independence. As a surveyor, he was able to provide accurate maps that enabled troop movement and the proper positioning of the American armies during the fighting. When the war was over, Erskine settled in his home in New Jersey and began a successful surveying business. He constructed the first house at Ringwood Manor and it became a showplace in the area. He lived there for the rest of his life and when he died, he was laid to rest in the small cemetery on the grounds. Apparently though, he does not rest in peace. Some say that Erskine had too many plans and too much activity in his life to settle into oblivion in the next world. For this reason, they say that he has returned and now interacts with those who visit his burial place.

The stories say that Erskine's ghost was released from the tomb when a brick fell out of the wall and was not replaced. He has been seen in this tiny graveyard ever since. Legends say that on the darkest nights, when the moon is new and the sky is black, Robert Erskine will appear on top of his cemetery vault, swinging a lantern in one hand. Some brave visitors to the graveyard even claim that Erskine will sometimes even escort them down the shadowy road to the old bridge that takes them out of the cemetery.

One night in the early 1970's, three young men visited the Ringwood Cemetery to see if the stories of the ghost were true. The young men had driven to the cemetery and entered through the gate, quickly finding Robert Erskine's grave. They sat around for awhile talking, never really expecting to see anything, and making jokes about the validity of the story. Just as they were getting ready to give up and leave, one of the boys noticed a hazy, blue light that had appeared above Erskine's burial vault. He pointed this out to the others and they fell into a stunned silence.

Finally, summoning up their courage, they walked around the crypt and looked carefully at every corner of it, thinking that perhaps someone had rigged the light to appear. However, there was no wire or artificial light to be found.... the blue glow still remained! That was enough to convince them that they should leave.

As they hurried toward their car, one of the young men looked back and saw that the light had left the crypt and was now moving after them. In a state of panic, they reached the car and fumbling with the keys, piled inside of it. Suddenly, the blue light was now directly in front of the car, hovering and thrumming with an electric glow. The driver quickly pulled away and drove off, but the light remained right next to them, slowing down and speeding up as they did. When they reached the main road though, the light vanished, as if it had never existed at all.

Although they were frightened, the boys really had little to be afraid of. It wasn't some malevolent spirit they had seen but simply, as the legends state, the courteous spirit of Robert Erskine escorting them out of the dark cemetery!

GRAVEYARD GHOSTS OF WASHINGTON

Our nation's capital is undoubtedly one of the most haunted cities in America. The ghosts of Washington are among some of the most famous in the annals of the supernatural and are made up of names that have shaped the country's history. Even the cemeteries and burial grounds of Washington have spellbinding stories to tell.

One of the most spirit-infested houses in the city is that of the Kalorama. There was a time many years ago when a large amount of Northwest Washington was occupied by the Kalorama estate, which was owned by Joel Barlow. The mansion was constructed in 1807 and stood on what is now the 2300 block of S Street, Northwest.

During the Civil War, Kalorama became a hospital for wounded soldiers. There were hundreds of them who were treated and cared for in the mansion and on the grounds of the estate. On Christmas Eve of 1865, the soldiers at the Kalorama Hospital decided to throw a party. Unfortunately, a defective stovepipe caused a fire to break out, which swept through the building. The flames spread through the entire east wing of the house before it was brought under control. The building was badly damaged but most of it was saved.

Soon, however, stories started to be told about the ruins of the east wing of the estate. It was said that screams and moans could be heard there, coming from the darkness. Some of the visitors to the hospital ruins told of hearing sounds and voices from the 'house's past' and of seeing strange lights appearing among the rubble of the damaged wing. The reports became more prominent as the years passed and a newspaper account in 1905 reported that 'the few people who lived in the vicinity were seized with cold tremors when they heard the howls and screeches that came from within the walls'. Occasionally, visitors would report cold spots in the house and unexplained odors that seemed to be the smells of blood, morphine, sweat and gunpowder.

Eventually, the growing population of Washington took over the Kalorama estate and what was left of the house was replaced with a newer home in the early 1900's. There are those who still say that even though the estate has vanished, the cold spots and the sickly smells still remain. Some believe that a few former patients of the Kalorama hospital are still lingering behind.

Although these tales are undoubtedly the most famous stories of the old estate, there is a legend of a haunted grave that was located here too. In the early 1800's, Kalorama was the home of General John Bomford, a close friend of Commodore Stephen Decatur and his wife, Susan. When Decatur was killed in a duel in 1820, Susan Decatur became a guest on the Kalorama estate for quite some time. Bomford even allowed Decatur's body to be buried in a tomb on the estate.

There is a legend about Decatur, besides the one that has his apparition haunting his former home, which says his ghost was unhappy at Kalorama and that blood from his wound would sometimes appear on the outside of the tomb. Some say that this is why Susan Decatur finally had the body removed to Philadelphia, where his parents were buried. They say this removal finally stopped the bloody stains from appearing on the stone walls of the crypt.

Located east of the U.S. Capitol building and along the banks of the Anacostia River is Congressional Cemetery, the final resting place of not only some of our nation's leaders but a number of historical figures of the past. The cemetery was started in the early 1800's when Congress purchased hundreds of lots at the Washington Parish Burial Ground of the Christ Episcopal Church. Back then, it was nearly impossible for bodies to be shipped back home, so any congressmen who died In Washington would be buried here. Special markers were even designed so that the graves would be uniform in appearance.

Later on, as it became possible for cadavers to be transported, many of those buried in Congressional Cemetery were claimed by their families and the remains were relocated home. The distinctive markers then became "cenotaphs", grave monuments erected in honor of someone whose body lies elsewhere. This has become the case with such men as

Presidents William Henry Harrison, John Quincy Adams and Zachary Taylor, among others.

However, many notables are still buried here and some, like John Phillip Sousa, allegedly do not rest in peace. Sousa was born in Washington in 1854 and music was always his life. By the age of thirteen, he had been apprenticed to the Marine Band, the official band of the President of the United States. Thirteen years later, he was appointed the leader of the prestigious band and it was during this time period that many of his most famous marches were composed. Among them were *Semper Fidelis* and of course, *The Stars and Stripes Forever*. Sousa later resigned and formed his own band.

The great musician was always a perfectionist and established a new level of professionalism for marching and concert bands. He was also a musical inventor, devising a tuba-like instrument that he called the "Sousaphone". He designed it from a large bass tuba with a circular coiling and an upright bell. He gave a "big bold brassy" sound to the marches that a traditional tuba could not match.

Sousa's tomb is located in the southwest corner of Congressional Cemetery and it overlooks a bridge that bears his name over the Anacostia River. Legends say that over the years, people have heard the sounds of a deep bass horn being played on foggy nights. The music comes from the cemetery and from the vicinity of Sousa's tomb. The stories say that it is the sound of John Phillip Sousa still trying to perfect the tones of the "Sousaphone".

Another reportedly restless spirit of this cemetery is that of the famed photographer Mathew Brady. He was at the height of his career when the Civil War began, with fashionable galleries and studios in New York and Washington. His reputation was so great that he was known world-wide and would, throughout his career, preserve the images of eighteen U.S. Presidents. When rumors reached Brady in 1861 that a battle was going to take place just south of Washington, he hastily equipped a wagon with equipment and supplies and, like many other curious residents of the city, set out for Manassas.

Mathew Brady and a group of his Photographers

During the war, Brady invested his own money in documenting the devastation following the battles. He financed twenty-two photographic teams in every theater of the war, a move that brought him not success, but financial disaster. By 1865, Brady had spent his entire fortune and was in debt for supplies that had long since been used. The views of the war were not good sellers amongst the general public. To make matters worse, the War Department, although it made use of the photographs, balked at paying for them and Congress failed to see that Brady was reimbursed for any of them.

By the end of the war, Brady was exhausted, depressed and disillusioned. His wife, Julia, was in poor health, his business was in ruins and his life in shambles. Now, younger photographers competed for business and misfortune seemed to plague Brady at every turn. Julia finally passed away in 1887 and while Brady mourned, he continued to work in his Washington gallery, hoping that his views of the war might someday gain wider acceptance.

In the summer of 1885, Brady began to talk of a New York exhibit that would feature his Civil War photographs. He believed it would be his long-awaited triumph and would restore his faltering reputation. Over the following winter, he moved to New York and began extensive preparations for the show. Tragically, Brady died of a kidney ailment in January 1896, never realizing the fame that would someday come. He died alone, in poverty, in the small room of a New York boarding house.

As if his lonely death were not enough, Brady would suffer another indignity. When his body was returned to Washington, he was not buried in the National Cemetery at Arlington where so many of the statesmen and soldiers whose portraits he had preserved had been laid to rest. Instead, he was buried in Congressional Cemetery, next to the very men who had fought to keep him from being reimbursed for his expenses during the war.

In the years after his death, legend had it that a frail, bearded man, dressed in a wrinkled overcoat and slouch hat, was seen wandering the cemetery. He walked about and peered at the inscriptions on the cenotaphs, reading the names of those whose photographs he took years before. These men were immortalized by a tragic figure who, in death, would become known as one of the greatest figures of the Civil War. They say that Mathew Brady's ghost walked for many years, never content in the fact that his legacy was never realized during his lifetime.... And some say that he still walks today.

THE MYSTERY OF EDGAR ALLAN POE & THE HAUNTED CATACOMBS

Located in Baltimore is one of the most compelling cemeteries on the east coast, although many people are unaware that a portion of it even exists. It is called the Old Western Burial Ground and it holds the remains of people like Edgar Allan Poe, the son of Francis Scott Key, the grandfather of President James Buchanan, five former mayors of Baltimore and fifteen generals from the Revolutionary War and the War of 1812.

Not all of the cemetery is easy to find, for the Westminster Presbyterian Church (now Westminster Hall), was built over a large portion of the cemetery. These graves and tombs date back to a century before the church was built. Much of the cemetery, where

Poe is buried, is still accessible above ground in the churchyard but a large portion of the graveyard can only be reached by way of the catacombs underneath the building. It is here where the ghosts of this eerie graveyard are said to walk. Strangely though, these restless spirits are not the most enduring mystery of the Western Burial Ground.

This famous and unsolved mystery involves a man who has been seen in the graveyard for more than fifty years. Whoever this strange figure may be, he is always described in the same way. Dressed completely in black, including a black fedora and a black scarf to hide his face, he carries a walking stick and strolls into the cemetery every year on January 19, the birth date of Edgar Allan Poe. On every occasion, he has left behind a bottle of cognac and three red roses on the gravesite of the late author. After placing these items with care, he then stands, tips his hat and walks away. The offerings always remain on the grave, although one year, they were accompanied by a note, bearing no signature, which read: "Edgar, I haven't forgotten you."

There have been many stories that claim the ghost of Edgar Allan Poe haunts his gravesite but the man in black seems to be quite tangible, although who he is remains a riddle. In addition, scholars and curiosity-seekers remain puzzled by the odd ritual he carries out and the significance of the items he leaves behind too. The roses and cognac have been brought to the cemetery every January since 1949 and yet no clue has been offered as to the origin or true meaning of the offerings.

The identity of the man has been an intriguing mystery for years. Many people, including Jeff Jerome, the curator of the nearby Edgar Allan Poe house, believe that there may be more than one person leaving the tributes. Jerome himself has seen a white-haired man while other observers have reported a man with black hair. Possibly, the second person may be the son of the man who originated the ritual. Regardless, Jerome has been quoted as saying that if he has his way, the man's identity will never be known. This is something that most Baltimore residents agree with. Jerome has received numerous telephone calls from people requesting that no attempt ever be made to approach the man.

For some time, rumors persisted that Jerome was the mysterious man in black, so in 1983, he invited 70 people to gather at the graveyard at midnight on January 19. They had a celebration in honor of the author's birthday with a glass of amontillado, a Spanish sherry featured in one of Poe's horror tales, and readings from the author's works. At about an hour past midnight, the celebrants were startled to see a man run through the cemetery in a black frock coat. He was fair-haired and carrying a walking stick and quickly disappeared around the cemetery's east wall. The roses and cognac were found on Poe's grave as usual.

Not in an effort to solve the mystery, but merely to enhance it, Jerome allowed a photographer to try and capture the elusive man on film. The photographer was backed by LIFE Magazine and was equipped with rented infrared night-vision photo equipment. A radio signal triggered the camera so that the photographer could remain out of sight. The picture appeared in the July 1990 issue of LIFE and showed the back of a heavyset man kneeling at Poe's grave. His face cannot really be seen and as it was shadowed by his black hat. No one else has ever been able to photograph the mysterious man again.

Legend has it that the ghost of Edgar Allan Poe has been seen near his grave and in the catacombs of the church. The author died mysteriously in Baltimore and thus came to be buried there. He had lived in the city years before, but had only been passing through when he perished under mysterious circumstances. At the time of his death, Poe had been on his way to New York to meet his beloved mother-in-law. He was bringing her back to Richmond, Virginia, where the author was to marry his childhood sweetheart. His first wife had perished from tuberculosis years before.

The trip came to a tragic conclusion when, four days after reaching Baltimore, Poe was found barely conscious and lying in a gutter on East Lombard Street. He was rushed to a hospital but he died a short time later.

The entire time in the hospital was spent with Poe crying and trembling and he once screamed the name 'Reynolds'... although who this could have been also remains a mystery. He died on October 7, 1849.

Some said Poe's death was caused by alcohol, others say that he was in a psychotic state and even rabies has been blamed. Other writers believe that he may have been drugged and murdered as the clothes that he wore were not his own and the walking stick he carried belonged to another man. There have been literally dozens of theories posed as to what caused Poe's death but no one will ever know for sure. Perhaps the fact that his death remains unexplained is the reason why Poe's ghost remains in the Old Western Burial Ground.

And it's not the only place associated with Poe that claims to have a ghost. For Poe's death to have come in Baltimore is strangely ironic as it was here in 1829 that he struggled to begin his writing career. He lived in a house on North Amity Street with his aunt and his cousin, Virginia Clemm, a young girl he married six years later. Poe's years in Baltimore were a time of poverty and debt and marked him for life. He lived in an attic room that is accessible by a narrow, winding staircase and a doorway so small that an average-sized adult is forced to crawl through it. Although visitors to the house have reported unexplained cold spots in the place, Poe's ghost is not believed to haunt it. However, there have been spectral sightings of a heavyset woman with gray hair and period clothing of the early 1800's.

The house was vacant between 1922 and 1949, when it became a historical site and museum. Since the 1960's, the sounds of hushed voices have been heard and visitors have reported being touched by invisible hands and have seen doors and windows open by themselves.

Without a doubt, while the mystery concerning Edgar Allan Poe is the most famous aspect of the Western Burial Ground, it is not the only one. The catacomb beneath the church holds secrets of its own. While restored and kept in good condition today, visitors to this place will still get an eerie chill as they walk about this gothic chamber of horrors. Graves and crypts hold the bodies of those long since deceased and yet stories of the not so distant past tell of unexplained disinterment and a strange fascination that drew a number of people to commit suicide here in the years between 1890 and 1920.

I was lucky enough to be able to visit this place a few years ago and found it to be both fascinating and spooky. While I had no supernatural encounters while roaming the catacombs and tunnels, others have not been so lucky. There are a number of stories told of visitors who have come here and who have felt icy spots that have no explanation, have felt the soft caress of unseen hands and have heard the startling whispers of voices that should not exist.

Guided tours of the subterranean cemetery are available on Sunday afternoons, but organized searches for ghosts here have been few. One outing, in August 1976, brought ten ghost hunters to the graveyard in search of the ghost of a little girl who has been reported here over the years. Robert Thompson, the leader of the group and at that time, behind a drive to restore the cemetery, stated that while the ghost hunters didn't spot the small spirit, the investigation did not come up empty. "We didn't see anything," he recalled in an interview, "but we sure heard things.... like footsteps. It scared the heck out of me is what it did".

· CHAPTER FIVE ·
PLACES OF REST
A COLLECTION OF HAUNTED
GRAVEYARDS ACROSS THE AMERICAN
SOUTH

The lore of the American South is filled with stories of ghosts, hauntings and graveyard specters. One of the things that has always intrigued me about this region is the fact that ghosts are a part of the accepted culture in the south. There does not seem to be a plantation house anywhere in the southern states that does not boast a ghost or two. In addition, restaurants, inns and cemeteries also appear to be infested with ghosts. In some southern cities, businesses even compete to see which place is the most haunted!

Graveyards in the South are also well known for their hauntings. This may be because of the culture and methods of burial here. In many locations, the ground is too wet for burial and the use of crypts and tombs are common. These crumbling structures now conjure up spirits, not only from the imagination, but from history as well. These places of rest also have some other peculiarities when it comes to their hauntings, as the reader will soon see. It is interesting to note how many of them seem to stem from either a curse or a lost love affair. It appears that the romance of the Old South is still very prevalent today in her culture and her hauntings alike!

PHANTOMS OF AQUIA CHURCHYARD

Fredericksburg, Virginia is said to be one of the most historic cities in America and, according to many, one of the most haunted as well. One could spend weeks tracking down ghost stories and strange reports in Fredericksburg, and you would soon find that the place is a treasure trove for history buffs and supernatural enthusiasts alike. Nearly every building in town claims at least one ghost and many of them are said to have several.

It is believed that most of them are spirits from the city's past, as little has changed here in years, remaining virtually the same as it was in colonial times. With that in mind, is it really a surprise that local folks often encounter the ghosts of those long dead?

One Fredericksburg haunting, the Aquia Church and adjoining graveyard, is located about twenty miles north of the city. It is high on a wooded hill that overlooks the town of Stafford and U.S. Highway 1. Since the middle 1700's, this beautiful chapel has withstood the changing force of history from the American Revolution and the War of 1812 to the Civil War. Inside, it has one of the only known triple-deck pulpits and rustic pews that have seen generations of families. These same families may have been the first to realize that there was something strange going on in the church. It soon became a tradition that no one went into the building after dark... and none dared set foot into the adjacent churchyard.

Construction was started on the church in 1751, but in 1754, it was severely damaged in a fire, just three days before it was to be completed. It took another three years for it to be finished. The hauntings here had their beginnings during the American Revolution. For decades, visitors have reported the sound of feet running up and down stairs, heavy noises of a fierce struggle and even the apparition of a terrified young woman standing at a window.

These frightening events reportedly stem from a night in late 1770's when a woman passing nearby was set upon by thieves. She managed to escape into the darkness and came upon the church. She tried to seek shelter but found that it was empty. The church was not used during the war and in fact, its precious silver, including an old dish, chalice, cup and plates were all buried for safekeeping. After her desperate pounding on the door failed to rouse anyone, she managed to slip the lock and get inside... but it was too late. The highwaymen found her hiding place and followed her into the building. Here, she was brutally attacked and killed. They dragged her body to the belfry and left her there, not knowing that it would remain hidden for years. When the skeletal remains were finally discovered, it was said that the woman's golden hair remained intact. Until the early 1900's, when a new cement floor was laid, the bloodstains where she had been slain were clearly visible.

The repeated events of that dark night are the most famous manifestations in the church but they are not the only odd things that happen here. There is another story about a prominent socialite who spent her summers in Stafford County in the 1920's and who became interested in the Aquia chapel because of the ghostly tales that she heard in the area. She decided to go and spend the night in the place, but found that she couldn't get any of the men from the vicinity to go into the chapel with her after dark. She refused to give up her plans and recruited two scientists from Washington who had a shared interest in the supernatural. After darkness fell, they entered the Aquia Church with the socialite leading the way. She had no more than walked in the door though when an unseen hand slapped her sharply across the face! The two men ran inside and searched the place but found no one there. They were unable to provide a logical explanation for what had happened. The mark remained on the woman's face for several days afterward. Could it have been the ghost of the murdered woman?

A much less angry spirit appears in a tale that was told about the church during the Civil War. The story was first told by William Fitzhugh, a Confederate soldier who stopped for rest at the church during a scouting mission. He credited the ghost here for saving the lives of he and another scout in 1863. The two young men had come to the church in search of a place to sleep. They had heard about the chapel being haunted but were too tired to care. At some point during the night, the two men were roused by what Fitzhugh described as "unmistakable footsteps at the rear of the church on some stone flagging". Then they heard someone sharply whistle the tune "The Campbells are Coming". The frightened men jumped up and struck a light, but they were in the place alone. One of them went to the door and looked out and saw a troop of Federal soldiers coming down the road. The soldiers were heading right for the church! They jumped out a window at the back of the chapel and escaped. Fitzhugh never forgot the ghost that saved his life!

Was this the same spirit who also slapped the socialite across the face? And if so, is she also the apparition that has been seen in the old churchyard? According to a former caretaker named Robert Frazier, ghosts are often seen here, flitting among the tombstones and appearing like white, blurry shapes. Frazier and his son recalled numerous sightings over the years in a past interview. Each of the sightings occurred at night and when the two Fraziers went over to see what the figures were, they vanished.

"Everybody says there are ghosts up here," he said. "Me and my son seen 'em! They're here!"

LEGENDS OF MEMORY HILL

Located in the very haunted town of Milledgeville, Georgia is Memory Hill

Cemetery, a small, twenty-acre piece of land that was set aside as a graveyard back in 1803. This historic site holds the remains of a number of people associated with Georgia history, including famed southern author Flannery O'Connor.

And, if the stories are true, it holds a few ghosts as well.

One unusual resident of the cemetery is William Fish, who once lived in the town of Hardwick, just outside of Milledgeville. In 1872, Fish's wife and daughter contracted typhoid and both of them died slow and agonizing deaths. In despair, Fish constructed a brick mausoleum in which they were interred. For the next several months, he continued to mourn, unable to overcome his depression. Not long after the mausoleum was finally completed, he placed his old rocking chair inside of it, closed the iron door, sat down in the chair and shot himself with a revolver. He was soon placed next to his wife and child and the three of them will be together for eternity. Although Mr. Fish has still been unable to rest. Legends of the cemetery say that if a visitor knocks on the iron door of this small crypt, sometimes an answering knock will be heard in reply!

Perhaps the most famous grave in this cemetery belongs to a "witch". The occupant, Dixie Haygood, was born in Milledgeville in 1861 and according to the stories, possessed amazing supernatural powers as a psychic medium. It was said that she could cause a piano to move about a room and chairs to rise up into the air. While in a trace, she could find lost objects for members of the audiences who came to seen her and she had an ability that could prevent five men from lifting her small body off the floor. On one occasion, Dixie was said to have lifted a table holding several men and she was able to command the chairs around it to leave the room. Her audience watched in amazement as one by one, the chairs slid off the stage. Some of the spectators even checked to make sure there was nothing physical propelling them. Dixie would often simply place her hands on the back of a chair and without holding onto it, make it rise from the floor. A dozen men were unable to break her hold on the object without twisting or jerking it away from her.

During her career, Dixie allegedly performed for the tsar of Russia, Queen Victoria of England, governors of Georgia and even United States presidents. She became a well-known southern medium but one day, it all came to an end. Stories say that Dixie eventually went crazy and records show that she was a patient at the Central State Hospital for the Mentally Insane when she died. She was then laid to rest next to her husband in Memory Hill Cemetery.

Since that time, her grave has become a popular spot for ghost hunters and curiosity-seekers because the legends say that her spirit still lingers nearby. Before her death, Dixie was said to have placed a curse on many of the local families, including the Yates family, whose burial plot is located next to hers. For the past century or so, a sinkhole has appeared in the Yates' plot every year just before Christmas. The hole is so bad that the gravestone of Mr. Yates and one of his daughters sinks out of sight. Many blame this odd phenomenon on the winter rains and in the past, city crews have filled the hole with cement, gravel and stones. No matter what they do, the hole always comes back.

Could it be, as legends say, the wrath of Dixie Haygood, still be felt from beyond the grave?

THE GRAVEYARD LIGHT

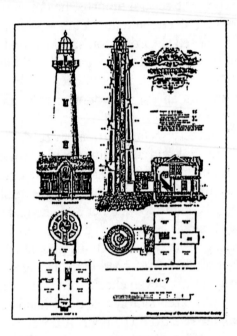

The St. Simons Island Lighthouse

There is no question that the state of Georgia is a very haunted place. Ghost stories here abound, both in the small towns and in the large cities. One haven for ghostlore is a line of islands that stretch along the southeastern shore of the state. These "Golden Isles" are filled with both history and hauntings but none of them can claim as many ghostly tales as St. Simons Island can.

There are a number of famous stories on the island that have been passed along for generations. There is the story of Mary the Wanderer, a grieving woman who roams the deserted roadways in search of her drowned lover. There are the ghosts of the Africans who were brought to America as slaves but chose to take their own lives rather than give up their freedom. Still wearing their chains, they walked off into Dunbar Creek and some say their chanting can still be heard along the water today.

Another haunted spot is the St. Simons Lighthouse and legends here say that the ghost of a former lightkeeper still walks up and down the metal staircase inside of the structure. His spectral footsteps have been heard here for many years. A past owner of the Kelvyn Grove Plantation also keeps a ghostly watch over his old property. His ghost is said to wander the grounds in search of the man who killed him.

But of all of these tales, there is no other account as famous as that of the light that appears in the Christ Church Cemetery. Today, there are few island residents who can remember the full name of the woman in the story. In spite of this, nearly all of them can tell you the legend of the woman whose fear of the dark prompted her husband to place a lighted candle on her grave every night.

According to the story, Emma, on whose grave the candle glows, was always afraid of the dark. Growing up, it had been her greatest childhood fear. Her father, who loved his daughter and indulged her every desire, took her fear lightly at first. He assured her that there was nothing to be afraid of but even a few moments alone in the darkness would have the little girl screaming in terror. At her insistence, a servant placed a lighted candle by her bedside every night. Emma's father went along with this for quite some time, always believing, as she grew older, that she would overcome her phobia. Finally, his patience at an end, he ordered her to be put to bed one night without the candle.

The servant reluctantly did as she was told. She put out the lamp and closed the door and then hurried from the house so that she would not have to hear Emma's screams. The child wailed and cried for hours but her father forbade his wife, or any other member of the household, to go and comfort her. At last, he could stand it no more and went to Emma himself. He was determined to harshly stop her crying, but when he found the girl in hysterical tears, he embraced her instead. Emma collapsed into his arms and his anger vanished. He left a candle burning next to her bed and quietly left the room. From that time on, a lamp was always left next to Emma's bed with a glowing candlestick inside.

Even as Emma grew older, her fear remained. She began to develop an anxiety about running out of candles in the house and she started hoarding the discarded stubs. She hid them away in her bureau until her mother found them and was going to throw them away. Emma was so upset that her mother allowed her to keep them in a box in the corner of the pantry instead.

Except for her incredible fear of the dark, Emma was a normal, happy and very attractive young woman. She had many friends and was invited to all of the social occasions on the island. Although her friends sometimes teased her about being afraid of the dark, they all accepted it as a rather romantic notion, especially with a lone candle burning in her window at night as if signaling some illicit lover.

One evening at a party, Emma met a young man named Phillip. He had recently moved to Brunswick, Georgia from the Carolinas to work in a cotton brokerage firm. He and Emma fell in love and not long after, they were married at Christ Church. Phillip soon learned to live with Emma's intense fear of the dark and never complained about the candle that was left burning beside their bed each night. They lived a very happy life and after a few months, moved from Brunswick to Frederica on St. Simons Island. Phillip went to work managing his father-in-law's plantation and his shipping company.

Time passed and one day Emma was busy making candles when she accidentally spilled hot wax on her arm. She was badly burned and for some reason, the wound did not heal properly. An infection set in and despite care from the local doctor, she came down with blood poisoning. In less than a week, Emma died.

Phillip was heartbroken. Only the kindness and caring of Emma's family got him through the funeral. That afternoon, he returned home and he sat in a chair on the porch and watched as the sun slipped from the sky. Twilight shadows were creeping across the lawn when Phillip went into the house and took a candle from a box that Emma had made. He walked down the road to the cemetery at Christ Church and went to his wife's grave. He pushed the candle into the soft dirt and lit the wick. The light flared up and Phillip managed to smile. "You'll always have a light," he whispered. "... always."

Every night, for as long as Phillip lived, he made a solitary journey to the graveyard and he placed a candle on Emma's grave. When the weather was rainy or windy, he placed it inside of a glass lamp, but he never failed to leave a light for her. His friends and neighbors sadly remarked on his faithfulness and they always explained the significance of the candle to strangers who asked about it.

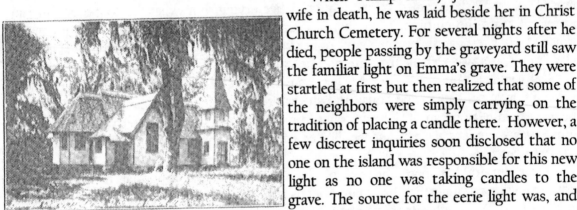

When Phillip finally joined his beloved wife in death, he was laid beside her in Christ Church Cemetery. For several nights after he died, people passing by the graveyard still saw the familiar light on Emma's grave. They were startled at first but then realized that some of the neighbors were simply carrying on the tradition of placing a candle there. However, a few discreet inquiries soon disclosed that no one on the island was responsible for this new light as no one was taking candles to the grave. The source for the eerie light was, and remains today, a mystery.

Christ Church on St. Simons Island

Since Phillip's death, literally hundreds of people on St. Simons Island have seen a glowing light that looks just like a candle flame appearing near an old grave in Christ Church Cemetery. A brick wall that has been built now hides the graves from those who pass on the road. However, those who walk back into the graveyard at night and stand beneath the Spanish moss that hangs from the ancient oaks still tell of occasionally seeing a strange, flickering light among the tombstones.

Emma still has her light... and she always will.

LOST SOULS OF OAKDALE CEMETERY

The shaded and tranquil surroundings of Oakdale Cemetery in Wilmington, North Carolina provide a peaceful illusion for the casual observer. Here, the moss-covered monuments and elaborate funeral art make the graveyard appear to be a calm and restful place. Below the surface though, restless spirits still walk here. For decades, ghost stories have been told about Oakdale Cemetery and there is much reason to believe that the dead here do not rest in peace.

The cemetery itself had dark beginnings. In the early and middle 1800's, the city of Wilmington was devastated by a number of epidemics. Yellow fever, typhoid and diphtheria all took a great toll on the population and with so much death, it soon became apparent that the local churchyards would not be able to hold the bodies of the dead. In 1852, a committee was appointed to locate a site for a new cemetery. Within two years, a parcel was chosen and sixty-five acres of land along Burnt Mill Creek were purchased for the new burial ground.

Dr. Armand J. deRosset, a prominent local physician, was chosen to serve as the first president of the cemetery board. Ironically, the first burial carried out in the new Oakdale Cemetery would be that of Dr. deRosset's own daughter, who was only six years old. The doctor was devastated by the loss and after her death, he gave up his medical practice. He was too shaken by the fact that his years of training could not save the life of his child.

Dr. deRosset would not be the only grief-stricken father to bury his child in Oakdale Cemetery and his little Annie would not be the only ghost who legends say still wanders this place. Another father was Captain Silas Martin, who buried his own daughter here a few years later.

Captain Martin was a wealthy Wilmington merchant and ship captain. In 1857, he set sail on a voyage to the Caribbean and took with him his daughter, Nancy, and his son, John. Soon after their departure, Nancy became ill and unfortunately, with no ship's doctor, there was little that could be done for her. Soon, her condition began to get worse and Captain Martin ordered the ship to the port of Cardenas, Cuba. By the time they arrived though, it was too late and Nancy had died. Captain Martin was a broken man. He could not bear to have his daughter buried on foreign soil and so far from home, nor did he want to have her buried at sea. He wanted to take his daughter home with him, but his business commitments would keep him at sea for some time to come. So, he had her placed inside of a cask of rum and then had the barrel sealed shut. In this way, Nancy's body would remain preserved until they could return to Wilmington.

Captain Martin's decision to continue his voyage turned out to be a tragic one. Several months after Nancy's death, in a terrific storm, the captain's son, John, was washed overboard and was lost. His body was never recovered. After this, the ship turned back and returned home, where Captain Martin had to break the horrible news to his wife that both of their children had died.

The distraught parents decided not to place Nancy's body in a coffin and they had her buried in the cask of liquor instead. The marker over her grave bears only the inscription "Nance", but her name and dates of birth and death appear on the family stone, just next to her brother's name, which is followed by the words "Lost at Sea".

Nancy's ghost has long been rumored to haunt this graveyard and it is not uncommon for visitors to report a forlorn young woman standing near her gravesite, the lonely echo of a life cut short.

The Civil War also left its mark on Oakdale Cemetery. There are the graves of nearly four hundred unknown Confederate soldiers here and legends say that some of these men still roam the burial ground today. In addition, Oakdale marks the final resting place of Rose O'Neal Greenhow, a spy for the Confederacy who was known in her day as "Rebel Rose". The stories say that may walk here as well.

During the height of the war, Rose was returning from England aboard a ship called the *Condor*. She was bringing with her over $2,000 in gold that she had earned from the publication of a book about her experiences as a spy. The gold was going to be added to the struggling coffers of the Confederacy in order to aid the war effort. As the ship neared the Carolina coasts, it ran into the Union blockade of the southern coastline and specifically the guns of the *U.S.S. Niphon*. In the pursuit that followed, the *Condor* ran aground and fearful of being captured by the Federal forces, Rose exited the ship in a small dinghy. The Captain begged her to stay on board, as the sea was rough and dangerous, but she insisted on trying to escape. Almost as soon as the small boat was lowered into the water, a wave crashed over it and the boat overturned. All of those aboard it were lost.

Rose Greenhow's body washed ashore a few days later and she was brought to Wilmington for burial. In tribute to her loyalty, her body was wrapped in a Confederate flag and she was buried with full military honors. Author Brooks Newton Preik writes that hundreds of people attended her funeral.

There have been many conflicting accounts about just what happened to the gold that Rose was carrying with her. Some claim that it was sewn into her clothing and others believe that it was placed in a purse and carried around her neck with a chain. All of them feel that it must have been responsible for her drowning though, although what became of it after her body was found remains a mystery. Perhaps this unsolved riddle is the reason that her ghost is still said to walk?

Local residents of the past are not the only spirits to haunt Oakdale Cemetery, for there are reports of a spectral dog as well. Many believe this ghost is that of old "Boss", who still guards the grave of his master, a riverboat captain named William A. Ellerbrook. The captain lost his life back in 1880 while fighting a fire in downtown Wilmington. According to those present, Ellerbrook's dog, Boss, stood back on the edge of the fire and then rushed fearlessly into the blaze when his master got into trouble. Those outside anxiously watched as the animal plunged into the fire and smoke but neither Ellerbrook nor Boss came back out again.

When their bodies were discovered, Captain Ellerbrook was lying face down, trapped beneath a smoldering timber. Nearby was Boss, who had been overcome by smoke while trying to pull the captain to safety. A torn piece of Ellerbrook's coat was still clamped in his jaws. It seemed appropriate to friends that the two long-time companions be laid to rest in the same coffin and so they were. On Captain Ellerbrook's monument is the sculpted image of a dog and the inscription, "Faithful Unto Death".

KENTUCKY'S GRAVEYARD GHOSTS

Kentucky is a state that is filled with legends and ghostlore and when it comes to graveyards, these locations are no strangers to spirits and hauntings. Many of the stories of the state are oral lore and legends that have been collected about cemeteries and haunted houses. Others have been recorded for many years and have long been a part of Kentucky's history.

One eerie tale was told by a man named Ronnie Bryant and was recorded by folklorist William Lynwood Montell. This family story occurred near a place called Little Sulphur Creek, not far from Tompkinsville. It recalls a man who was plowing his corn field one day, just a short distance from an old cemetery, one of the oldest in the county. As the story goes, he happened to look up toward the cemetery and saw a lady and a young girl standing among the tombstones. The woman was quite beautiful and both she and the girl wore dresses the color of roses. Even though this story took place around 1910, the clothing worn by the two of them was old-fashioned. The rose dresses were of a "hooped" design, commonly worn in the era of the Civil War.

The woman and the girl had appeared so suddenly in the graveyard that the man in the cornfield was startled. Always known as a level-headed man though, he began to plow closer to the cemetery, curious about the two figures he saw there. He watched them as they stood near the gravestones, seeming to sway to and fro and they walked about. They seemed to be looking for the graves of their departed loved ones, the man thought. He drove his mules a little closer and then closer yet. Finally, he mustered his courage and laid his plow aside, determined to walk up to the woman and her daughter. Instead, as he got closer, he realized there was no one woman and girl there at all, but a large rose bush that had become tangled in a smaller one as they gently blew in the wind.

This story continues to live on today, even after nearly a century. People who still live in the vicinity of Little Sulphur Creek claim that even though the cemetery rose bush has long since died and has been cut down, the "Rose Lady" can still be seen at certain times of the year.

Another Kentucky graveyard story comes from a cemetery that rests on a hillside in Pulaski County. According to old-timers in the area, this burial ground holds the grave of a witch. Visitors here will find the grave to be isolated from the rest of the stones here and an iron fence with a gate surrounds it. The old, weather-beaten tombstone bears the name of Katherine Tyler. She died, it reads, in 1899 at the age of only nineteen.

A large oak tree has grown up alongside the fence, its roots twisting and gnarling toward Katherine's gravestone. The tree's branches also reach out for the grave of another, located a few yards away from the enclosure. This gravesite belongs to John Tyler, Katherine's father, and the man who abandoned her not long after the death of her mother.

Katherine gained her reputation as a "witch" when she was about twelve years old. She began making predictions about her neighbors, which came eerily true, and seemed to possess the power to read minds. She always seemed to know when a farm animal was going to get sick or die, when crops would fail, what neighbor was going to have an accident and other things that no ordinary child would know. Not surprisingly, soon after Katherine began to exhibit her strange gifts, people began to avoid the Tyler farm and talk among some of the locals turned threatening. Fearful, John Tyler abandoned his daughter and his farm and left the area. He would not return until after her death.

Katherine began to spend more and more time alone. She walked and wandered in the woods for hours and even days at a time. The stories said that the animals were not afraid of her and that she became a part of the forest herself. Gradually, as time passed, her hair grew long and her eyes wild and feral. The Tyler farm slowly crumbled and so did Katherine's mind. It was said that neglect and loneliness caused her to go insane.

As her sanity slipped away, strange things began to happen in the neighborhood. Cows refused to give milk, crops failed, farm animals died for no reason, large snakes, of an unknown species, were seen and huge birds began to appear in the area. After a few years of these unnatural occurrences, the superstitious locals decided that Katherine was a witch. They were determined to either drive her out of the area, or kill her. They would do anything to save their farms and homes.

A group of men gathered one night and they went out to the old Tyler farm. The house and the outbuildings had fallen into disrepair over the past several years and now lay huddled at the edge of an overgrown clearing. No lights burned in the windows of the house. They called out for Katherine, but she did not appear. Gathering their courage, they broke open the door and went inside. What they discovered makes this particular story even stranger....

They found Katherine inside of the house. She was dead and her body was lying on the bed. Strangely, the frightening wild woman was gone and had been replaced by an angelic-looking young woman who was dressed in beautiful, expensive clothing that no one had seen before. It was as if Katherine had, in her death, turned back the hands of time and the past seven years had been erased. No one ever learned what caused her death, or how the change to her appearance had taken place.

Because of their fear, the locals refused to have Katherine buried in the local graveyard. When John Tyler learned of his daughter's death, he returned to the area and buried her, with his own hands, a few yards outside of the graveyard. It was he who built the iron fence around the site but it was the locals who erected the pointed gravestone over her resting place. This type of stone is said to be the indication that a witch is buried there.

The stories go on to say that the oak tree over Katherine's grave began to grow a few months after her burial. They say that the long limb of the tree that reaches out toward the grave of John Tyler is a manifestation of the girl's love for the father who abandoned her. She still reaches out to him, they say, from beyond the grave.

In 1938, stories of a "killer ghost" began to be told in eastern Kentucky. Even though no one ever saw this malevolent apparition, it was said to have caused five very similar and unexplained deaths.

In June of that year, a man named Carl Pruitt came home from work one night and found his wife in bed with another man. After her lover escaped by jumping out of a window, Pruitt strangled his wife with a small piece of chain. Immediately after, perhaps having just realized the depth of his madness, he committed suicide. He was buried in a separate cemetery from his wife.

A few weeks after he was buried, visitors to the cemetery began to notice the pattern of a chain that was slowly forming on Pruitt's gravestone. The "chain" was caused by an unusual discoloration in the stone and slowly, it gained links until it formed the shape of a cross. At that point, it stopped growing. A number of local residents suggested that perhaps the supernaturally marked tombstone should be removed from the graveyard and destroyed, but officials scoffed and nothing was done about it.

A month or so after the chain stopped growing; a group of boys were riding their bicycles past the cemetery one afternoon. One of them, a boy named James Collins, decided to throw a few stones at Pruitt's "cursed" gravestone, probably just to prove that he wasn't afraid and had little use for spooky stories. Whatever the reason for his actions, the hurled rocks managed to chip several spots from the stone. As the young men started home, Collins' bicycle suddenly began to pick up speed, to the point that he could no longer control it. It veered off the road and collided with a tree. Then, in some unexplained way, the sprocket chain tore loose and managed to wrap itself about the boy's neck, strangling him. Rumors quickly spread about this remarkable occurrence, especially after an examination of the Pruitt tombstone revealed that no marks or chips marred the surface of it. The other boys knew what they had seen however and their breathless accounts only fueled speculation about a vengeful ghost.

James Collins' mother was especially heartbroken over her son's death. Less than a month after his accident, she went out to the cemetery and destroyed the Pruitt gravestone with a small hand axe. She pounded and hacked at the stone until it lay in dozens in pieces. The following day, she was hanging the family wash on the line. Ironically, the clothesline was made from small linked chain rather than the usual rope or wire. Somehow, she slipped and fell and her neck became entangled in the chain. She twisted and tried to get free, but it was no use and she strangled to death. The legends say that after she died, the Pruitt tombstone showed no signs of destruction!

Needless to say, news of this most recent incident spread. A short time later, a local farmer and three members of his family were driving a wagon past the cemetery. For some reason, the farmer announced that he had no fear of ghosts and fired several shots at the Pruitt stone with his revolver. Chunks flew from the marker and immediately, the horses pulling the wagon began to run. Their hooves pounded faster and faster, until the wagon was out of control. The family members all jumped to safety but the farmer hung on, frantically pulling on the reins. Just as the wagon veered around a curve in the road, the farmer was thrown from his seat and he tumbled forward. His neck snagged on one of the trace chains and the motion of the horses snapped his neck. Once again, Pruitt's stone showed no signs of the damage that had been done to it.

The local residents were now convinced of the fact that the grave marker was cursed. Things got so bad that the local congressman was contacted and two police officers were sent out to the cemetery to investigate the stories. When they arrived at the graveyard, one of the men began to laugh about the stories and made fun of the idea of so-called "ghosts and curses". Regardless, they took several photos of the stone and then left to go and talk with the witnesses to the events surrounding it. As they were leaving, the doubting officer happened to look into the car's rearview mirror. In it, he saw a bright light coming from the direction of the Pruitt tombstone. At first he assumed that it was just a reflection from the car's tail lights, but then it began to get closer to the car. Startled, he began to drive faster, but the light kept coming. He drove faster and faster, always watching his mirror. His partner pleaded with him to slow down, but it was no use. The light was still coming!

Just then, the car swerved off the road and crashed between two posts. It rolled over and over again several times. The officer on the passenger side was thrown clear of the wreck and was only slightly hurt. Shaken, he climbed to his feet and went to his partner's aid. He found that his friend was dead... but he had been killed before the car had wrecked. As the car had passed between the two posts, a chain that had been hanging between then had shattered the car's windshield and had wrapped around the driver's neck. The force was so great that it had nearly severed his head!

After this death, residents began to avoid the cemetery altogether. Only one man, Arthur Lewis, dared to go there. He was determined to prove that the stories of a "cursed" tombstone were nothing but superstitious nonsense. One evening, after telling his wife what he intended to do, he went to the graveyard with a hammer and chisel and began to methodically destroy the grave marker. The sounds of the hammer and the shattering stone could be heard by all who lived near the cemetery... and they also heard the bloodcurdling scream that filled the night too! Several men grabbed lanterns and went down to investigate. When they arrived, they found Lewis dead with the long chain that had been used to close the cemetery gate wrapped about his neck. Apparently, something had frightened him and he had started running, forgetting about the chain that barred the entrance gate. Oddly, even though ten or fifteen people had heard the sound of the man breaking Pruitt's gravestone, there were no marks of broken places on it.

After this last death, other bodies in the cemetery were removed and buried again in other locations. People gradually moved away and the small burial plot was forgotten. Since Pruitt had no family left to care for his grave, the site became overgrown and tangled with weeds. In 1958, it was destroyed for good by a strip-mining operation. The five strange deaths, all linked by chains, were never explained.

THE GIRL BY THE GRAVE

The small community of Mansdale, Mississippi is located about fifteen miles north of Jackson. In this small town is a gothic church, the Episcopal Chapel of the Cross, and beside it is a churchyard. It sits on a small knoll and is nearly hidden from the road by a grove of trees.

This shaded cemetery is the final resting place of a man named Henry Vick, a tragic figure in Mississippi history. The graveyard is also the place where Vick's lover, Helen Johnstone, came to grieve for him in the weeks and months following his death in May 1859. Some say that she grieves here for him still....

The story of Helen Johnstone and Henry Vick began during the holiday season of 1855. Helen and her mother, Margaret Johnstone, were spending Christmas with Helen's sister, Mrs. William Britton, at Ingleside, the home that John Johnstone had built as a wedding gift for his oldest daughter. The house had been Johnstone's first construction project, which was to have been followed by a manor house called Annandale, his own estate. The plans for the house had been delayed by his wife's insistence that they first build a chapel though and sadly, Johnstone died before the chapel could be completed. Mrs. Johnstone went ahead with the plans however and personally supervised the building of the church. When it was consecrated in 1852, her husband's body had been moved into the small churchyard behind it. Three years later, she also ordered the construction of her husband's Annandale and work had just begun before the holiday season.

One night, just before Christmas, the family was seated to dinner when a knock came on the front door. The servant who answered it returned to the dining room to inform Mr. Britton that a young man named Henry Vick wished to speak with him. Vick, spattered with mud, was there to ask for help in getting his carriage repaired. While servants tended to the carriage, Vick became a guest at Ingleside. He stayed for several days and while he was there, he and Helen fell deeply in love.

In fact, he had charmed the entire family and Helen's mother approved of their match. Vick came many times to the Johnstone home over the next three years. As Helen had only been sixteen when they met, her mother requested that they wait to be married. A date was eventually set for May 21, 1859 and the location would be the family's Chapel of the Cross. A reception would be held at Annandale.

A week before the wedding, Vick boarded a steamer in Vicksburg. He planned to travel to New Orleans to buy a suit for the ceremony. Soon after his arrival, he stopped in a billard room where he had a chance meeting with James Stith, a former friend that had caused him many problems in the past. A passing insult from Stith led the two men to get into a heated argument and an altercation. Vick, in the heat of the moment, challenged the other man to a duel. Stith quickly accepted.

Hours later, when his passions had cooled, Vick regretted his hasty actions and sent a friend to try and cancel the duel. Stith refused to back down however and the illegal affair was scheduled to take place in Alabama within days. They traveled to Mobile with their seconds and assembled one morning at a place called Holly's Garden. This was to be one of the last duels ever fought in the city and the weapons were Kentucky rifles, fired from thirty paces. The duel ended with Vick being shot in the head. He fell, dead before he hit the ground.

Stith and his friend escaped back to Mobile but Vick's second, A.G. Dickinson, was delayed by an undertaker who had to take charge of his friend's body. Before he could leave Mobile, the authorities issued a warrant for his arrest. He took refuge in the home of friend who was a local physician and managed to avoid the search for a few days. Finally though, guilt-ridden over his part in Vick's death, Dickinson sent a message to the Mobile chief of police, Harry Maury, and confessed to his role in the duel. He asked that he be permitted to take his friend's body back to Vicksburg. Maury was so impressed by the man's honesty that he sent his own carriage to take Vick's body to the riverfront docks.

The body was taken to New Orleans and then loaded onto a packet going upriver. Ironically, on this same boat were the caterer, the cooks and the helpers who were on their way to Annandale for Helen and Vick's wedding dinner. Their supplies were loaded right alongside Vick's coffin.

Helen and her family buried her betrothed in the same graveyard where her father's body was put to rest. His grave was marked with a simple granite cross and small statues of his hunting dogs. Day after day, Helen sat on an iron bench near the grave and wept for her beloved fiancée. When darkness fell, some member of the family would gently lead her home, but she would return early the next morning to resume her vigil. She was said to have made her family promise that the grave space next to Vick would always remain empty. She wanted it saved for herself and wanted no one else to ever be buried there.

Months passed and Mrs. Johnstone, fearing that Helen would never recover, took her to Europe so that she would have time for her broken heart to heal. They remained away for many months and by the time they returned, Helen had recovered from her depression. She later married Reverend George Harris, but never forgot about Henry Vick. She and her husband later moved to the northern part of the state and Helen died in 1916.

The space next to Vick's grave at the Chapel of the Cross remains empty today but the ghost of Helen Johnstone still appears there to weep for her lost love. Many visitors to the secluded cemetery have told of seeing a young woman kneeling in grief beside Vick's stone cross. When they try to approach her, she looks up and then vanishes before their eyes. Some still wonder if the gravesite beside Henry Vick is vacant after all....

FROM A STEAMBOAT TO THE GRAVE

The Bladon Springs Cemetery in Bladon Springs, Alabama is the burial place of a man named Norman T. Staples, a steamboat captain and ship designer who committed suicide in 1913. He is buried here with the bodies of his wife and several of his children and legend has it that Staples haunts this place, protectively watching over the graves of his family. If his ghost does still walk though, the cemetery was not the first place where his spirit appeared... nor was it the most tragic one!

Norman Staples was born in 1869 and was raised along the banks of the Tombigee River in Alabama. From his early days, he was fascinated with steamboats and when the time came for him to select his life's work, he chose the river. He got a job on a riverboat and soon became a skilled navigator on the Tombigee. In no time, he was offered his first command and became an accomplished pilot. His family was impressed with his career, but it was his sister Mary who was able to actually help him succeed. She had married a wealthy man named Fred Blees and she convinced him to finance her brother so that he could build his own boat. Fred agreed with the only stipulation being that the boat would be named in Mary's honor.

Mary's confidence in Norman paid off and soon the *Mary S. Blees* became one of the most profitable vessels on the river. Staples was able to repay his brother-in-law's generous loan in less than two years and so they worked together to commission another ship, the *Mary E. Staples*, which was named after Norman's mother. Soon, the new boat was also traveling up and down the river, carrying passengers and cargo and making a large amount of money for the owner. Staples continued to create new and bigger plans for his greatest ship yet. In 1908, he built his dream vessel, a huge and impressive ship called the *James T. Staples* in honor of Norman's father.

By this time, Staples was a wealthy and successful businessman and a few years before had married Dora Dahlberg. Unfortunately, his family life did not go as well for him as his career did. Staples was an inattentive husband and rarely home. When he was, he was usually occupied with some piece of business. In spite of this, Staples and his wife soon had two children, a boy named James Alfred and a little girl they called Mable Claire. Unfortunately, before Dora could recover from James' difficult birth, the boy had gotten sicken and had died. They grieved but this did not stop them over the next few years from having four more daughters, Beatrice Alice, Bertha, Melanie and Mary Faye, and a stillborn son, who was buried next to his brother. The deaths of his sons forced Staples to concentrate even harder on his business and he and his wife began to see less and less of one another. He loved all of them very much but his drive for success continued to overshadow everything else.

In 1907, Staples was desperately trying to complete the *James T. Staples* but then tragedy struck his family. During that cold winter, all of the children came down with a fever. Bertha and Mable would not survive it and the Staples marriage barely did. Rather than being closer together in their grief, the deaths drove Norman and Dora even further apart. Dora was heartbroken but she knew that her other children needed her. Norman became even more involved in the construction of his new vessel.

Every penny had gone into the construction of the ship and little did Staples know, but the heyday of the steamboat was just about to end. To make matters worse, a company called the Birmingham and Gulf Navigation Co. was putting small operators out of business. They were determined to own and operate all of the remaining boats on the river and soon began undercutting the small businessmen like Staples. This forced to Staples to also lower his rates, putting him even deeper into debt. At this same time, a new railroad spur was constructed that ran right next to the river. Many companies that had once shipped by riverboat now turned to the railroads instead, chipping away even more at Staples' failing business.

Somehow, he managed to keep the company operating until December 1912. Shortly after Christmas tough, his creditors called in his loans and effectively shut Staples down for good. On January 2, 1913, Captain Staples committed suicide, unable to cope with the loss of his lifelong dream. His wife and two daughters wept bitterly as his body was lowered into the grave. Staples had been able to bear the deaths of his children, but the loss of his steamship company had simply been too much for him to withstand.

The creditors who had taken away the *James T. Staples* were having problems of their own trying to operate the ship. No one wanted to work the boat without Captain Staples, who had been considered a good and fair man and a friend to many on the river. Finally, a crew was assembled but then several of the ship's firemen claimed to see the ghost of Norman Staples lurking around the boiler room. The shadowy figure was clearly recognizable as the late captain and the firemen stated that he moved around the boiler room with a purpose, as though he belonged there, and then suddenly he vanished. Frightened, the firemen all quit their jobs and after hearing the story, many of the other workers left too.

With great difficulty, the new owners got another crew together. This time, it was made up of men who had never worked with Staples and knew nothing about the sighting of his ghost on the boat. A few hours before the vessel was scheduled to depart, when the passengers and their luggage were being loaded on board, the crew members noticed something very strange taking place. All of the rats, which were common on any boat, suddenly began pouring out of the hold and scurrying off the ship. It was as if they knew, or sensed, that something terrible was about to happen. A few of the more superstitious crewmen regarded the evacuation of the rats as an ominous omen and many of them abandoned their posts.

New crew members were hired over the next few hours and the passengers were assured that everything was operating normally. Soon, the boat departed from Mobile and headed north. The trip proceeded uneventfully until they reached Powe's Landing, a port about one hundred miles from Mobile. The crew was unloading freight and the passengers were taking their noon meal. All was calm and then suddenly, one of the boilers in the ship's bow exploded with a tremendous roar! The steaming hot water shattered the decking and gushed over the crew and passengers, killing many of them instantly. The front of the ship burst apart and the river became a frothing, writing scene of horror. Dozens were killed, including the captain and first mate, scalded beyond recognition.

In what seemed like moments, the *James T. Staples* burst into flames and began drifting out into the river as the ropes securing it to the dock slowly burned. With fire dancing up from the hull, the ship sluggishly moved down the Tombigee until it came to a point almost in line with the Bladon Springs Cemetery, where Norman Staples was buried. Then, with a great shudder, the vessel sank to the bottom of the river. Twenty-six people had died in the disaster and another twenty-one had been seriously injured.

A full-scale investigation of the accident followed and the *James T. Staples* was hauled up from the riverbed and inspected. The conclusion was reached that the boilers had malfunctioned, but no one was able to explain why. They had been inspected in December and had been in perfect working order. Strange stories soon came to be told. Many remembered the sightings of Norman Staples' ghost in the boiler room of the ship. They believed that his spirit was determined not to let his enemies operate his beloved boat. Could the ghost have actually damaged the boilers and caused them to explode?

With the ship gone, the ghost of Captain Staples apparently left the river and took up residence in the Bladon Springs Cemetery. Over the years, visitors to the graveyard have reported the apparition of a man matching his description near his gravesite. They say that he sits there, holding his head in his hands as if he has some great regret. They wonder what keeps the ghost here, watching over the graves? Could it that he wishes he had spent more time with his children in life, or something much worse?

There are those who say that Captain Norman Staples will never rest. Eternal peace will always elude him because of his actions in 1913 that caused the deaths of passengers on the *James T. Staples*... actions carried out from a place beyond this world. .

THE KNEELING WOMAN

According to author Alan Brown, stories of tombstones that bear ghostly images are somewhat common in Alabama. Some of them are even supposed to show the person who is buried in the grave. For example, there is a story from Red Level that tells of a man who was riding his horse along a desolate stretch of road one night and he accidentally got his head caught in the fork of an overhanging tree branch. Shortly after he was buried, the image of a hanging man appeared on his gravestone.

One of Alabama's most famous tombstone images is the impression that appeared on the eight-foot obelisk marking the grave of Robert Musgrove. He is buried in the Musgrove Chapel churchyard in Winfield, Alabama. The image that appeared on his tombstone was not one depicting his death however, but of a testament to the love that was felt for him by a woman.

Robert Musgrove was born in 1866 and was raised in Fayette County, Alabama. He grew up loving trains and as a young man, he began working for the railroad. He was a hard worker and well-liked and started working his way up through the ranks from conductor to brakemen to fireman. After a number of years, he was promoted to the rank of engineer on the St. Louis and San Francisco Railroad. The train on which he was an engineer ran between Memphis and Amory, Mississippi and Robert's good looks had women waiting for him in both destinations. He became involved with a number of women of questionable character until one night when he was attending a party in Amory. There, he met a stunning young woman named Maude and it wasn't long before the two of them fell in love. Within six months, they were engaged to be married.

Both families were delighted with the engagement and arrangements were made for the two of them to be married at Musgrove Chapel, a church that had been built by Robert's family in Winfield.

Unfortunately, their wedding plans were cut short one night in April 1904. Somehow, something had gone wrong and crossed signals had two trains approaching each other head-on along the same route. One of them was speeding toward Amory and the other was headed on the same track toward Memphis. They collided and Robert was killed instantly in a massive explosion.

The railroad sent Robert's remains back to Alabama and a funeral service was held at Musgrove Chapel, where Robert and Maude's wedding was to have taken place. Instead of joyous nuptials though, Maude was a mourner at her lover's funeral. Shortly after he was buried, Maude walked over to his grave, knelt down and prayed. As she was getting up, someone standing nearby heard her whisper, "I'll be with you always".

It was said that Maude never married and each year, on the anniversary of Robert's death, she came to the cemetery and placed flowers on his grave. She cleared away the undergrowth and made sure the site was never neglected. This continued up until the time of her death... and then people began to notice that something unusual had happened at the grave.

One day in 1962, as people were leaving Musgrove Chapel, someone walking past the graveyard noticed what looked like the silhouette of a woman on Robert Musgrove's obelisk. Other people gathered around the tombstone and agreed that it did appear to be a woman's shadowy form on the marker. One of the parishioners remarked that perhaps it was Maude, still watching over her lover's grave. Soon, word quickly spread about the strange tombstone and people from all over the area came to see it.

The Musgrove family was justifiably disturbed by the groups of strangers who were traipsing through the cemetery and so they went out to the graveyard and tried to remove the images with soap and water. They scrubbed and scoured the stone with brushes, but it did no good. When these efforts failed, they hired a stonemason to try sandblasting it. Although this method did erase the shadow, the spectral image of a woman returned after a year and is still visible on the marker today. Visitors who go to the cemetery can find the outline of a grieving girl still kneeling in prayer over her lost love.

Is it merely a coincidence? A trick of the eye? No one really knows but Maude did state that she would never leave her lover's side. And perhaps she hasn't....

NEW ORLEANS' HAUNTED CEMETERY

The cemeteries of New Orleans are much like the city itself. The graveyards are a mirror to the opulence and desecration of a mysterious and enchanting city. As one of America's most haunted cities, New Orleans has perhaps more than its share of ghosts. The cemeteries of this historic place boast not only hauntings, but strange stories as well. The "Flaming Tomb" of Josie Arlington is an earlier chapter is just one of these tales but perhaps the most terrifying tales center on New Orleans' most infamous graveyard, St. Louis Cemetery No. 1.

The cemetery was created because of the decay and overcrowding of the city's earlier burial grounds. The first cemetery was created in 1725, but burials had already been taking place here for decades. Nearly all of these burials ran into problems because the original site of New Orleans, which is the French Quarter today, had a water table just beneath the soil. The highest area in the region was along the banks of the Mississippi. The natural levees there had been created by years of soil being deposited by the river's current. This was the first site chosen for burial of the deceased. During floods (which came often) though, the bodies of the dead would wash out of their muddy graves and come floating through the streets of town. Obviously, this was considered a problem.

In 1725, a new graveyard was created outside of the city but it could only be reached by a winding path from town. This was not done for aesthetic reasons, but for ones of health. It was commonly believed that graveyards exuded a noxious odor that carried disease. Combined with the marshy soil of the area, it was considered to be an unhealthy place. For this reason, the cemetery was placed outside of town as a precaution against infection in a town already known for its high death rate.

The cemetery was known as St. Peter Street Cemetery. Most of the burials here were below ground and space was reserved for the clergy and the wealthy and distinguished of the city. In spite of this, the cemetery, which has long been built over, was said to be as shabby and dirty as New Orleans itself in those days. The cemetery remained a prime burial spot for many years, until finally, it was simply filled to capacity.

During the years of 1787 and 1788, New Orleans saw much in the way of death and hardship. The city was rocked with plague and disease, claiming many lives. Malaria, smallpox and influenza took their toll on the city and hundreds died. St Peter Street Cemetery became so overcrowded that reports claim the bones of the dead commonly protruded from the ground. There was simply no other place to put the newly departed.

The following year, a fire broke out on Good Friday and swept through the city, destroying homes, buildings and the parish church of St. Louis. A few months later, a hurricane wiped out another huge portion of the city. Hundreds more lives were taken.

A new graveyard was desperately needed and the St. Peter Street Cemetery closed down for good. St. Louis Cemetery No. 1 was officially opened in 1789. The new cemetery was a walled enclosure with its main entrance off Rampart Street. The poor were buried here in unmarked graves until the middle 1800's and as available space filled, the level of the soil began to sink. Contracts for dirt were frequently bid upon and city chain gangs shoveled it evenly throughout the graveyard, making room for more bodies. It is believed that beneath the grounds of the cemetery, there are layers of bones several feet thick.

Is it any wonder these labyrinths of the dead breed tales of ghosts?

For all but the indigent though, above ground tombs were the rule. The reasons were obvious as the wet ground of Louisiana caused the graves to fill with water. The coffins would often float to the surface, despite gravediggers placing heavy stones or bricks on the lids. Such conditions made funerals a somewhat terrifying affair. Caskets were often lowered into gurgling pools of water and oozing mud. As often as not, the coffin would capsize as the water began to leak in, causing newly buried and half-decomposed cadavers to float to the surface of the grave... to the horror of those attending the funeral, of course.

There are a number of different types of tombs in the cemetery, from family crypts to society tombs to the "oven vaults" that are located inside of the cemetery walls themselves. The tombs are often used and re-used over a period of years by different members of the same family. They are closely crowded together inside of this walled cemetery, creating narrow paths and cornered avenues that can become an eerie maze after darkness falls.

While the cemetery holds the tombs of many famous former citizens and notable of New Orleans, perhaps the most famous person buried anywhere in the cemetery is Marie Laveau. Despite long-running controversies as to whether or not Marie is really buried here, the tomb is the most frequently visited site in the graveyard. It has been generally accepted as her burial place and generations of curiosity-seekers and Voodoo devotees have visited the crypt. Many of them have left offerings behind that include anything from coins, to pieces of herb, beans, bones, bags, flowers, tokens and just about anything else. All of them are hoping for good luck and the blessings of the Voodoo Queen.

The actual religion of Voodoo, or "Voudon", originated from the ancient practices of Africa. Voodoo came about most likely in Santo Domingo (modern day Haiti) where slaves devoted rituals to the power of nature and the spirits of the dead. For many enslaved Africans, such spiritual traditions provided a means of emotional and spiritual resistance to the hardships of life. In time, slaves from the Caribbean were brought to New Orleans and they brought Voodoo with them.

These slaves, most of whom spoke no French, had brought with them their religions, beliefs, charms and spells from Africa and Haiti, but soon learned that they were forbidden to practice their own religions by their masters. Many of them were baptized into the Catholic Church and later, the use of these Catholic icons would play a major role in their new religion of Voodoo. These icons would take their place in the Voodoo hierarchy and be worshipped as if they were praying to the God of the Catholic Church. Many of the Catholic saints would become "stand-ins" for important Voodoo deities and if you go into a Voodoo shop today, you will see statues, candles and icons depicting various Catholic images. There are in fact, Voodoo symbols as well.

Soon after the introduction of the African slaves to New Orleans, Voodoo began to play a major part in the traditions, and fears, of the general populace. It was not long before the white colonists also began to hear of it and to feel its power. Soon, Voodoo was firmly entrenched in the culture of New Orleans. The religion was practiced by the slaves and the free blacks as well and so strong was the power held by the upper echelons of the religion that they could entice their followers to any crime, and any deed. Whether or not these priests held supernatural power or not, the subtle powers of suggestion and of secret drugs made Voodoo a force to be reckoned with.

Marie Laveau was the undisputed Queen of Voodoo in the city. During her lifetime, she was the source of hundreds of tales of terror and wonder in New Orleans. She was born on Santo Domingo in 1794. Her father was white and she was born a free woman. The first record of her in New Orleans was in 1819, when she married Jacques Paris, another free black. He died in 1826 and Marie formed a liaison with Christophe Glapion, with whom she had she bore a daughter, also named Marie, in February 1827. During her long life (she lived until 1881) she gave birth to fifteen children.

That same year, Marie embraced the power of Voodoo and became the queen of the forbidden but widely practiced culture. She was a hairdresser by trade and this allowed her access to many fashionable homes in the city. In this way, she and her daughters had access to an intelligence network that gave Marie her "psychic" powers. She knew everything that was going on in the city just by listening to her customers tell of gossip and scandals.

Marie became a legend in New Orleans. She dealt in spells and charms, for both white and black customers, and produced "gris-gris" bags to cure their ailments. The small bags would be filled with an assortment of magical items and curative roots and could be used to work both good and bad magic. She was a clever and astute businesswoman who knew how to use her beliefs, and the beliefs and fears of others, to her own advantage.

One tale of Marie Laveau has reached legendary status in New Orleans. During the height of Marie's power, a young man from a wealthy family was arrested and charged with a series of crimes. While the young man himself was innocent, the true perpetrators had been several of his friends and they had let the blame fall upon their unlucky companion. The grief-stricken father sought out the assistance of Marie and explained the circumstances of the case to her. He promised a handsome reward if she would use her powers to obtain his son's release.

When the day of the trial came about, Marie placed three peppers into her mouth and went into the St. Louis Cathedral to pray. She remained at the altar for some time and then gained entrance to the Cabildo, where the trial was to be held. Before the proceedings could begin, she managed to deposit the three peppers beneath the judge's chair. They were in a spot where they could not be seen by the spectators, but couldn't be missed by the judge when he walked into the courtroom. One can only imagine his feelings over spotting the peppers and then spying the recognizable face of Marie Laveau among the people in the courtroom!

After a lengthy deliberation, the judge returned to the courtroom after hearing all of the unfavorable evidence against the young man and pronounced him to be "not guilty". Was it the supernatural power of Voodoo at work... or did the judge fear what might happen to him if he found the man to be guilty? Remember that Marie possessed the secrets of many of the most influential people in the city. Did the judge have his own secrets to hide? No matter how she had managed it, the father of the freed youth was ecstatic over the verdict and in return for her help, he gave her the deed to a cottage at 1020 St. Anne Street, between Rampart and Burgundy. It remained her home until her death a number of years later.

Marie died in June of 1881 but many people never realized that she was gone. Her daughter stepped in and took her place and continued her traditions for decades to follow. Today, Marie and her daughter still reign over the shadowy world of New Orleans Voodoo from the confines of St. Louis Cemetery No. 1. Both are entombed in this cemetery in two-tiered, white stone structure. Or are they?

The actual site where Marie Laveau's remains are located has been the subject of controversy for many years. Most believe the crypt in St. Louis Cemetery No. 1 holds the bodies of Marie and her daughter, Marie II, but there are many others who do not think so. You see, there is also a "Marie Laveau Tomb" in St. Louis Cemetery No. 2. There are also tales that claim Marie is buried somewhere else altogether, including Girod Street Cemetery, Louisa Street Cemetery and Holt Cemetery.

Some believe the confusion started after the body that was originally buried in the

Laveau tomb was later moved. It is said that Marie was first buried in St. Louis Cemetery No. 1 but that her spirit "refused to behave". People became so scared that they refused to go near the cemetery so another priestess, Madame Legendre, and some relatives, moved Marie to Holt Cemetery. She was re-buried in an unmarked grave so that her name would not be remembered. The ghost stayed put from that point on, the story said, but her name has yet to be forgotten.

Regardless, New Orleans tradition holds that Marie is buried in St. Louis Cemetery No. 1 and literally thousands have come here in search of her crypt. The tomb looks like so many others in this cluttered cemetery, until you notice the markings and crosses that have been drawn on the stones. Apart from these marks, you will also see coins, pieces of herb, bottles of rum, beans, bones, bags, flowers, tokens and all manner of things left behind in an offering for the good luck and blessings of the Voodoo Queen. Once, in the 1940's, a sexton of the cemetery told author Robert Tallant that he had found a pair of false teeth that had been left behind here!

But does Marie's spirit really rest in peace? Many believe that Marie returns to life once each year to lead the faithful in worship on St. John's Eve. It is also said that her ghost has been seen in the cemetery and is always recognizable thanks to the "tignon", the seven-knotted handkerchief that she wears.

It is also said that Marie's former home at 1020 St. Ann Street is also haunted. Many claim that they have seen the spirit of Marie, and her ghostly followers, engaged in Voodoo ceremonies there.

Perhaps the most unusual sighting of Marie's spirit took place in the 1930's when a man claimed to be in a drug store near St. Louis Cemetery No. 1. He was speaking to the druggist when an old woman in a white dress and a blue tignon came and stood next to him. Suddenly, the druggist was no longer listening to him, but looking in terrible fear at the old woman instead. Then, he turned and ran to the back of the store. The man turned and looked at the old woman and she started laughing "like crazy", he said. He thought that perhaps the druggist had been frightened of this "poor crazy woman" who lived in the neighborhood.

Finally, the woman looked at the man and asked if he knew her. He replied that he didn't and she laughed some more. Then, she turned and looked behind the counter. "Where the drugstore man go at", she questioned the young man, now seeming very angry. He shrugged and at that, she slapped him across the face. Moments later, she turned and ran out the door and, to his shock and surprise, vanished over the cemetery wall. Stunned, the man then stated that he "passed out cold".

When he woke up, the druggist was pouring whiskey down his throat. "You know who that was?" he asked the man but the other was still unable to talk. "That was Marie Laveau. She been dead for years and years but every once in awhile people around here see her. Son, you been slapped by the Queen of Voodoos!"

Another tale of the cemetery, and Marie Laveau, springs from the 1930's. According to the story, a drifter with no money or prospects decided to sleep in the cemetery one night. He scaled a tomb and slept fitfully for several hours before being awakened by a strange sound. Thinking that perhaps vandals or grave robbers would injure him, he decided to make his escape to the streets. As he rounded the corner of a row of crypts, he saw a terrible sight. Positioned in front of Marie Laveau's tomb was a glowing, nude woman with her body entwined by a serpent. Surrounding her were the ghostly forms of men and women, dancing in mad but silent abandon. Needless to say, the drifter fled for his life.

But is Marie Laveau the only restless ghost of St. Louis Cemetery No. 1? Many don't believe that she is because one of the most famous "vanishing hitchhiker" stories in the South is connected to this graveyard. The stories also say that in the 1930's, New Orleans taxi cabs avoided St. Louis Cemetery No. 1 whenever possible.... or at least they never stopped to pick up a young woman in white who hailed them from the graveyard's entrance!

One driver had picked up just such a young girl one night and drove her to the address that she gave him. Once they arrived, she asked him to go up and ring the bell, then inquire for the man who lived there. The man came out, but when the driver told him of the girl waiting in the cab, he immediately asked for her description. When the driver described the girl to him, the man shook his head sadly. This was obviously not the first time that a driver had appeared on his doorstep. The young girl, he explained to the taxi driver, was his wife... but she had died many years ago and had been interred wearing her bridal gown at St. Louis Cemetery No. 1. That was when the driver suddenly realized the white gown the woman was wearing had been a wedding dress!

He raced back to the cab and jerked open the door but the woman was gone. The driver fainted away on the spot. After that, young women in white stood little chance of hailing a cab near the entrance to the graveyard.

And some say they still don't stand a chance today!

· CHAPTER SIX · THE LAST SHOWDOWN

SOME OF THE MOST HAUNTED GRAVEYARDS OF THE AMERICAN WEST

Ghosts and hauntings are no more visible in any other part of America than in the vast region of the West. The Old West and the frontier of the late 1800's have long been a part of the popular imagination with tales of six-guns, shoot-outs and cowboys. Ghosts have also long played a major role in the lore and lure of the western states. In this open land, the supernatural takes every form and is associated with old houses and buildings of every type from hotels to theaters to mansions, as well as with old forts, deserted stretches of highway and yes, even graveyards. Ghost lights here abound and so do tales of mysterious bones, lost Hollywood legends and lonely spirits from a time long past.

One strange tale from the western state of Oklahoma is among the most chilling in the state. It dates back a number of years and involves a cemetery that is located in the town of Arapaho. It follows along the line that some ghosts are not seen, but only heard.

This one in particular is said to cry out the words, "Oh no! Oh, my god! Robina has not been saved!"

When the voice was first heard, it was identified as that of a recently departed local named George Smith, a pious and religiously devout man. In 1936, his daughter was killed in an auto accident when she was only 19 years old. He never really recovered from the loss of his child and to make matters worse, the fact that she had not achieved salvation from the church haunted him until the day that he died. After Smith's death in 1972, visitors to the graveyard began to report an eerie disembodied voice coming from his gravesite. The stories quickly made the rounds and people began coming from all over to hear the words, lamenting the fact that Robina was not "right with God" when she died. Locals in the area report that the voice can still sometimes be heard today.

Witnesses vary in credibility, but even one minister claimed to hear the voice. In March of 1979, while holding a funeral service at a nearby gravesite, the pastor was startled by the sound of Smith's voice. In 1980, a couple named Cecil and Sharon Rutherford came forward with their own experience. They had been putting flowers at a grave that was located nearby when they heard a deep groan and then a bawling voice that cried that Robina had not been saved. Not knowing the ghostly tale of the cemetery, they thought someone might be playing a trick on them. They looked around but found no one else in the vicinity.

A few years ago, a geologist and part-time ghost hunter named Arthur Turcotte, attempted to find a natural explanation for the strange phenomena. He studied the gravesite and ran every test that he could possibly think of. Not only did he find no logical explanation for the voice, but he was also stunned to clearly hear it himself. The strange voice remains unexplained!

GRAVEYARD HAUNTS OF HOLLYWOOD

Los Angeles, the fabled "City of Angels".... Home to the rich and famous, palm trees, sandy beaches, orange groves, Disneyland and most of all, to that wonderful place of the American Dream known as Hollywood. America has always been fascinated by the glamour, the glitter and the decadence of old Hollywood. But like the city of Hollywood itself, the legends of the place have a dark side.

The lure of "Tinseltown" has been a part of America since the first silent film makers came west to the small town of Los Angeles at the turn of the century. What began as a scheme for movie maker Mack Sennett to make some extra money with a low-cost housing area called "Hollywoodland" became a movie colony for artists, writers and actors who came west to make it big. Today, Hollywood remains not so much a place as a state of mind. In fact, it has not even been incorporated as a city since 1910, when it joined Los Angeles to share its water supply. However, it still retains a strange allure for those with an interest in history and hauntings and for those interested in the screen legends of long ago.

The history of the region is a dark journey through tales of crime, corruption, death, murder, and of course, Hollywood-style scandal. Nearly every tale of ghosts and hauntings in Hollywood involves some sort of terrible crime or an unsolved murder. Why is this? Well, we don't really know for sure, but perhaps there is something about the region itself that attracts both the brightest lights and the darkest shadows to its streets.

The dark tales of Hollywood's most haunted cemetery are no exception.

If you are looking for movie stars in Hollywood, you can always find plenty of them along the legendary Walk of Fame, where celebrities both past and present are paid tribute by their fans and admirers. You can also find plenty of former legends in the local graveyards. For instance, Forest Lawn Cemetery in Glendale, is often referred to as the "Disneyland of the Dead", thanks to all of the stars who are interred here. There are no tombstones at Forest Lawn for only bronze nameplates are allowed to mark the graves and crypts of the occupants. Celebrities buried here include Clark Gable, Spencer Tracy, Errol Flynn, Humphrey Bogart, Jean Harlow and dozens of other Hollywood greats.

One of the most persistent legends of Forest Lawn concerns the final resting place of Walt Disney. For years, rumors have circulated that Disney was immediately frozen after his death in December 1965. He was then placed into cryogenic suspension so that, in case a cure was ever discovered for cancer, the beloved figure could be brought back to life. Author William Poundstone, in researching a book on secret stories, not only heard that Disney was frozen but that his body was hidden away below the "Pirates of the Caribbean" at Disneyland! While the story is not true (unfortunately... Walt was cremated two days after his death), there are a number of reasons why it has endured for so long.

First of all, Disney loved new technology, dating all the way back to his pioneering use of sound and color in animation and in his fascination with life in the future. According to some of his biographers, Disney also expressed an interest in cryonics, but probably more out of curiosity than anything else did. In fact, he never made any final funerary arrangements and even after entering St. Joseph's Medical Center in Burbank, he had no idea how serious his condition was. His doctors and his family reportedly never even told him that his surgery to rid him of lung cancer was unsuccessful or that his condition was terminal. With that in mind, he never would have been able to arrange to be preserved.

Another reason the story has persisted is probably because of Disney's rapid succession of decline in health, death and burial. The general public never even knew he was ill and news of his death and burial came after the fact, which seemed mysterious to many. There was no news coverage of his funeral and it was attended by close friends and family only. The news that Disney had died and was already buried fueled speculation about the manner of his final arrangements.

How the rumor about Disney being frozen got started is uncertain. However, many things lent credibility to the story. The family and studio never officially denied the rumor and both refused to comment on Disney's death in any way. Many people took this as a non-denial of the story, thus meaning it must be true. In addition, while his gravesite is not a closely guarded secret, its location is relatively unknown. It can be found at the left corner of the "Freedom" mausoleum, against the wall, and partially obscured by a tree. Conspiracy theorists point to the fact that it is one of the few markers in the cemetery that bears no dates.

While Forest Lawn may have the largest number of celebrity internments, a more classic graveyard is Hollywood Memorial Park. It boasts the graves of many silent film stars and legends of the silver screen like Douglas Fairbanks, Rudolph Valentino, Tyrone Power, Cecil B. DeMille, Clifton Webb and others. This park is so geared to the celebrity of Hollywood that it even passes out maps to the star's graves at the front office. And some say that if you stay in the cemetery after dark, you might even be able to get your map personally autographed! You see, Hollywood Memorial Park is one of the most haunted sites in the area...

One ghost who wanders this cemetery is that of actor Clifton Webb, who was best known for playing "Mr. Belvidere" in the film *Sitting Pretty* and as newspaper columnist Waldo Lydecker in *Laura*. Webb is said to divide his time between haunting the graveyard and his former home in Beverly Hills. Webb was a long-time believer in life after death and hosted many seances in his home. Many later owners of the house, and visitors to the cemetery, claim to have encountered his spirit.

If Clifton Webb does haunt this place, he does not do so alone. The hauntings at Hollywood Memorial Park are reportedly so strong that they have even affected Paramount Studios, which is located next door!

One haunted spot in the cemetery is the grave of actress Virginia Rappe, a barely remembered starlet who would be completely forgotten today if not for her unwilling part in one of the greatest Hollywood scandals of all time. But what tragic events have caused her spirit to linger behind? To answer that question, we have to look back to the doomed history of the man who was accused of her murder, Fatty Arbuckle.

Roscoe "Fatty" Arbuckle was an overweight plumber in 1913 when Mack Sennett discovered him. He had come to unclog the film producer's drain but Sennett had other plans for him. He took one look at his hefty frame and offered him a job. Arbuckle's large appearance, but bouncing agility, made him the perfect target for Sennett's brand of film comedy, which included mayhem, pratfalls, and pies in the face. He was soon making dozens of two-reelers as a film buffoon and audiences loved him. He made one film after another, all of them wildly successful, and also made a rather substantial fortune, going from a $3-a-day job in 1913 to over $5000 by 1917, when he signed with Paramount.

Virginia Rappe came to Hollywood around 1919. She was a lovely brunette model who caught the eye of Mack Sennett and he offered her a job with his company. She soon went to work on the studio lot, taking minor parts and apparently, sleeping around. This fact became so well known that rumor had it Virginia passed along a rather sensitive infestation to so many of Sennett's crew that he closed down the studio and had the place fumigated. Soon however, she earned a part in the film *Fantasy* and later met Fatty Arbuckle and appeared with him in *Joey Loses a Sweetheart.*

Fatty Arbuckle... Funny Fat Man!

Soon, Virginia was noticed by William Fox, shortly after winning an award for "Best Dressed Girl in Pictures" and he took her under contract. There was talk of her starring in a new Fox feature called *Twilight Baby* and Virginia certainly seemed to be on her way. Fatty had taken a shine to Virginia soon after meeting her and insisted that his friend, Bambina Maude Delmont, bring her along to a party celebrating his new $3 million contract with Paramount. Fatty decided to hold the bash in San Francisco, which would give him a chance to try out his new custom-made Pierce-Arrow on the drive up the coast. On Labor Day weekend, two car loads of party-goers headed up the coast highway, including Fatty, several friends and an assortment of starlets. They arrived in San Francisco late on Saturday night, checking into the luxurious Hotel St. Francis. Fatty took three adjoining suites on the 12th floor.

Shortly after arriving, Fatty made a call to his bootleg connection and the party was on, lasting all weekend. On Labor Day afternoon, which was Monday, September 5, 1921, the party was still going strong. The crowd had grown to about 50 people, thanks to Fatty's "open house" policy. Virginia and the other girls were downing gin-laced Orange Blossoms; some of the guests had shed their tops to do the "shimmy"; guests were vanishing into the back bedrooms for sweaty love sessions; and the empty bottles of booze were piling up.

Around three in the afternoon, Fatty who was wearing only pajamas and a bathrobe, grabbed Virginia and steered the intoxicated actress to the bedroom of suite 1221. Bambina Maude Delmont later testified that the festivities came to a halt when screams were heard in the bedroom. She also said that weird moans were heard from behind the door. A short time later, Fatty emerged with ripped pajamas and he told the girls to "go in and get her dressed...she makes too much noise". When Virginia continued to scream, he yelled for her to shut up, or "I'll throw you out the window".

Bambina and another showgirl, Alice Blake, found Virginia nearly nude and lying on the unmade made. She was moaning and told them that she was dying. Bambina later reported that they tried to dress her, but found that all of her clothing, including her stockings and undergarments were so ripped and torn "that one could hardly recognize what garment s they were."

A short time later, Virginia slipped into a coma at the Pine Street Hospital and on September 10, she died. The cause of her death almost went undiscovered. The San Francisco Deputy Coroner, Michael Brown, became suspicious after what he called a "fishy" phone call from the hospital, asking about a post-mortem. He went over personally to see what was going on and walked right into a hasty cover-up. He was just in time to see an orderly emerge from an elevator and head for the hospital's incinerator with a glass jar containing Virginia's female organs. He seized the organs for his own examination and discovered that Virginia's bladder had been ruptured, causing her to die from peritonitis. Brown reported the matter to his boss and both agreed that a police investigation was called for.

The hospital staff was grilled as to what they knew and they reluctantly reported the strange incidents that brought Virginia to the hospital. Soon, the newspapers also carried the story and Fatty Arbuckle was charged with the rape and murder of Virginia Rappe. The authorities blamed her death on "external pressure" from Arbuckle's weight being pressed down on her during sex. Soon, the newspaper stories spun out of control. It was no longer just sex, they told a nation of stunned fans of the "happy fat man", but "strange and unnatural sex". According to reports, Arbuckle became enraged over the fact that his drunkenness had led to impotence, so he ravaged Virginia with a Coca-Cola Bottle... or was it a champagne bottle... or could it have been a piece of ice? Others claimed that Fatty was so well endowed that he had injured the girl, while others stated that the injury had come when Fatty had landed on the slight actress during a sexual frolic.

Needless to say, a lot of guessing was being done and a lot of insinuations were being made about Fatty Arbuckle and Virginia's tragic death. The public was in an uproar and soon, Arbuckle's films were pulled from general release.

Held without bail, Fatty waited in the San Francisco jail while his lawyers sought to have the charges reduced from murder to manslaughter. Film tycoon Adolph Zukor, who had millions at stake with Arbuckle, contacted San Francisco District Attorney Matt Brady in an effort to make the case go away. Brady was enraged and later claimed that Zukor offered him a bribe. Other friends of Fatty called the D.A.'s office and suggested that

Arbuckle was being punished because some starlet drank too much and died. They assumed they were helping Fatty's case, but the result was just the opposite. Brady grew angrier with each call on Fatty's behalf and by the time the case went to trial, he was livid.

The trial began in November 1921 with Arbuckle taking the stand to deny any wrong-doing, although his attitude toward Virginia was one of indifference. He never bothered to express any remorse or sorrow for her death. His lawyers were even more to the point, making every effort to paint Virginia as "loose", suggesting that she slept around in New York, South America, Paris and of course, in Hollywood. After much conflicting testimony, the jury favored acquitting Fatty by 10-2 after 43 hours of deliberating. The judge declared a mistrial.

A second trial was held and this time, the jury was hung at 10-2 for conviction. Fatty was now out on bail and was forced to sell his Los Angeles home and fleet of luxury cars to pay his lawyer fees.

Despite the hard work of Brady, who wanted to convict Arbuckle very badly, Fatty was finally acquitted in his third trial, which ended on April 22, 1922. Thanks to confusing testimony by 40 drunken witnesses and no physical evidence (like the infamous bottle), Fatty was finally a free men. In fact, the jury issued this statement: "Acquittal is not enough for Roscoe Arbuckle. We feel a grave injustice has been done him and there was not the slightest proof to connect him in any way with the commission of any crime."

Fatty may have been free, but he was hardly forgiven. Paramount soon canceled his $3 million contract and his unreleased films were scrapped, costing the studio over $1 million. Fatty's career was finished and he found himself banned from Hollywood.

Arbuckle would never act in the movies again and the public would never allow him to forget his fall from grace either. People shouted "I'm Coming, Virginia" when they recognized him on the street and laughter often greeted him in restaurants and shops. In his forced retirement, Fatty also took to drinking quite heavily and finally, he died in New York on June 28, 1933.

Innocent or guilty? We'll never really know for sure, but in the state of mind called Hollywood, it didn't really matter. Arbuckle had managed to change the image of Hollywood from one linked to dreams to that of one forever linked to scandal.

And now we return to Hollywood Memorial Park.... and the ghost of Virginia Rappe. I would imagine that there is little doubt in the mind of the reader as to why Virginia's spirit may be a restless one. In addition to losing her life during the horrifying incidents of that fateful Labor Day, Virginia lost her reputation as well. The press was nearly as cruel to her as they were to Fatty Arbuckle.

So, it's not surprising that her ghost still lingers behind. Visitors who come to Hollywood Memorial Park have reported hearing a ghostly voice that weeps and cries out near Virginia's simple grave. It is believed by many to be her ghost, still attached to this world, and still in anguish over her promising career, which was cut short... just like her life.

Ghosts in Hollywood are not confined to the cemeteries. Many of the old-time movie studios have their own ghostly tales but without a doubt, the most haunted of them is Paramount. Over the years, the ghostly sightings and strange reports here have become as much a part of the legend of the place as the movies themselves. Being the last major studio actually located in Hollywood, Paramount makes the perfect setting for ghostly activity. It is located right next door to Hollywood Memorial Park, which is no stranger to ghost stories itself, serving as the final resting place for many of the stars who worked for Paramount in days past. The stories say that some of their spirits have been seen walking directly through the walls from one lot to the next.

Hollywood Memorial Park is located closest to stages 29 through 32. The reports of spirits seen entering the studio lot describe them as wearing clothing from the 1930's and 40's. Out of all of sound stages in that area, Stages 31 and 32 seem to have the most activity. Footsteps are often heard tapping through stages that have been secured for the night and it is not uncommon for equipment to turn on and off and operate by itself.

Paramount Studios has many entrances and some of them are walk-in gates, like the one at Lemon Grove, located a few feet from the cemetery. It is here where many of the ghosts from the graveyard are also said to enter the studio lot. Some of them, according to guards posted here, actually appear as heads that poke through the cemetery wall and then disappear. Others actually walk through the gate itself, like the ghost of silent film star Rudolph Valentino.

Valentino was considered the greatest Latin heartthrob of the 1920's. He made a number of successful films but died early in his career at the age of only 31.

Rudolph Valentino

When news leaked of his death in 1926, crowds of adoring fans mobbed the funeral home where his services were held, people everywhere were heartbroken and several passionate admirers even committed suicide.

Not surprisingly, a number of legends have sprung up around Valentino and his ghost. One such legend grew up around his crypt in Hollywood Memorial Park, where he was buried. It seems that since the demise of the star in 1926, a "Lady in Black" has put in an appearance at his tomb and each week, leaves a fresh bouquet of flowers. There is no way to know if this might be the same woman after all of these years, but regardless, the flowers have never stopped coming. I visited Hollywood Memorial Park a few years ago and visited the crypt. Not surprisingly, fresh flowers were still appearing each week.

There are also the "spirited" tales as well. In fact, Valentino may be the most well-traveled ghost in Hollywood. He is reported to haunt his former home in Beverly Hills, "Falcon's Lair", Valentino Place, an old apartment building that used to be a speakeasy in the 1920's and a place frequented by the actor, his former beach house in Oxnard, and of course, Paramount Studios. Valentino was a driving force at Paramount in his day and rumor has it that he was buried in his white costume from the film, *The Sheik*, for which he is best remembered. Whether he was or not, it is in this costume that his ghost is sometimes reported.

In addition to Valentino, other Hollywood Memorial ghosts sometimes appear at the gates. This does not please the security guards at all, especially those who work the night shift at the Lemon Grove gate. The gate is located at the northeast corner of the studio lot facing Lemon Grove Avenue and a wall is all that separates it from the cemetery. It is here where most of the uninvited visitors are usually seen but these sightings are mostly harmless, leaving the officers confused over where the "trespasser" disappeared to. These sightings can also leave a few rattled nerves however.

One night, a veteran security guard was working the late night shift. Most of the guards know everyone who comes in an out of the gates because they see them every day. On this evening, the guard noticed an unfamiliar face lurking about. He followed the man to a corner of the wall to the cemetery and thinking he had him cornered, he waited for the suspicious visitor to come out. After a minute or two, he looked around the corner... just in time to see the man vanish into the cemetery wall! From that time on, he refused to work the Lemon Grove gate at night.

FATHER PADILLA'S BONES

The deserts of New Mexico are filled with ghostly tales. Many of them concern the colonial days of the Spanish Missions and the men who came to bring God to the native population. One such ghost story involves the bones of one of New Mexico's early priests, Father Juan F. Padilla. He was murdered in 1756, although accounts vary as to his violent method of death. One story says that Indians near Gran Quivira killed him, while another claims that he was stabbed to death by a jealous husband who believed that the priest was his wife's lover.

Regardless of how he died though, Father Padilla was wrapped in a shroud and buried beneath the altar of one of the region's greatest churches, the now ancient mission at Isleta Pueblo. In this dark alcove, the priest's body rested for nearly twenty years, then in 1775, his remains inexplicably rose up through the hard-packed earthen floor. How this may have been accomplished in unknown, but it must have proved to be a startling event to those who witnessed it. What was even more astonishing though was the macabre condition of the priest's body. According to the accounts, it had not decayed at all but was actually soft and pliable and had a pleasant, earthy smell. Even though such a thing was surely supernatural, it was said that no one, not even the little children, were frightened by the sight of the corpse.

The parishioners of the church had no idea what to make of this bizarre event but some speculated that perhaps the priest no longer wished to be buried in the bare earth. With that in mind, they fashioned a coffin for him from the hollowed-out trunk of a cottonwood tree and placed the body inside. He was buried again and this time, remained beneath the altar for the next forty-four years. Then, in 1819, he rose through the floor again!

An account of the 1819 "resurrection" was discovered by Father Angelico Chavez, a historian and a restorer of the early missions, and he published an article about it in 1947. Apparently, parishioners and priests carried out an investigation after the body appeared again. The wooden casket that had been built years earlier accompanied the corpse, which was now mummified. The investigators examined both but could find no explanation as to why it had again come through the floor. An overnight wake was held and Father Padilla was again reburied.

The good padre was not heard from again for seventy-six years. During the time that he remained in his resting place, a wooden floor was added to the church. On Christmas Eve 1895, the priest made his most dramatic appearance yet. During a series of Indian dances that preceded the midnight mass, Father Padilla began knocking from beneath the wooden floor. The rapping and knocking continued for some minutes until it put a halt to the performers. Someone finally noticed that the church altar was shaking and rocking back and forth. The bumping noises seemed to be coming from underneath it!

The ceremony was halted and several of the men pried up the floorboards. Beneath them, they discovered the coffin of Father Padilla had once again arisen from the hole in which it had been placed. It had been banging against the underside of the altar!

In the presence of the Bishop of Santa Fe, the Most Reverend Placido Luis Chapelle, the casket was opened once more. The mummified body was now examined by Dr. W.R. Tipton. They were all understandably perplexed and again, no explanation could be reached as to why this strange event was happening. After much in the way of discussion and suggestion, Father Padilla was buried for the fourth time.

Father Chavez's 1947 article was also unable to offer a suitable explanation for the odd appearances of the body and the coffin. He believed that it might have been possible for the wooden coffin to be buoyant in the shifting sand, thus forcing it upward over a period of time. Of course, this does not account for the priest's first post-mortem appearance, nor does it explain why none of the other bodies buried beneath the altar never rose out of the ground.

Author Jack Kutz has suggested that perhaps Father Padilla was simply restless as his life ended so suddenly and prematurely. He may have been trying to attract attention to the fact that his work on earth was unfinished, a classic reason for a ghost to continue to haunt. But whatever the reason for his return, the night in 1895 was Father Padilla's last appearance and he has rested quietly ever since.

THE WELL-READ GRAVEYARD GHOSTS

In earlier chapters, we discussed a number of places that have become haunted after being built on top of a burial ground. The Sweetwater County Library in Green River, Wyoming is no exception to that rule! The library opened back in 1980 and has gained a reputation for being one of the spookiest locations in the state. This comes as no surprise when you learn that it was constructed on top of the city's oldest cemetery.

The graveyard was started back in the 1860's but most of the area's early citizens rested peacefully in unmarked graves until 1926. It was in that year, as so often happens with old cemeteries, that the town decided to expand and use the land where the cemetery was located. The bodies were exhumed and then moved to the site of the current graveyard. That was the intention anyway, but they soon discovered that a few of the occupants got left behind!

In the 1940's, housing for World War II veterans started being built in the area where the cemetery had been and it soon became obvious that not all of the bodies had been discovered twenty years before. Each time that a new set of bones was found, they were moved to the new graveyard, but many of the workers wondered just how many they might have missed. That question was answered (at least in part) in 1978 when the library purchased the land for a new building. As soon as the groundbreaking took place, workers made more grim discoveries in the form of eight to twelve bodies in unmarked graves.

Architect Neal Stowe from Salt Lake City noticed a heavy tractor moving back and forth, loosening the soil. He later stated in an interview that "I walked right through the middle of the site, where something that looked like a deteriorated coconut was sitting on top of some freshly churned dirt. I picked the thing up, turned it around, and recognized it as part of a skull. Little tufts of brown hair were still clinging to it."

Stowe immediately stopped work at the site and summoned city officials in order to try and determine the extent of the burial ground. Unfortunately, there were no records or physical clues to say just how many bodies might have been left behind. Workers from the crew started probing the area with hand shovels and discovered pieces of rotted wooden caskets, as well as bits and pieces of human bones. The bones were collected and these remains were also moved to the new cemetery.

While this was going on, new rumors began to spread around town concerning the cemetery. Remembering that scraps of Oriental cloth had been found during earlier excavations, some claimed this had been a Chinese graveyard, even though one exhumed corpse had red hair. Others insisted that the bones belonged to smallpox victims from a long-ago epidemic and that the library construction was now endangering the entire town by exposing the infected remains. This rumor also proved to be groundless. While there had been a smallpox epidemic among Green River railroad workers in the 1860's, the victims had all been buried in a part of the graveyard that had not been disturbed.

What would soon be disturbed however was the well being of the new library's staff! Almost as soon as the place was opened, they began experiencing some pretty strange things and unfortunately, the discovery of human remains around the building would continue. This might possibly explain why the building continued to be actively haunted.

In the spring of 1983, landscaping work was done outside the front doors and one of the contractors uncovered what was thought to be old wood. When the landscapers looked closer, they realized they were bones. Since not all of the remains could be removed without tearing up the sidewalks, only portions of the skeletons were reburied in the local cemetery. The rest of the bones remained behind. Also, in 1985, structural work was necessary on the library, as a section of it had started to sink. When the construction crews began drilling into the foundation, one said that they found a small coffin with the body of a child inside. It was said that the body was perfectly preserved, although the "flesh was like gelatin".

Not surprisingly, such grisly finds were unsettling to library staff members, who were also making some strange discoveries of their own. They were beginning to realize that many of the strange sounds and events in the building could not easily be explained away. Library director Helen Higby first heard about the events that other staff members and maintenance workers were already talking about in late summer of 1986. She later described a security gate that people have to pass through when they leave the library. If a book is not checked out properly, an alarm will sound. There was also a bypass gate for people in wheelchairs to pass through. This gate was made from wrought iron and stood a little over waist-high.

"One night, two of my staff were the only ones left in the building," she told author Debra Munn, "and at ten minutes to nine, they were getting ready to close up. Each one was at least fifteen feet from this bypass, but all of the sudden, it slammed as hard as it could, swung open again and then oscillated back and forth for several seconds until it came to a stop.... that was the first that I'd heard about any unexplained phenomena and the two women were so upset that they didn't want to talk about it. But afterwards, I started hearing about other weird things that had happened."

Many of the staff members spoke of events involving electrical disturbances, like lights turning on and off by themselves. One maintenance worker turned off the lights one evening in the multi-purpose room and then returned ten minutes later to find them on again. He was the only person in the building at the time.

Another maintenance worker spoke of trying to operate a vacuum cleaner one evening. He was sweeping between the stacks of books and accidentally went too far and pulled the plug from the wall. He then switched it off and went to plug it back in again at a more accessible outlet. After he plugged it back in, he walked back over to machine. Before he could switch it on though, the vacuum turned itself back on again! He immediately turned it off, unplugged it, rolled up the cord and went home for the evening.

Nearly all of the staff members reported feeling as though they were being watched in the library, especially in the multi-purpose room. A worker was vacuuming in there one day and noticed that the curtains were open on the adjoining stage. A community event was coming up soon and the stage had already been set up for it. As she was sweeping, she happened to look up again and this time noticed that the curtains were closed. An electronic switch operated the curtains and the cleaning woman guessed that the staff members at the circulation desk were playing tricks on her. She called their bluff... only to learn after confronting them that the only switch for the curtains was in the multi-purpose room itself!

Strange sounds often occur as well. One night, according to librarian Judy McPhie, they were closing up on a Friday and several staff members were present. "We heard a noise like someone hammering on a door, trying to get out. It seemed to come from the back part of the building... but we couldn't find anyone."

Another maintenance worker once heard the voices of a man and woman arguing violently in the multi-purpose room. He could only catch an occasional word, but it was obvious that they were having a very heated discussion. Curious, because he had just passed through that room taking out some trash and no one had been in it, he went to the door and opened it. Immediately, the muffled voices come to an abrupt stop. He looked around but there was no one in the room and no place that anyone could have disappeared to. It turned out later that he was not the only person to hear the voices. One former assistant was so terrified that she refused to talk about them.

As most of the strange events seemed to happen in the evening, director Helen Higby rearranged schedules and made it a rule that no one worked alone. After that, little out of the ordinary was reported, either because the activity stopped or because no one was around in the evening to hear it. But had it really stopped altogether?

One night, not long after the new policy went into effect, the library's business manager came in to do some work on a holiday. As she was going to be by herself, she brought her Doberman pinscher along. After she was in her office for awhile, her dog suddenly stood up and went over to the door. He cocked his head as if someone were outside and then sat back down again. For the rest of the evening, he stared at the door, completely alert, as if someone were in the hallway that his master could not see.

So, what goes on at the Sweetwater County Library? Are the strange things that occur here merely figments of the imagination or are they manifestations of spirits, angry at having their graves disturbed? Ask the staff members here and see what they think. I believe that you'll find that most of them are more than a little open-minded to the possibility of library patrons from the other side!

GHOSTS OF BUCKSKIN CEMETERY

Colorado is a state infested with ghosts. There's really no other way to put it. It seems to be a predictable by-product of a rich historical past. Many have found that one of the most beautiful and history-filled states in the Union is also one of the most haunted. There are dozens of tales of hauntings in Colorado and even a handful that are connected to graveyards. In fact, two very mysterious tales are connected to same small burial ground near Fairplay.

Gold was discovered in a narrow valley located a few miles west of Fairplay in August 1860 by Joseph Higginbottom, David Greist, M. Phillips, W.H.K. Smith, D. Berger and A. Fairchild. A district and town were named "Buckskin Joe" for Higginbottom, a mountain man and trapper who had long been known by this nickname. The camp kept this name for many years, although it was sometimes just known as "Buckskin" and for awhile as "Laurette", a combination of the names of the only ladies here in 1861, Laura and Janette Dodge. As word of the gold discovery spread, more women came to the area but the men in the area still outnumbered the ladies by seventy to one. Even then, most of the women attracted to this mining camp were "soiled doves" and as rough as the men who flocked to the gold strike.

One story of the cemetery involves a man named J. Dawson Hidgepath, who came to Buckskin to find gold and a wife in 1863. He became a nuisance to most of the working girls as he attempted to get them to marry him. He even approached married women, arriving at their homes uninvited and unconcerned about their husbands. Trouble seemed to follow him everywhere. His professed love for a singer and dancer named Julia Cotton got him tossed in the creek. His adoration for Lulu Wise, a working girl, got him a beating from her employer. His advances toward a woman staying at the Argyle House only gained him a knock on the head from her husband's revolver. In addition, his gold claim never seemed to pay off as others nearby did, making Hidgepath all the more miserable. In the end, his search for love and wealth ended in disaster.

On July 23, 1865, Hidgepath's broken and lifeless body was found at the bottom of the west side of Mount Boss, where he had apparently fallen several hundred feet while trying to prospect on the mountainside. The eccentric character was laid to rest in Buckskin Cemetery but he didn't stay at rest for very long. Soon after he was buried, Dawson's bones were discovered on the bed of a dance hall girl in town. How they could have gotten there, no one knew, but assuming that it was some sort of tasteless prank, they were returned to his grave in the cemetery.

In the following months, Hidgepath's bones began appearing about town on a regular basis. It was as though the lovesick miner refused to stay in his grave. The skeleton was reportedly found in women's kitchens, parlors and even in their beds. Some of the women claimed to hear a voice asking them to be Hidgepath's wife, while others stated that the bones were accompanied by a sprig of flowers. Each time, the men of Buckskin reburied the mysterious bones. Once they dug a deeper grave, but it didn't matter. Next, they placed a large, flat rock over the hole, but somehow they managed to escape again.

Eventually, as the mines played out, the town of Buckskin faded into obscurity. However, this did not stop the roving skeleton. Now, the bones sought out women in the town of Alma, a boomtown less than two miles from Buckskin that had sprang up in 1872. Soon, the ladies here also began to receive amorous visits from the now-legendary bones. By this time, they had become the talk of the state and each time they managed to escape from the grave, the story was told in every saloon in the region!

By 1880 though, the local folks decided that the incidents had gone on long enough. Late one night, a handful of men removed Hidgepath's skeleton from his grave and took it to Leadville, where the bones were tossed into an outhouse. What happened next is anyone's guess, but according to the legend (or is it a tall tale?) Hidgepath's bones are resting today in the Buckskin Cemetery. How they managed to get back there is unknown but perhaps a young lady of Leadville got a little more than she bargained for when she went to use the outhouse one day....

Another tales from Buckskin's heyday is bit more on the romantic side. It begins shortly after the town was started in 1861 when a lovely young woman was touring Colorado's opera houses and theatrical halls. Her real name is forgotten today but her stage name was "Silverheels", thanks to the fact that she had a popular song-and-dance routine that she performed while wearing a pair of silver-heeled shoes.

After performing in Fairplay, she traveled over to Buckskin and sang and danced for the miners. Needless to say, they were enthralled. In those days, the sight of any woman was a welcome one in the camp but Silverheels was different than any woman they had ever seen before. She was said to have been very beautiful and had a voice like an angel. She stayed for several nights in Buckskin and then prepared to leave for performances in other towns. The men in town begged her to stay though and lavished her with gifts. Finally, Silverheels agreed to stay on for a few more nights. According to legend though, she left the camp before dawn the next morning so that she wouldn't have to disappoint the men who had been so kind to her.

The miners never saw Silverheels perform again, but they never forgot about her. One day, about a year later, word reached Buckskin that Silverheels had died. The legends say that she visited a town that was afflicted with a smallpox epidemic and rather than flee, she stayed there to care for the sick. Eventually, she contracted the disease herself and perished. In any event, the men in Buckskin were saddened and they grieved for the performer who had brought beauty into their lives. They held a memorial service for her and named the mountain above the town "Mount Silverheels" in her honor. This rugged peak still bears that name today.

In 1870, a cemetery was laid out on a ridge not far from the town. It can still be visited today and is a rustic location with a collection of scattered graves that are nestled beneath the pines and aspens. Here, the miners who died in accidents and of illnesses were buried for years. Even after Buckskin died out in 1872, the people of Alma continued to use the small burial ground and it was these folks who began to witness the incredible apparition of Buckskin Cemetery.

Over the years, visitors stated that the ghost of a beautiful woman often appeared at twilight in the small cemetery. She always wore a white dress and she walked along peacefully through the tombstones and wooden crosses. Some even claimed that she sometimes sang in a sweet, ghostly voice that would echo into the shadows as darkness began to fall. They all knew who she was, of course. The radiant ghost was Silverheels, returning to embrace the long-dead miners who were once her greatest admirers.

THE GHOST LIGHTS OF SILVER CLIFF

One mile south of the little town of Silver Cliff, Colorado sits an old graveyard that has become one of America's greatest sites for unexplained phenomena. During the daylight hours, the Silver Cliff Cemetery is a tranquil place and gives no indication that many unsolved questions have plagued the burial ground since 1880. It is not until darkness falls that the cemetery becomes quite eerie and it is not until then that the "ghost lights" begin to appear!

These mysterious lights have been observed in the old miner's cemetery for more than a century, intriguing several generations of tourists and the residents of Silver Cliff, which is located in the Wet Mountain Valley. Silver Cliff is little more than a ghost town today, boasting only a few hundred inhabitants, but in its heyday, it was a bustling town of more than 5,000 people. Once the mines stopped producing though, the population dwindled but the ghost lights remained.

The lights, which appear as white balls of illumination, have been talked about for years. In the earlier days, the stories were spread by word of mouth, but in 1956, an article appeared about them in the *Wet Mountain Tribune*. It wasn't long before people from all over Colorado began coming to the small cemetery. The reports rarely varied and described tiny, dim lights that would flash on and off, popping up and then vanishing. Sometimes they would be little more than a twinkle and other times they would move about horizontally. If a visitor tried to approach them, they would always stay out of reach and no source could ever be determined as to their origin.

Skeptics dismissed the lights as nothing more than reflections, but in the older parts of the cemetery (where the lights usually appear), there are no reflective stones. Still, in order to counter this explanation, residents of Silver Cliff, and even those in nearby Westcliff, deliberately agreed to shut off their lights for an evening. Even the streetlights were shut off, plunging the area into blackness.

"But the graveyard lights still danced," recalled Judge August Menzel.

A Denver scientist named Charles H. Howe had tried to discover a source for the lights in 1895. He journeyed to Silver Cliff in the company of a photographer, Joseph Collier, and an electrical engineer named John Crawford. They studied the lights for an entire week in May and saw the lights on two of the seven nights. On both nights, the sky was overcast and there were no light reflections from town.

Other have tried to explain the lights as being nothing other than the reflections of the stars overhead. In 1988, a reporter and an electrical engineer investigated the phenomenon and stated that the lights were just that, obvious overhead reflections. Unfortunately, this did not take into account the sworn statements of witnesses who had seen the lights on overcast evenings or, like Silver Cliff resident Bill Kleine, had observed them on nights when there had been a thick fog.

Another explanation maintained that the lights were merely "swamp gas" or "will-o'-the-wisps", effects caused by marshy places and decaying matter. Ray de Wall, the publisher of the *Wet Mountain Tribune*, adamantly disagreed. He stated that the cemetery was on a dry ridge and that yucca and cacti grew on the graves. This would rule out wet conditions causing the lights to appear.

So, if we agree that the lights remain an enigma, why are they appearing? Many of the old-timers of the area believe that the ghost lights have a supernatural, rather than a natural, explanation. According to the legends, the cemetery became the burial ground for many of the men who died while working in the mines of the region. The flickering lights of the graveyards are said to be the small lights that used to be worn on the miner's hats. They appear because they are manifestations of the restless souls of the miners... still looking for the bonanza they never found during their lifetime.

The Silver Cliff lights gained national attention in August 1967 when an article was published about them in the *New York Times*. This got the attention of *National Geographic* Magazine and assistant editor, Edward J. Linehan.

Miners did brutal, back-breaking work below the earth and scores of them died during the many strikes in Colorado.

He featured a piece about the lights in the August 1969 issue of the magazine. Linehan drove to the cemetery in the company of Bill Kleine, the mentioned area resident and the proprietor of the local campground. Kleine had seen the lights on many occasions and he directed the writer to park the car. They climbed out and stood in silence for several minutes.

"Do you believe it?" Linehan asked. "About the lights in the graveyard?"

"I've seen them plenty of times," Kleine replied. "This is a good night for them... overcast, no moon".

The two walked closer to the old cemetery and slowly, the vague outlines of the tombstones appeared through the haze. That was when Bill Kleine's voice harshly whispered. "There!", he hissed, "and over there!"

Linehan looked and saw the lights appearing. "Dim, round spots of blue-white light glowed, ethereally among the graves", he later wrote. He and Kleine walked about in the cemetery, pursuing one ghost light after another, for the next fifteen minutes. No matter how hard they tried, they were unable to catch them.

Strangely, the lights remain just as elusive today as they were in 1969. Even the most logical and persistent seekers of an explanation for the lights have been forced to admit that they have no answers. No one had been able to get close enough to examine them and despite many attempts, the lights refuse to be photographed.

Over the years, many attempts have been made to discredit the supernatural powers of the lights but until a logical explanation can be reached, the more romantic of us will still wonder about the signal lights of the lost miners. As Edward Linehan wrote in the conclusion of his article about the ghost lights:

> "No doubt someone, someday, will prove there's nothing at all supernatural in the luminious manifestations of Silver Cliff's cemetery. And I will feel a twinge of disappointment. I prefer to believe they are the restless stirrings of the ghosts of Colorado, eager to get their Centennial state on with its pressing business: seeking out and working the bonanzas of a second glorious century."

THE ALBINO WOMAN OF KANSAS

The vast and open landscape of Kansas is "haunted" by ghost stories and legends and not surprisingly, the graveyards of the state are good places to find them. In fact, one of the greatest cemetery haunts in America can be found around an abandoned church and cemetery in a small Kansas town. And there are other ghosts here as well....

One of the strangest legends of the state is that of the Albino Woman who haunts the Rochester Cemetery in Topeka. Over the course of at least three generations, she has been a figure of terror to residents of Topeka, north of the Kansas River. She has become such a part of the mythological landscape that stories have been invented in her honor. One such tale says that if you cross the bridge over the river at night and stare into the black water, you will see the face of the Albino Woman looking back at you. Another story claims that when staring into a darkened mirror, you can say "Albino Woman" three times and she will appear in the glass and scratches will materialize on your face.

This ghostly woman has long been a part of local lore and the Albino Woman is said to be a startling apparition with white skin, red-rimmed eyes and tangled pure-white hair that falls to her waist. She is usually seen wearing a long white dress and is often accompanied by a dog. She wanders the area surrounding Rochester Cemetery and has also been seen along back roads and in isolated spots in the vicinity. But who is she? No one really seems to know, although older residents of North Topeka recall a real albino lady who lived and worked in the area in the 1930's and 1940's. In addition, people who live near

Rochester Cemetery also remember a "crazy lady" with white hair who lived in the neighborhood for some time. Many believe these two individuals may have "merged" to create the stories that are still told today about a supernatural being.

The stories of the Albino Woman have changed many times over the years. In the early accounts, she was always seen as a benign figure, a wandering soul who may have been a real person but was seen as an outcast because of the odd way that she looked. It was always said that she roamed the streets, never talking to anyone, and that in the mornings, she stood in her yard and silently watched the children pass by on her way to school. A woman named Mrs. Cook, a resident of Lower Silver Lake Road, once told a reporter that an albino woman lived next door to her at one time and that neighbors largely avoided her because of her unfriendly demeanor. The local children often taunted the woman, although they were deathly afraid of her. Mrs. Cook added that the woman had lived alone and had no relatives.

The very real albino woman died in 1963 and after that, the stories of the legendary creature took a different turn. These new tales had the Albino Woman as a ghostly apparition. Stories emerged from people who claimed to see her white figure drifting along roadways at night. The sightings usually occurred on a route from the Seaman district to the cemetery where the woman was buried.

On April 11, 1966, a man named Paul Bribbens reported that a white ghost appeared in the front yard of his home along this same road. "It kept talking in a woman's low monotone," he said. "I couldn't make out a word of it. Like she was stark raving mad or something." Paul's dogs, at the sight of the apparition, climbed underneath his front porch and could not be coaxed out. Bribbens called the sheriff's department, but by the time the officers arrived, the ghost had vanished.

Reports continued to come in from area residents, visitors and people who worked in the neighborhood. They stated that a "glowing white woman" was walking the streets at night. Several employees of the local Goodyear Tire Factory and the Boy's Industrial School saw the ghost regularly as it walked along the banks of Soldier Creek. A long-time Topeka resident, who lived just west of the school on Highway 24, reported that whenever the ghost came near, "everything would become very quiet". He said that animals in the vicinity always seemed to know it first and would cower in fear. He warned others about being out alone and on foot when the Albino Woman was nearby.

The ghost was also sighted quite often in Rochester Cemetery, but the most famous sighting connected with the place later turned out to be a hoax. An article in a student newspaper at the time claimed to have a first hand account from a man named George Sanderson, Jr. who was supposedly the cemetery caretaker in 1968. The story went on to say that one night in the fall, he and his wife were returning home from dinners at the Elk's Club. As they turned into the driveway of the caretaker's home on the edge of the cemetery, Sanderson's wife pointed at something through the windshield. In the headlights of the car, the couple saw a thin, white figure running among the headstones. At first thinking that it must be a prank, he turned the car so that the headlights washed over that section of the graveyard. Illuminated by the lights, Sanderson saw a woman kneeling at one of the graves.

The caretaker opened his door and got out of the car. As he did, the woman turned around and glared at him and then walked further into the cemetery. Sanderson admitted that he and his wife were badly shaken by the eerie event and although he called the police, investigators found no trace of the woman. Whoever she was, she had completely vanished, the article claimed. The story was the admitted invention of a student writer, who also changed the name of the cemetery to "Rockingham", a change that has caused a lot of confusion with ghost hunters over the years.

In the 1970's and 1980's, the stories changed again. Up until this point, the ghost of the Albino Woman had always been a little frightening, but never threatening or violent. All that was about to change though. She had now become a more terrifying apparition and malevolent in her actions. The legend now incorporated the idea that she was searching for her lost children (perhaps a hybrid of the Hispanic legend of La Llorona?). If she didn't find her own though, well, anyone's children would do!

The fearsome spirit was said to be attacking and scaring young couples parked in cars too. They would often be terrified by a rapid tapping on the window, only to look up and seen a white, red-eyed face on the other side of the glass. Often, motors stalled and headlights failed when the ghost was lurking nearby, which could prove hazardous to the drivers and passengers in the automobile.

In recent times, the legend of the Albino Woman has faded somewhat. Perhaps people have started to realize the changing versions of the story have the ring of the true "urban legend" or perhaps the ghostly woman herself has indeed moved on. Who knows? Regardless, the Albino Woman will always be at least a small part of the ghostly lore of Kansas.

A GATEWAY TO HELL?

There are graveyards across America, places with names like Bachelor's Grove and Stull Cemetery, that defy all definitions of a "haunted cemetery". They are places that go beyond the legends of merely being haunted and enter into the realm of the diabolical. They are places said to be so terrifying that the Devil himself holds court with his worshippers there... and in the case of Stull Cemetery in Kansas, is one of the "gateways to hell" itself!

But just how terrifying are these places? While there are few of us who would challenge the supernatural presence of a place like Bachelor's Grove (see the next chapter), there are some who claim that Stull Cemetery does not deserve the blood-curdling reputation that it has gained over the years.

Stull Cemetery, and the abandoned church that rests next to it, is located in the tiny, nearly forgotten Kansas town of Stull. There is not much left of the tiny village, save for a few houses, the newer church and about twenty residents. However, the population of the place allegedly contains a number of residents that are from beyond this earth! In addition to its human inhabitants, the town is also home to a number of legends and strange tales that are linked to the crumbling old church and the overgrown cemetery that can be found atop Stull's Emmanuel Hill. For years, stories of witchcraft, ghosts and supernatural happenings have surrounded the old graveyard. It is a place that some claim is one of the "seven gateways to hell."

The Devil himself is said to make an appearance at Stull Cemetery!

The legends say that these stories have been linked to Stull for more than 100 years, but none of them made it into print until the 1970's. In November 1974, an article appeared in the University of Kansas student newspaper that spoke of a number of strange occurrences in the Stull churchyard. According to the article, Stull was "haunted by legends of diabolical, supernatural happenings" and the legends asserted that the cemetery was one of the two places on earth where the devil appears in person two times each year. It said that the cemetery had been the source of many legends in the area, stories that had been told and re-told for over a century.

The piece also went on to say that most students learned of Stull's diabolical reputation from their grand-parents and older individuals, but that many of them claimed first-hand encounters with things that could not explain. One student claimed to have been grabbed by the arm by something unseen, while others spoke of unexplained memory loss when visiting the place. Like many other locations of this type, the tales of devil worship and witchcraft also figured strongly into the article.

But were the stories actually true?

Not according to the residents of Stull, who claimed to have never even heard the stories before. They were bemused, annoyed and downright angered that such things were being said about their town. The pastor of the new church in Stull, located right across the road from the old one, indicated that he believed the stories to be the invention of students at the university.

But such stories have a strong hold on people, as evidenced by the reaction to the article that claimed that the devil would appear in Stull Cemetery on the night of the Spring Equinox and again on Halloween. On March 20, 1978, more than 150 people waited in the cemetery for the arrival of the devil. The word also spread that the spirits of those who died violent deaths, and were buried there, would return from the grave. Unfortunately, the only spirits that showed up that night came in bottles and cans... but this did not stop the stories from spreading.

All through the 1980's and up until today, stories have been told about Stull Cemetery and as time has passed, most have grown more horrifying and hard to believe. The problem seems to be that the cemetery has a lack of real, documented accounts of strange activity. The weird tales seem to be little more that "urban legends" and second-hand stories from teenagers and college students.

One story told of two young men who were visiting Stull Cemetery one night and became frightened when a strong wind began blowing out of nowhere. They ran back to their car, only to find that the vehicle had been moved to the other side of the highway and was now facing in the opposite direction. Another man claimed to experience this same anomalous wind, but inside of the church rather than in the graveyard. He claimed that the sinister air current knocked him to the floor and would not allow him to move for some time. Incidentally, it is inside of this same church where "witnesses" say that no rain will fall... even though the crumbling building has no roof!

The legends also say that the Devil has been appearing here since the 1850's and insist that the original name of the town was "Skull" and that the later corruption of that into "Stull" was simply to cover the fact that the area was steeped in black magic. It was said that the witchcraft-practicing early settlers were so repentant about their past deeds that they changed the name of the town. In truth, the town was called "Deer Creek Community" until 1899, when the last name of the first postmaster, Sylvester Stull, was adopted as the name of the village. The post office closed down in 1903, but the name stuck.

In 1980, an article appeared in the *Kansas City Times* that added further fuel to the rumors about Stull Cemetery and the abandoned church. The article was quoted as saying that the Devil chose two places to appear on Earth every Halloween. One of them was the "tumbleweed hamlet" of Stull, Kansas and the other, which occurs simultaneously at midnight, is someplace on the "desolate plain of India." From these sites, according to the article, the Devil gathers all the people who died violent deaths over the past year for a prance around the Earth at the witching hour.

But why in Stull? The article adds that he appears in Stull because of an event that took place in the 1850's, when "a stable hand allegedly stabbed the mayor to death in the cemetery's old stone barn. Years later, the barn was converted into a church, which in turn was gutted by fire. A decaying wooden crucifix that still hands from one wall is thought to sometimes turn upside-down when passersby step into the building at midnight..." The story neglects to mention that, historically speaking, neither the Deer Creek Community nor Stull have ever had an official mayor.

Author Lisa Hefner Heitz has collected numerous legends that have added to the mythology of Stull Cemetery. Some of them include the "fact" that the Devil also appears at Stull on the last night of winter or the first night of spring. He comes to visit a witch that is buried there. Coincidentally, an old tombstone bearing the name "Wittich" is located fairly close to the old church. It should also be mentioned that there are rumors that an old tree in the graveyard, which was cut down a year or so ago, was once used as a gallows for condemned witches. There is also said to be a grave in the cemetery that holds the bones of a "child of Satan", who was born of the Devil and a witch. The child was so deformed that he only lived for a few days and the body was buried in Stull. Some say that his ghost may walk here, as there supposedly was a photo taken a few years ago that shows a "werewolf-like boy" peering out from behind a tree.

One of the strangest stories about Stull supposedly appeared in *Time* magazine (it didn't) in either 1993 or 1995 (depending on the version you hear). This story claims that Pope John Paul II allegedly ordered his private plane to fly around eastern Kansas while on his way to a public appearance in Colorado. The reason for this, the story claims, was that the Pope did not want to fly over "unholy ground".

The Abandoned Church at Stull Cemetery (Photo by Rene Kruse)

The legends grew and by 1989, the crowd at the graveyard on Halloween night had become so overwhelming that the Douglas County sheriff's department had to station deputies outside to send people on their way. They handed out tickets for criminal trespass to anyone caught on the property. It was believed that nearly 500 people came to the cemetery on Halloween night of 1988, doing damage to the church and gravestones, prompting a police response the following year.

As time passed, the local residents grew more irritated that vandals and trespassers were wreaking havoc in the cemetery where their loved ones and ancestors were buried. Finally, a chain link security fence was installed around the grounds and although the area is still regularly patrolled, the visits have died down somewhat, at least outside of October. In addition, there have been the signs posted against trespassing here and locals have made it clear that visitors are not welcome.

So, what about the stories? Were they true or the work of some student writer's imagination? Is the cemetery at Stull really haunted.... or is the "haunting" merely the result of an "urban legend" gone berserk? That's a hard question to answer. Although undoubtedly the vast majority of the tales about the cemetery have been manufactured from horror fiction, they still beg that now-familiar question of how such stories got started in the first place? Is there a grain of truth to the dark tales? Did some isolated supernatural event take place here that led to embellishment over the years?

We have no idea and local residents are not talking. Strangely, although property owners have spoken out against both vandals and the macabre stories, they have done little to try and end the legends for good. For example, as so many of the paranormal events supposedly involve the ruin of the old church, why not tear it down? The building has been standing vacant 1922 and it has been badly damaged by vandalism over the years. In 1996, the remnants of the roof blew off and once exposed to the elements, the interior walls have been damaged by both weather and graffiti. Recently, a large crack also opened in one of the stone walls after the church was struck by lightning. So why not tear it down before it falls down on its own? Wouldn't this bring an end to the demonic tales circulating about the place?

To make matters worse, why chase away those who come to the cemetery at midnight on Halloween to see the Devil appear? Why not simply "control the chaos" and allow the curiosity-seekers to see that no spirits will run rampant on that fateful night? On Halloween night of 1999, reporters from a local newspaper and a television news crew joined a group of onlookers at the cemetery. Sheriff's deputies were on hand, but did not ask anyone to leave until 11:30pm. Why?

At precisely this moment, an unknown representative for the cemetery owners appeared and ordered everyone to leave the property. The officers had no choice but to go along with their wishes and the reporters and spectators had to leave. As Stull Cemetery and the land around it is private property, there was no option but to comply. The owners stated, through the representative, that they did not want media attention brought to the graveyard because it attracts vandals. But couldn't they have furthered their cause by allowing the camera crew to show that the Devil did not appear at midnight, thus debunking the legend forever?

Makes you wonder, doesn't it?

CHAPTER SEVEN ·
THE BECKONING END...
THE MOST HAUNTED GRAVEYARDS IN AMERICA'S HEARTLAND

What is it about the American Midwest that seems to invite such darkness? Are we startled to find that the place is so haunted, because ghosts here seem to appear where we least expect them? The Heartland certainly hides its secrets well among the blowing fields of grain, the shadows of the forest, the ramshackle farm houses, and of course, in the quiet graveyards. It is here where hauntings arise with great frequency, dashing the idea that cemeteries are not good place to find ghosts. Without a doubt, the graveyards of the Heartland have **many ghosts indeed!**

These graveyard ghosts are strange and often perplexing and the many stories run the entire gamut between entertaining folklore and authentic accounts of the supernatural. One such account, which seems to combine elements of both, involves a place called White

Cemetery in northern Illinois. This small graveyard, and the surrounding Cuba Road area near Barrington, has gained a rather strange reputation in recent years.

White Cemetery is a small burial ground that is located just east of Old Barrington Road. It dates back as far as the 1820's, but no records exist to say when it started to gain the attention of those with an interest in the unexplained.

For many years, it has been reportedly haunted by eerie, white globes of light that have been seen to hover and float among the tombstones. Witnesses to these anomalies have ranged from teenagers to average passersby, many of whom have gone to the local police and have described not only the glowing lights, but hazy figures too. The lights are said to sometimes float along through the cemetery, drift over the fence and then glide out over the surface of the road. The hazy human-like figures have been spotted along the edge of the fence and lingering near stands of trees. They tend to appear and then vanish at will. Both types of the phenomenon have been investigated and studied by ghost hunters and researchers for some time, but no explanation has been discovered as to their source.

There have also been many stories told about nearby Cuba Road itself. Most of them involve a phantom black automobile that appears near the cemetery and an old house that is seen and then vanishes nearby. The house is believed to have actually existed many years ago and legends say that it burned down under mysterious circumstances. It has been repeatedly spotted over time, often by people who have no idea that the house no longer exists. Some of the sightings also involve a spectral old woman who carries a lantern and flags down passing motorists. When someone stops and tries to help her, she disappears along the edge of the roadway.

STRANGE LEGENDS OF STEPP CEMETERY

Elements of folklore and the supernatural also pervade the story of one of the most famous haunted cemeteries in the state of Indiana. Located off of Old State Highway 37 in the Morgan-Monroe State Forest is a small, abandoned cemetery around which a number of eerie legends have appeared.

It is called Stepp Cemetery and it is a desolate and lonely place that can be found at the end of a narrow, dirt trail that winds back into a veritable wilderness. Such a place would have long been forgotten if it wasn't for the weird tales that are still told about it. Only two dozen of so grave markers remain here and all of them are old and crumbling, as no one has been buried in this tiny graveyard in decades. Along the southern edge of the grounds is a row of tombstones and nearby is a worn tree stump that looks to be vaguely in the shape of a chair.

Depending on which version of the Stepp Cemetery legend that you hear, one of these graves seems to be the focus of the paranormal activity in the cemetery. Does the grave marker belong to that of a child? A road worker who was killed before his time? Or a teenager who met a tragic end? The stories vary, but one part of them all stays the same... each of them tells of a ghostly woman who watches over the gravesite, and the cemetery, in the darkest hours of the night. Over the years, scores of people have claimed that she is seen in the darkness, seated on the old tree stump that is found nearby. There, she waits silently, watching over and protecting the grave of her loved one.

The history of this cemetery is nearly as mysterious as the ghost who is found here. No one really seems to know when the burial ground was started, or by who. Forest rangers will tell visitors that some area families founded it, but local rumors state that a now defunct religious cult called the "Crabbites" may have had some connection to it. Apparently, this peculiar sect conducted services that included snake handling, speaking in tongues and sex orgies. Local lore has it that a deputy from the area once stated that he had been called to the cemetery late one night to break up a particularly bizarre Crabbite ritual. The story says that he had to use a bullwhip to settle things down!

The legend of the spectral woman is just as strange. In his book *Haunted Indiana*, author Mark Marimen tells of a young woman who came to the region from the east. Her husband went to work in one of the local quarries and they settled down and had a daughter. One afternoon, her husband was killed in a dynamite explosion at the quarry and was buried in Stepp Cemetery. After that, her daughter became her entire life and she watched over her constantly as she got older, attended school and later met a young man of her own. But unfortunately, her happiness was not to be. One rainy night, when coming home from a date, the young couple was killed in auto accident. In a repetition of the earlier tragedy, the daughter too was buried in Steep Cemetery. Her mother would never recover from the girl's death.

Soon, she began to make nightly treks to the cemetery, where she would sit for hours, talking to her dead husband and daughter as if they were still alive. An old tree stump that was near to the graves made a comfortable, makeshift chair for her visits. It was here where locals who passed by the cemetery began to see a woman in black sitting and weeping as the sun fell from the sky. It was said that if anyone approached her, she would run away and hide in the woods and would not return until they had gone. Soon, local residents began to avoid the graveyard, as it was believed the woman was crazy.

Eventually, she too died and, according to the legend, was also buried in Stepp Cemetery. Her spirit is still said to be restless today though, lingering in the graveyard and watching over the remains of her family. Many people believe that her ghost can still be seen at Stepp on nights of the full moon, when the woman in black returns to the stump **and is visible to those of us still among the living. Those who doubt the legend to be true** should take into account the many strange sightings that have taken place over the years. The most chilling encounters take place when visitors leave the cemetery shaken after having seen a black figure rise from the old tree stump and turn toward them in the darkness. The descriptions they give of the woman in black are strikingly similar as well. She is said to have long, white hair, although she is not old, but rather the color was bleached from her hair by shock.

Those who do not see the mournful apparition still often have their own tales to tell. It has been said that strange sounds sometimes emanate from the cemetery grounds. Law enforcement officials and park rangers are said to have received reports of a woman sobbing in the cemetery at night. When they go to check and see if anyone is injured or ill, they find that no one is there.

Descriptions of the ghostly woman and her heartbreaking cries have not changed much over the years, but the origins of the phantom often vary with each teller of the tale. There are a variety of different stories that supposedly explain the mysterious appearance of the spirit and here are a few of them:

- In the 1950's, a young girl was murdered in the vicinity and her body was dumped at Stepp Cemetery. The girl's mother never gave up the search for her daughter's killer, even after death. Her ghost now returns to the graveyard and watches over the girl's grave, waiting to revenge herself on the murderer.

- When they were building the Morgan-Monroe County Forestry many years ago, a man was killed working construction. He was buried in Stepp Cemetery and his wife came there to watch over his grave. Her ghost still returns to the spot today.

- A young child was killed in an auto accident in the 1920's and blaming herself, the little girl's mother would come to the cemetery to mourn at her grave. Distraught, she disinterred her daughter's body so that she could hold it one last time. She was found the next day, having committed suicide. Her ghost still haunts the cemetery today.

In more recent times, the story of the woman in black has taken on some of the elements of the classic "urban legend" tales. In one version, she appears as the mythical "Hook" (which was discussed in an earlier chapter). The story goes that a woman and her son were involved in a horrible auto accident. The little boy was killed and buried in Stepp Cemetery and his mother's hand was severed at the wrist and was replaced with a metal hook. The boy had always been afraid of the dark and his heartbroken mother came to his grave and watched over him every night. She continued to do so even after death and her ghost now warns away strangers, waving her hook at those who come to close to the grave.

Another story also serves as a warning to teenagers who park in cars. In this tale, a young couple goes for a drive in the state forest at night. While they are driving, the girl tells her boyfriend that she no longer loves him and doesn't want to see him anymore. Angry, the boy forces her to get out of the car and he drives away, leaving her alone in the dark woods. The girl vanishes without a trace and her mother begins endlessly searching the forest for the girl until she too vanishes. Today, her ghost appears in the vicinity of the cemetery and prowls about in the darkness. The ghost of the girl's mother allegedly frightens teenagers who come there to go parking. It is said that her face suddenly appears outside, peering into the windows.... looking to see if her daughter might be in the car!

While the stories have changed many times over the years, it does seem possible that the story of the woman in black may have been based on a real event that occurred many years ago. True or not though, Stepp Cemetery has become a landmark in the Morgan-Monroe State Forest and is a popular stop for ghost hunters, curiosity-seekers and those with an interest in eerie folklore.

Many of those who come here wonder if the story of the ghostly woman can be true? Perhaps the story is just a compelling piece of Hoosier folklore, or perhaps not. Those who are convinced that the tale is merely the creation of someone's imagination often confess to a feeling of doubt when they see the twisted tree stump that looks remarkably like a chair on the far side of the cemetery. If the old stump truly exists, they ponder, can they woman in black exist as well?

THE STORY OF STIFFY GREEN

They say that there is nothing unusual about hearing a dog barking in a cemetery at night, unless you happened to be in Terre Haute, Indiana. If you are anywhere in the area around Highland Lawn Cemetery at night, and hear a dog bark, you may just be hearing the legendary voice of Stiffy Green, Indiana's favorite graveyard ghost.

In the early 1900's, Stiffy Green was a familiar character around Terre Haute. He was the constant companion of a man named John Heinl, an elderly gentleman who was well-liked in town. He too was familiar figure as he strolled about the city each day in the company of his little bulldog. Stiffy Green was so named thanks to his unusual, stiff-legged walk and the fact that he had startling, green-colored eyes. The little dog was friendly, yet fiercely protective of his master, never allowing strangers to get too close.

In 1920, John Heinl passed away. While his death was a cause for sadness in the community, no one was hit harder by it than Stiffy Green. The poor creature was heartbroken and he refused to leave his master's side, even during the funeral services and after Heinl was entombed at Highland Lawn. Eventually though, two of Heinl's friends decided to take in the dog and care for him. They took him to their house in Terre Haute and introduced him to his new home.

Within a few days, Stiffy Green had gone missing. He was found a few hours later lying in front of the door to the Heinl mausoleum, silently watching over his master's burial place. John's friend placed a leash on the dog and took him back home again but less than a week later, the dog was missing once more. He was always discovered again, several miles away, in the cemetery. Over the next month or so, this became a standard routine. If the dog could not be found around the house anywhere, his new owners always knew where he was. Eventually, they just gave up and let Stiffy Green take up residence in the graveyard. They brought him food and water and allowed him to stay there.

Not long after this, they began to realize that the dog was not eating. He paid little attention to the bowl of water either, preferring to sit nearly motionless at the entrance to the tomb, barring anyone from entering it. He stayed there in the rain and cold and never shirked what he seemed to feel was his duty. And it was there, on the cold stone step, that the body of Stiffy Green was eventually found.

As word of the loyal dog's death spread, Heinl's friend pondered what to do with the animal's body. They certainly didn't want to simply dispose of their friend's constant companion but they weren't certain he should be entombed as a human would be either. Finally, they reached a compromise. A fund was established and the dog's body was taken to a local taxidermist. The dog was then stuffed and mounted into the sitting position that he had maintained outside of the tomb for so many months. His eyes were left open and his bright green eyes were replaced with glass ones that managed to capture the gleam of the originals. When the task was completed, Stiffy Green was placed inside of the Heinl tomb, right next to the crypt that held the remains of his beloved companion.

And seemingly, this would be where our story ends... but it's not.

Several months after Stiffy Green's death, a caretaker was leaving the cemetery on a warm evening. Just as he was opening the door to his car, he heard the bark of a dog from the direction of the Heinl mausoleum. Thinking that something about this seemed odd, he decided to go and have a look. As he neared the tomb, the sound got louder and then he suddenly realized why the bark seemed so strange, and so eerily familiar. He had heard this dog barking before. It was the bark of Stiffy Green!

But that was impossible, he realized, the poor animal had died many months ago. The bark must have been his imagination, he decided and walked back to his car. He would think no more about this until other people started to report the same barking from the area around the tomb.... and they would report something else too.

According to the legends, many people have heard the barking of a small dog in Highland Lawn Cemetery in the evening hours. It always seems to come from the direction of the Heinl mausoleum. A few of them have also reported that Stiffy Green does not wander the cemetery alone. They also claim to have seen the figure of an elderly man strolling along between the tombstones, sometimes smoking a pipe and sometimes just smiling as he looks away into the distance. While the old man's description sometimes varies, the witnesses never disagree about the fact that he is always accompanied by a small stiff-legged bulldog... with piercing green eyes.

MYSTERIES OF THE GRAVE

Located in a remote and secluded area of the Midwest is a graveyard that may be the most mysterious place discussed anywhere in this book. Unlike other dark and horrifying burial grounds, with tales of murder, death and black rituals, this cemetery seems to have no obvious reasons for being haunted... and yet it is. But do the spirits who walk here have any real connection to the place?

Or are they merely passing through, so to speak, using the wooded graveyard as a way station between this world and the next?

Anderson Cemetery is not a place that you are going to find on any maps. It is a typical rural cemetery that is well hidden by curving back roads, thick woods and wind-swept fields of grain. It's not a place that most people would go to, or would care to find, unless they had relatives buried there and had a reason to visit. Unlike other cemeteries in this book, it is not vandalized and is in fact in good condition, well maintained by the local township crew and still in use today.

Over the years, I have visited literally hundreds of places that are alleged to be haunted, but by all indications, Anderson Cemetery may be one of the most actively haunted spots that I have been to. Strangely though, its history suggests nothing that would have made it become that way. It is located on land that once belonged to a local farmer named Tavner Anderson. Prior to 1867, the graveyard was nothing more than a wooded section of his property. It did not become a burial ground until the internment of a small child took place there. A family that was passing through the area on their way west came to the Anderson house with a child that had fallen ill and died. They asked if the child might be buried somewhere on the farm. Anderson selected a clearing in the woods where a high knoll was located and on this site the cemetery was started. The small hill can still be seen in the cemetery today, although any grave marker made for the young girl has long since deteriorated over time.

I first heard about this cemetery several years ago from a man who had grown up in the area where it is located. For some time, there had been stories about people reporting strange lights and unusual sounds in the cemetery at night. It is very isolated and surrounded on three sides by heavy woods, so it was unlikely these lights and noises were coming from a nearby farmhouse or road. There were also several stories (of the "urban legend" variety) that had been told about an abandoned, stone house near the cemetery. It was also supposed to be haunted, a claim that was met with much skepticism by the man who told me about it.

It was not until his made his own trip the cemetery that he began to believe there might be something behind the tales that he had been told. One night, he drove out to the graveyard and stayed for several hours. A short time after he arrived, he got his first glimpse of one of the eerie lights. It floated up from behind one of the graves, flashed for a moment, and then vanished seemingly into nowhere. Soon, he saw several more of them but could find no explanation as to what they might be. Stunned, he attempted several times to photograph them, but he was sure that his camera and reflexes were too slow to catch them. When his film was developed though, he got the surprise of his life!

The finished photos showed what can only be called a number of "misty shapes and apparitions". What these unusual anomalies might be is anyone's guess! Many believe that they are ghosts, but whatever they are he swears there was nothing like that present in the cemetery that night. If they are ghosts, how can they be captured with an ordinary camera? And why did these odd images appear on film when they could not be seen with the human eye? No one really knows that for sure, despite many decades of research into spirits and spirit photography. Some believe that perhaps this "spirit energy" moves too fast to be seen by the human eye, while others maintain that the energy is made up of a different spectrum of light that only a camera can pick up. It does this by freezing a moment of time and space in a way that we cannot do. Regardless of how it happens, there are a fairly large number of unusual photos out there that cannot easily be explained away or debunked.

I confess that when I saw these photographs and heard the man's stories about Anderson Cemetery, I was intrigued. In fact, I was intrigued enough to accompany a group of ghost hunters to the cemetery on several occasions for their own research. These outings also were rewarded with some pretty strange photographs, a few of which I took with my own camera. One of them shows what clearly appears to be a white-human-like face that is looking directly into the camera! It was pretty unnerving to say that least and some time later, it was sent to the Kodak Laboratories for an explanation. However, they had no idea what the weird image might be.

About a year after my first visit to Anderson Cemetery, I returned there in the company of several other ghost researchers, including Tim Harte and Mike Hollinshead, creators of a sophisticated computer tracking system. The device was designed to take readings in an alleged haunted location and then analyze the gathered data and determine the nature of the haunting. The system reads changes in electro-magnetic fields, temperature changes, visible light, seismic vibrations and other areas. The experiments with this system are closely controlled and monitored with motion detectors and video cameras. The experiment at Anderson Cemetery was done in much the same way as past investigations, except this time, the system was used to monitor activity in conjunction with an old-fashioned seance.

A table was set up and a small group of average (non-psychic) people gathered around it with a Ouija board. These people were completely unaware of the past history of the place and were asked to simply try and communicate with anything that might be present. Whether you believe in the validity of Ouija boards or not, it was a fascinating, and somewhat chilling, experiment. In a relatively short time, the sitters claimed to be in contact with something supernatural. Later, they would say that at times, the pointer on the board was moving so fast that their fingers were not even touching it! Stranger still, this spirited communicator claimed to be that of a small child who had been buried there before it was a cemetery. What was so strange about this is that, as you might remember, the first burial that took place here was that of a little girl who had died while passing through the area. Not a single one of the people involved in the seance knew this at the time! I was the only person who possessed this information! Coincidence? Perhaps, but it seems unlikely.

It seems especially unlikely when considered in connection with the results achieved by Tim and Mike's computer system. According to the read-outs and graphs, there were things occurring in the cemetery during the seance that could not be explained! These anomalous spikes and dips were totally out of the ordinary and showed severe fluctuations in electro-magnetic radiation that could not be explained by natural means. Even stranger still was the fact that these fluctuations were occurring in response to the questions asked by the sitters! It seemed as though some sort of intelligent energy was present in the graveyard.

"I couldn't explain why this was happening," Tim Harte later told me in an interview. "The readings were completely unexplainable. Whatever was going on, it seemed to occur at the same time the people at the table would ask a question. The computer would show a massive change then, pause for a moment, and then spike again. It was almost like something was answering."

In addition, cameras and other equipment that was present picked up a number of unusual images and totally inexplicable temperature drops that simply should not have occurred. It seems impossible that, on a warm summer evening, high-tech equipment would register temperature drops of seventy degrees and more!

In my opinion, something supernatural occurred that night in Anderson Cemetery. Was it ghosts? I don't know, but whatever it was, I have never forgotten it. To this day, the graveyard remains a peculiar and curiously haunted place. The strangeness of the haunting is rivaled only by the fact that it really seems to have no reason to be haunted, and yet it is.

Could this graveyard be a stopping point or "way station" between this world and the next? I have no idea, but I suppose it is as good an answer as any.

THE GRAY LADY OF CAMP CHASE

For many years, fresh flowers have mysteriously appeared on the grave of Benjamin Allen, a soldier in the Confederate Army, who is buried in the Camp Chase Confederate Cemetery in Columbus, Ohio. The mysterious flowers have also been found on the grave of an unknown soldier here. Who leaves these offerings behind remains a mystery, Are they gifts from some unknown southern sympathizer? Or are they tokens of grief from beyond this world?

During the Civil War, Camp Chase was located on Livingston Avenue near Columbus. It was used for a variety of things during the conflict. In the early days of the war, it was a training camp and then a mustering-out point for Union soldiers but as prisoners-of-war began to tax the facilities on both side, it became a Confederate prison camp. Camp Chase was considered a pretty horrible spot, as most of the prisons were during the war. Some 2,000 prisoners died there of disease and malnutrition and so it is not surprising that the place has come to be considered as haunted. Many of these soldiers who died were buried in the prison cemetery and it is here that the famed 'Lady in Gray' still walks and leaves gifts of flowers behind.

She is said to be a young woman who wears a gray traveling suit in the style of the Civil War era. She walks through the cemetery with her head bowed and appears to be weeping. She has been observed walking directly through trees and through the iron cemetery gates.

Who this woman may be is unknown, but she is most likely the widow of one of the men who died here. Even after the war ended, many of the men who fought and died remained missing. Mass burials had taken place at the battlefields and at prisons like Camp Chase, which had created the Confederate cemetery here. Many women from the South journeyed to the northern camps in hopes of finding the resting place of their dead husbands.

The legends say that the Gray Lady was one of these widows. She came to the cemetery at some point in the years following the war, most likely around 1870. Only one burial in the graveyard, No. 46, had recorded the dead man as "Unknown" but the widow who searched the weed-choked grounds could find no grave for her husband. Sadly, the cemetery was in poor condition and the wooden markers had deteriorated and were rotting away. Many of them had already been lost. In these bitter days after the war, few in the North carried about the graves of Confederate soldiers.

The lonely widow came and went from the cemetery each day, looking for a name on a fallen grave marker that might belong to her husband. She became a familiar sight to those who lived in the area and the people who passed by often saw her walking through the cemetery in her gray dress, a wrinkled handkerchief clutched in her hand. She was soon dubbed the "Gray Lady of Camp Chase".

One day, the widow disappeared and was never seen in the graveyard again. She most likely gave up her search and went home, although someone conceived the romantic notion that she had died of a broken heart. She would not be seen again for many years and even then, it would be in a spectral form.

As the years passed, the cemetery continued to decline. The grave markers, now mostly rotted away, had fallen down and a great number had become lost. Weeds and brush overran the grounds and the place had been largely forgotten. Around 1900, a Confederate veteran named William H. Knauss took notice of the Camp Chase Cemetery. Thanks to his efforts the grounds were cleared of the tangled brush and a stone wall was built around the grounds to replace the old wooden fence. New headstones were also placed, as accurately as possible, based on the poor burial records. Knauss also organized memorial services for the dead, inviting local officials, other Confederate veterans and members of the Daughters of the Confederacy. His plans did not please everyone in the area and a number of newspaper editorials railed against him. The services brought many threats to those who attended and guards had to be posted to insure that order was kept. Over time though, the cemetery was saved and because of Knauss has been preserved for history.

Not long after the cemetery was restored, local people began to notice a strange figure walking through the cemetery day after day. Many of the older folks remembered the story of the Gray Lady who had once searched the graveyard for the burial site of her husband. Could this be the same woman after all of the years? And is so, how could she look so young? Then, passersby noticed something that gave the most hardened disbelievers a cold chill down the spine... The Gray Lady of Camp Chase was apparently a ghost! Far too many people began to tell of seeing her walking among the new gravestones, only to suddenly vanish without a trace! The tales would go on to say that she was seen walking directly through trees and passing like a wisp of fog through the cemetery wall.

For many years, the stories have continued to be told about the Gray Lady. She still walks in Camp Chase today, they say, and many have encountered her. In the summer of 1988, during a Civil War re-enactment, many of the people present heard the sounds of a woman crying. There was no woman present but the weeping sounds were unmistakable.

Could this forlorn cry have belonged to the Lady in Gray? Doe she still grieve, after more than a century, for the lost love of a forgotten soldier?

THE MOST HAUNTED TOWN IN OHIO

If there is any town that might qualify as the most haunted place in Ohio, it would probably be Athens, a sleepy community in the southeastern part of the state. Besides being home to the Ohio University, it is also nestled into the Appalachian Mountains, which for centuries has been considered a region of magic and ghostly folklore. There are many stories to Athens... and many ghosts.

The ghost stories and legends here are numerous and include everything from the hauntings of an abandoned mental hospital to stone angels who shed tears in local cemeteries. There is also the tale of the headless train conductor near Lake Hope who tries to flag down passers-by with his lantern. The story dates back to a time when the citizens of local Moonville were quarantined because of a measles outbreak. The food and supplies in town were running low and this man went out to flag down a train that might bring help. Tragically, he was struck by the train and killed. He has haunted this stretch of tracks ever since.

There are also many haunted houses as well. One of them is cursed with a large drum that is dotted with holes and is used in front of a luckless Athens residence as a flower pot. Apparently, this drum never leaks, no matter how much water is poured into it. The stories say that it was used by a local college professor to dispose of his wife's body in the lake after he murdered her. Her ghost is still said to be lingering here, much like the ghost of an old woman who refused to ever leave her home when she was alive. After he death, her spirit never left either and she is still seen today peering out the second-story window of her house.

For many years, Athens has been plagued, not only with tales of ghosts, but tales of cults and strange rituals also. For many, these stories are simply a part of the Appalachian folklore of the area, but for others, these stories are terrifyingly real. There have been many stories recounted in Athens about satanic groups and odd religious cults. It is believed that many such cults meet in areas that are regarded to be haunted, or are "power spots", and Athens certainly has more than its share. These cults (if they exist) have given birth to many related legends, especially in the graveyards of the surrounding area.

During the 1970's, these stories became especially widespread, perhaps corresponding with what became known as the "Hocking Hill Murders". Over a span of about eight years, a number of animals in Hocking County were mutilated and then left to die in fields and farm lots. Often the animals were discovered bleeding to death with their heads or their genitalia severed off. Although rumors were rampant about cult rituals, the authorities were reluctant to pursue this angle. The cases remained unsolved and the activity mostly died out in the 1980's.

This may have been the peak in Athens modern occult activity, but stories of local cults and ritual activities are countless and date back many years. This may be because of the huge influx of Spiritualists who came to the area many years ago. Their faith must have seemed strange to local residents and one thing is certain, many strange tales came about during their heyday in the Athens area.

Mt. Nebo, one of the highest mountain peaks in Athens County, is one of the most famous of the haunted spots. Apparently, at some point in the late 1800's, the British Psychical Society named Athens, and Mt. Nebo, one of the most haunted spots in the world, possibly because of the extraordinary events that were linked to it. The Spiritualists began arriving in the area the late 1840's, claiming to be searching for an area of spiritual significance. They settled around Mt. Nebo, believing that it was a source of psychic energy, as did the Shawnee Indians, who had considered it a sacred place. The area became most famous in 1852 when a local farmer named Jonathan Koons received word through a Spiritualist medium that he and all of his eight children were to be given the ability to communicate with spirits. He built a large house on top of a hill, according to directions he received from beyond, and the place became famous for its many seances and strange events.

Koons supposedly contacted the spirit of a pirate named John King, the head of a huge family of deceased persons. Over time, all of them were said to have made appearances at the Koons' house. More than 56 members of the King family reportedly manifested, but the most famous was his daughter, Katie, who went on from Ohio to make appearances at Spiritualist gatherings all over the world. Her most astonishing appearances, however, took place in relation to British medium, Florence Cook. Reportedly, her ghost materialized at many of Cook's seances and was seen by dozens of reputable witnesses.

Even outside of Mt. Nebo, there are other ghosts in Athens and a number of stories are connected to the Ohio University campus. One such haunted spot is the Zeta Tau Alpha house. This is one of the oldest houses in town and legend has it that during the years of the Civil War, it was used as a hiding place along the Underground Railroad, the secret route that led escaped slaves out of the south. Apparently, Confederate soldiers once raided the house and shot and killed an runaway slave named Nicodemus, who was hiding in the basement. The place has been reported to be haunted by his ghost ever since. Residents of the house have reported hearing scratching and whining sounds behind the wall where the slaves once hid, creaking noises and footsteps, the unlocking of doors and even the apparition of a man in tattered clothing.

This is not the only building on campus that is said to be haunted either. Another is Wilson Hall, which is home to the ghost of a student who died mysteriously there in the 1970's. The student died in room 428 and for years after, residents of the room claimed to hear footsteps and strange sounds and witnessed objects moving about the room on their own. The room has since been closed off and it is not given out to new students anymore.

Strangely, Wilson Hall is said to rest in the very center of one of Athens' most enduring legends. The building apparently falls in the middle of a huge pentagram that is made up by five of the area's cemeteries. The graveyards are located in the Peach Ridge area and allegedly, when the positions of each are plotted on a map, they actually do form the shape of a pentagram, the occult symbol of magic and power. The stories say that an Ohio University student once computed the actual distances to create the pentagram and found that the distance of the side actually matched up to within less than one-quarter mile of each other. Could this be why the area seems to have attracted so many tales of the unknown?

The five cemeteries are the largest ones in the area and are Simms, Hanning, Cuckler, Higgins and Zion. Of these five, Hanning and Simms are the most famous, and perhaps the most haunted. According to the stories, Simms Cemetery is said to have a rocky cliff on one side from which a tree protrudes outward. This was once used a gallows for executions and the rope scars can still be found marring the trunk. Local historians claim that John Simms, for whom the cemetery was named, may have once been the local hangman. This leads some people to believe that some of the reported ghosts of Peach Ridge many be spirits of those executed here. It is also said that John Simms himself is sometimes seen in the graveyard, perhaps still carrying out his duties from the other side.

Hanning Cemetery is another reportedly haunted spot. The ghost who has been seen here is an old man who wears a long robe. He is usually accompanied by the disembodied sounds of screams that echo into the night. There have been a couple of locally famous seances conducted at the burial ground, including one in 1969, when the heavily padlocked gate of the cemetery unlocked and opened on its own during the proceedings. During another seance in 1970, the spirit of David Tischman, a deceased Ohio University student was supposedly contacted by a group of his friends.

Another infamous graveyard in the area is Bethel Cemetery, located in nearby Troy Township. The cemetery is located near the border of Athens and Meigs County and is noted, not only for its ghost stories, but also for the strange way in which some of the graves are laid out. In most cemeteries, the graves are laid in an east-west direction to face the rising sun. At Bethel Cemetery, a whole plot of graves, that are more than one hundred years old, are inexplicably laid out in a north-south direction. Despite searches through old records, and accounts from long-time residents, no one seems to know why this section is placed differently from the rest of the graves in the cemetery.

Haines Cemetery on Lurig Road is also said to be haunted and this time by the ghost of a Civil War officer who went insane after the war. After returning home, he killed his entire family, burned down his house and then committed suicide. He and his family are buried in Haines Cemetery and his spirit still reportedly haunts the place, restlessly pacing back and forth. Those who might come face to face with him are supposed to have bad luck for years to come.

GHOSTS UNDER MAIN STREET

The South Main Street antique district in St. Charles, Missouri is a quaint, historic area with a number of old, original buildings and a distinguished past. This small town, alongside the Missouri River, dates back more than two centuries and the footsteps of history have certainly left their mark on the brick streets and cobblestone walks. This may be one of the reasons why the town is considered so haunted and why South Main Street has so many ghosts. But it's not only the passage of time that has left spirits behind here... some believe an old cemetery may have something to do with it as well!

The first settlers came to St. Charles in 1769 when a French Canadian trapper named Louis Blanchette arrived in the area. He started a small settlement and called the region "Les Petites Cote" or "The Little Hills". Blanchette became the first commander of St. Charles, under Spanish rule, but the area was soon filled with French settlers. In 1800, Spain gave the Louisiana Territory to France and then in 1804, it was sold to the United States under Thomas Jefferson. The president then established an expedition to explore the new region and to chart the course of the Missouri River. Jefferson put the command of the expedition into the hands of Meriwether Lewis and William Clark. In May 1804, the two men outfitted their journey in St. Charles and then departed for the western frontier. Another famous explorer was Daniel Boone, who came to St. Charles from Kentucky in 1795. He joined his sons, who had a homestead south of town. Boone continued to explore the region and a trail that he created here, Boone's Lick Road, became the starting point for both the Oregon and Santa Fe Trails.

As St. Charles began to grow, it saw an influx of German settlers, thanks to reports that the area resembled the Rhine Valley back in Germany. German businesses began to spring up all over town, including a tobacco factory and a brewery. In 1821, when Missouri became a state, the first capitol was located in St. Charles. It was located here for five years while a permanent building was constructed in Jefferson City.

Despite all of this, it is the old cemetery that is blamed for many of the hauntings on South Main Street. In 1789, the St. Borromeo Cemetery was established in the 400 block of this district. Although the bodies were exhumed and moved to a newer graveyard on Randolph Street in the 1800's, many people believe that a number of bodies were left behind. One of those people is John Dengler, the owner of the reportedly haunted Farmer's Home Building. Dengler is a past president and board member of the South Main Preservation Society and a member of the St. Charles Historical Preservation Society. He is sure that many of the bodies buried in the old cemetery were never found.

"Evidently, that cemetery was pretty good-sized and went all the way up to Third or Fourth Street," Dengler stated. "There were bodies there, and in fact, they are still there."

He distinctly recalled some work that was being done behind a corner building that is sometimes called the Armory or the French Armory. A construction crew was excavating to enlarge a nearby structure and when they dug into the hillside, they found a large number of bodies that had not been removed. At another site, a cluster of forgotten bones was encased in concrete when the floor of the building was laid.

"Almost every building on South Main Street has a story to tell," Dengler once wrote in an article for *St. Charles Living* Magazine, "and sometimes these ghostly happenings are more apparent."

One such building with a story to tell is Dengler's own place, the Farmer's Home Building, where he owns a tobacco shop. This building was constructed directly on top of where the old cemetery once stood. I have had several opportunities to visit with this charming and delightful man and he never shies away from recounting the hauntings of the shop, even though he maintains a healthy skepticism about the supernatural.

The building was constructed around 1815 and up until 1856, it was the Farmer's Tavern, a popular hotel and restaurant. John Dengler's Tobacco Shop, which has been in operation since 1917, is located in what was once the ladies' dining room of the inn and sometimes the smell of ham and green beans wafts through the air, even though no one is cooking.

Dengler and his wife, Tru, use the second floor of the building as living quarters, while he rents out the other shops on the first floor. The other staff members in the building have also had some rather strange encounters that they have trouble explaining away. Peggy Behm of "Country Stichin'", once accused John of playing a prank on her. She was walking down a staircase in the back part of the building and distinctly felt a hand fall on her shoulder. Then, a voice whispered eerily in her ear. "Peggy, Peggy", it said. Startled, she hurried down the steps to find Dengler just walking in the door from a meeting that had kept him out of the building all morning. Even though she first assumed that he had played a trick on her, she quickly realized that she had no explanation for what had just happened.

They have also heard heavy footsteps on the same stairs and in the hallways of the building. Dengler's daughter, Laura Dengler Muench, was once terrified by the sound of laughter that came from nowhere and Tru Dengler had another strange experience while painting one day. "For about four days, "said John Dengler, "a French-speaking apparition seemed to delight in playing tricks of floating cigarette packs in the air and hiding them. Unexplainable too was how the KMOX radio talk show would suddenly be switched to rather unusual classical music without the dial being changed. On the fifth day of the Frenchman's visit, a baby was heard to be crying, whereupon it was soothed by a calming French voice."

So, who are the ghosts that haunt the Farmer's Home building? Are they former guests of the hotel or the spirits of those left behind from the St. Borromeo Cemetery? John Dengler has no idea but as far as he is concerned they are welcome to stay... "but they've got to behave themselves", he said with a smile.

HAUNTED CEMETERIES OF ILLINOIS

In his book *Mysterious America*, author Loren Coleman, in a discussion of regional anomalies, pointed to the fact that the state of Illinois seems to have an inordinate amount of graveyard hauntings. Why this might be, I have no idea, but it is certain that cemetery ghosts are plentiful here, as has been seen in earlier chapters and in the remainder of this one.

One of my favorite graveyard ghost stories involves the old cemetery that was once used by the Bartonville Insane Asylum near Peoria, Illinois. The hospital opened around 1900 and fell under the leadership of a man named Dr. George Zeller, a pioneer in mental health during that time. He was instrumental in bring health care for the insane into modern times and turned the Bartonville hospital into one of the finest institutions in the state. The hospital implemented what was called the "cottage system" and 33 different buildings were used to house patients. There was also a dorm for the nursing staff, a store, a power house and a domestic building with a laundry, bakery and kitchen. Dr. Zeller also supervised the creation of cemeteries, where the bodies of unknown patients could be buried. Eventually, the burial grounds grew to include four different graveyards although the oldest cemetery would mark the location of the first ghost story to ever be associated with the hospital.

And this is no mere rumor or folk tale, but a documented account of a supernatural event. The teller of the tale was Dr. George A. Zeller himself!

Shortly after organizing the cemeteries for the hospital, Dr. Zeller also put together a burial corps to deal with the disposal of the bodies of patients who died. The corps always consisted of a staff member and several of the patients. While these men were still disturbed, all of them were competent enough to take part in the digging of graves. Of all of the gravediggers, the most unusual man, according to Dr. Zeller, was a fellow called "A. Bookbinder". This man had been sent to the hospital from a county poorhouse. He had suffered a mental breakdown while working in a printing house in Chicago and his illness had left him incapable of coherent speech. The officer who had taken him into custody had noted in his report that the man had been employed as "a bookbinder". A court clerk inadvertently listed this as the man's name and he was sent to the hospital as A. Bookbinder.

Dr. Zeller described the man as being strong and healthy, although completely uncommunicative. He was attached to the burial corps and soon, attendants realized that "Old Book", as he was affectionately called, was especially suited to the work. Nearly every patient at the hospital was unknown to the staff so services were performed out of respect for the deceased and not because of some personal attachment. Because of this, everyone was surprised during the first internment attended by Old Book when he removed his cap and began to weep loudly for the dead man.

"The first few times he did this," Dr. Zeller wrote, "his emotion became contagious and there were many moist eyes at the graveside but when at each succeeding burial, his feelings overcame him, it was realized that Old Book possessed a mania that manifested itself in uncontrollable grief." It was soon learned that Old Book had no favorites among the dead. He would do the same thing at each service and as his grief reached its peak, he would go and lean against an old elm tree that stood in the center of the cemetery and here, he would sob loudly.

Time passed and eventually Old Book also passed away. Word spread among the employees and as Book was well liked, everyone decided they would attend his funeral. Dr. Zeller wrote that more than 100 uniformed nurses attended, along with male staff members and several hundred patients.

Dr. Zeller officiated the service. Old Book's casket was placed on two cross beams above his empty grave and four men stood by to lower it into the ground at the end of the service. As the last hymn was sung, the men grabbed hold of the ropes. "The men stooped forward," Dr. Zeller wrote, "and with a powerful, muscular effort, prepared to lift the coffin, in order to permit the removal of the crossbeams and allow it to gently descend into the grave. At a given signal, they heaved away the ropes and the next instant, all four lay on their backs. For the coffin, instead of offering resistance, bounded into the air like an eggshell, as if it were empty!"

Needless to say, the spectators were a little shocked at this turn of events and the nurses were reported to have shrieked, half of them running away and the other half coming closer to the grave to see what was happening.

"In the midst of the commotion," Dr. Zeller continued, "a wailing voice was heard and every eye turned toward the Graveyard Elm from whence it emanated. Every man and woman stood transfixed, for there, just as had always been the case, stood Old Book, weeping and moaning with an earnestness that outrivaled anything he had ever shown before." Dr. Zeller was amazed at what he observed, but had no doubt that he was actually seeing it. "I, along with the other bystanders, stood transfixed at the sight of this apparition... it was broad daylight and there could be no deception."

After a few moments, the doctor summoned some men to remove the lid of the coffin, convinced that it must be empty and that Old Book could not be inside of it. The lid was lifted and as soon as it was, the wailing sound came to an end. Inside of the casket lay the body of Old Book, unquestionably dead. It was said that every eye in the cemetery looked upon the still corpse and then over to the elm tree in the center of the burial ground. The specter had vanished!

"It was awful, but it was real," Dr. Zeller concluded. "I saw it, 100 nurses saw it and 300 spectators saw it." But if it was anything other the ghost of Old Book, Dr. Zeller had no idea what it could have been.

A few days after the funeral, the Graveyard Elm began to wither and die. In spite of efforts to save it, the tree declined over the next year and then died. Later, after the dead limbs had dropped, workmen tried to remove the rest of the tree, but stopped after the first cut of the ax caused the tree to emanate what was said to be 'an agonized, despairing cry of pain". After that, Dr. Zeller suggested that the tree be burned, however as soon as the flames started around the tree's base, the workers quickly put them out. They later told Dr. Zeller they had heard a sobbing and crying sound coming from it.

Eventually, the tree fell down in a storm, taking with it the lingering memories of a mournful man known as Old Book.

WHERE THE DEAD WALK

Located in the southern part of Decatur, Illinois and just a stone's throw away from the Sangamon River, is the city's oldest and most beautiful graveyard, Greenwood Cemetery.

There is a chance that Greenwood Cemetery is the most historic location in all of Decatur.... but regardless of whether or not it is the most historic, it is, without a doubt, the most haunted.

The beginnings of Greenwood Cemetery are a mystery. There is no record to say when the first burials took place in the area of land that would someday be Greenwood. It was not the city's first official burial ground, but the Native Americans who lived here first did use it as a burial site, as did the early settlers. The only trace they left behind were the large numbers of unmarked graves, scattered about the present-day grounds.

There was also an incident that took place many years ago that marked the beginning of the cemetery's strange and mysterious history. The precise year of this event is unknown but it is believe to have taken place in the late 1820's. A small group of settlers were encamped near the Sangamon River and had constructed a crude liquor still and were hard at work making 'moonshine' from corn alcohol. A group of Indians passed by where they were working and caught the attention of the moonshiners. No one knows the reason, but the settlers shot and killed the Indians and buried their bodies in a shallow ravine at the edge of the burying grounds. They heaped a number of stones on top of them and vanished. The makeshift grave can still be seen on the side of a hill in the southwest part of Greenwood Cemetery. The story of the settlers and the Indians has been largely forgotten over the years but folk legends have it that these murders may be the reason why the cemetery is so haunted.

It would be another ten years after this event before the general populace would begin to regard this area as a full-fledged cemetery. During the decade of the 1830's, it is believed that local settlers did use this area and legend has it that even a few runaway slaves who did not survive their quest for freedom were buried on the grounds under the cover of night.

In March 1857, the Greenwood Cemetery Association was organized and the cemetery was incorporated into the city of Decatur. By 1900, Greenwood had become the most fashionable place in Decatur in which to be buried. It had also become quite popular as a recreational park and it was not uncommon to see noontime visitors enjoying their lunch on the grassy hills. Unfortunately though, by the 1920's, the cemetery was broke and could no longer be maintained. It was allowed to revert back to nature and it wasn't long before the cemetery began to resemble a forgotten graveyard with overgrown brush, fallen branches and tipped and broken gravestones. Hundreds of graves were left unattended and allowed to fall into disrepair. The stories and legends that would "haunt" Greenwood for years to come had taken root in the desolate conditions that existed in the oldest section of the graveyard. Tales of wandering spirits and glowing apparitions began to be told about the cemetery and decay and decline came close to bringing about the destruction of the place. The cemetery became a forgotten spot in Decatur, remembered only as a spooky novelty.

The next decades however would bring a great change. At this point, the cemetery was nearly in ruins. The roads were now only partially covered mud and cinder tracks that were so deeply rutted that they were no longer passable. The oaks, which had added beauty to the cemetery, had now become its greatest curse. The falls of leaves, which had not been raked away in years, were knee-deep in some places. Fallen branches from the trees littered the grounds, which were overgrown and tangled with weeds and brush. Water, time and vandals had wreaked havoc on Greenwood's grave markers. Years of rain, harsh weather and a lack of care had caused many stones to fall at angles and many more were simply lost altogether. Others lay broken and damaged beyond repair, having given up the fight with the elements.

In 1957 though, ownership and operation of the cemetery was taken over by the city of Decatur and the township crews would now maintain it. The city could not handle the cost of the city's restoration, so a number of organizations and private individuals volunteered to donate time and labor to save it. The restoration was largely a success and despite a few setbacks, Greenwood Cemetery has managed to prosper over the years. Despite this, the place has not lost its eerie reputation and the stories of ghosts and the unexplained still mingle with fact and fiction, blending a strangeness that is unparalleled by any other location in the haunted heart of Illinois.

There have been nearly as many legends and strange stories told about Greenwood as there have been people buried here. They are the stories of the supernatural, of ghosts, phantoms and things that go bump in the night and what follows is a sampling of these eerie tales. Just don't forget, as you are reading them... keep looking back over your shoulder. You never know who might be coming up behind you!

The story of Greenwood's most famous resident ghost, the Greenwood Bride, begins around 1930 and concerns a young couple who was engaged to be married. The young man was a reckless fellow and a bootlegger, who was greatly disapproved of by his future bride's family. One summer night, the couple decided not to wait any longer to get married and made plans to elope. They would meet just after midnight, as soon as the young man could deliver one last shipment of whiskey and have enough money for their wedding trip. Unfortunately, he was delivering the bottles of whiskey when he was murdered. The killers, rival businessmen, dumped his body into the Sangamon River, where two fishermen found it the next morning.

The young woman had gone to the arranged meeting place the night before and she had waited until daybreak for her lover. She was worried when she returned home and devastated when she later learned that he had been killed. She became crazed with grief and began tearing at her hair and clothing. Finally, her parents summoned the family doctor, who gave her a sedative and managed to calm her down.

She disappeared later that night, taking with her only the dress that she planned to wear in her wedding. She was found wearing the bridal gown the next day, floating face down in the river, near where her lover's body had been pulled ashore. She had taken her own life near the place where her fiancee's had been lost, perhaps hoping to find him in eternity.

A funeral was held and her body was laid to rest on a hill in Greenwood Cemetery. It has been said however, that she does not rest here in peace. As time has passed, dozens of credible witnesses have reported encountering the 'Greenwood Bride' on that hill in the cemetery. They claim the ghost of a woman in a glowing bridal gown has been seen weaving among the tombstones. She walks here with her head down and with a scrap of cloth gripped tightly in her hand. Occasionally, she raises it to her face, as if wiping away tears.

Could this sad young woman still be searching for the spirit of her murdered lover? No record remains as to where this man was laid to rest, so no one knows where his spirit may walk. Perhaps he is out there somewhere, still looking for the young woman that he was supposed marry many years ago?

There have been many accounts of ghosts and spirits in Greenwood Cemetery that are not of the friendly variety and a number of anecdotes like the one that follows. It is a good example of the kind of story that has been told about Greenwood for years. The first accounts come from the 1920's, when the cemetery was an easy shortcut for those people who lived in the south end of the city. Rundown neighborhoods circled the graveyard in those days and it was often quicker to cut through the graveyard at night than take the longer route around it. On many occasions, these late night visitors told of hearing footsteps following along behind them as they walked along. Often the phantom footsteps would crunch in the leaves or disturb the tall grass as the unseen entity passed by.

One such story took place about two decades ago. A man was cutting through the cemetery one winter's night on his way to a friend's house. He was walking along a cemetery roadway when he heard the distinctive sound of hard-soled shoes following behind him. He looked back several times, but saw no one in the gloom. Finally, unnerved by the continuing sound, he veered from the paved road and set off across the cemetery grounds. The sounds followed him! Although his pursuer was still unseen, he could hear their footsteps pounding behind him, sinking through the hard crust of the snow. The footsteps got closer and closer.... but whoever was chasing him remained invisible!

Finally, he arrived at his friend's house, breathless and scared. It wasn't long though before his friend managed to calm him down and to make him realize that the so-called "chase" had been all in his mind. To prove the point, his friend accompanied him to the cemetery the next morning. They soon found the place where the man had left the road and got quite a surprise when they examined the surface of the snow! They easily found the man's footprints, but behind them was a second set of tracks that followed the first to the edge of the cemetery... then abruptly disappeared!

Another strange entity of Greenwood is no less mysterious for the fact that it made a single appearance more than 20 years ago. In fact, this one may be even more frightening!

Jack Gifford, a former Decatur resident, told me about a night when he decided to venture alone into the cemetery. He waited until after dark and then climbed the back fence. That night was in 1977, but Gifford has not been back to Greenwood since then!

He walked out among the tombstones, hoping to make his way by the light of the moon. He crossed the road and started up a small hill, then spotted a figure standing among the gravestones a short distance away. Gifford froze in his tracks, sure that he was about to be caught. The cemetery closes at sunset and he knew that he could be arrested for trespassing. He ducked behind the largest tombstone that he could find and decided to wait until the other man walked away.

After waiting a few minutes, he heard nothing, so he decided to look and see if the man was still standing there. He poked his head around the end of the stone and saw that he was still in the same spot. The man appeared to be staring at something, but he wasn't looking in Jack's direction. Gifford described the man as very tall, thin and rather ordinary-looking. He said that the man then turned slowly around, facing in his direction. "But he didn't really turn," Jack corrected himself. "He just seemed to rotate... and that was when I saw his eyes!"

The mysterious man looked toward where he hid behind the tombstone and Gifford saw that he was staring with what appeared to be empty eye sockets!

"They were like black holes.. but they sorta glowed a little, like the moon was shining through the back of his head," he told me and he chuckled self-consciously as if he were embarrassed by his suggestion. "I took off running then and I don't have any idea if the man chased me, but he wouldn't have caught me anyway!"

One of the cemetery's most enduring legends is the story of the "ghost lights" that appear on the south side of the burial grounds. These small globes of light have been reported here for many decades and are still reported today. I saw these lights myself a few years back and while I have no logical explanation for what they are, or why they appear here, the lore of the cemetery tells a strange and tragic story.

The legend tells of a flood that occurred many years ago, most likely around 1900-1905, which wiped out a portion of the cemetery. The Sangamon River, located just south of the cemetery, had been dammed in the late 1800's and was often prone to floods. During one particularly wet spring, the river overflowed its banks and washed into the lower sections of the cemetery. Tombstones were knocked over and the surging water even managed to wash graves away and to force buried caskets to the surface. Many of them, as these were the days before Lake Decatur had been formed, went careening downstream on the swollen river.

Once the water receded, it took many days to find the battered remains of the coffins that had been washed down the river and many were never found at all. For some time after, farmers and fishermen were startled to find caskets, and even corpses, washing up on river banks some miles away. There were many questions as to the identities of the bodies and so many of them were buried again in unmarked and common graves. These new graves were placed on higher ground, up on the southern hills of Greenwood.

Since that time, it has been said that the mysterious lights have appeared on these hills. The stories say that the lights are the spirits of those whose bodies washed away in the flood. Their wandering ghosts are now doomed to search forever for the place where their remains are now buried.

Dozens of trustworthy witnesses have claimed to see the "spook lights" on the hill, moving in and out among the old, weathered stones. The mystery of the lights has managed to elude all those who have attempted to solve it. Many have tried to pass them off as reflections from cars passing over the lake... but what of sightings that date back to before Lake Decatur ever existed? In those days, a covered bridge over the Sangamon River took travelers along the old county highway and for many years, not a single automobile crossed it, as motorcars had not yet come to Decatur.

Whether the cause is natural or supernatural, the lights can still be seen along the edge of the graveyard today. Want to see them for yourself? Seek out the south hills of Greenwood some night by finding the gravel parking lot that is located across the road from the cemetery fence. Here, you can sit and observe the hills. You have to have a lot of patience, and may even have to make more than one trip, but eventually, you will probably be lucky enough to see the "ghost lights". It's an experience that you won't soon forget!

Located on the edge of the forest that makes up Greenwood's northwest corner is an old burial plot that sits upon a small hill. This is the plot of a family named "Barrackman" and if you approach this piece of land from the east, walking along the cemetery's narrow roads, you will find a set of stone steps that lead to the top of a grassy hill. There are four, rounded stones here, marking the burial sites of the family. Little is known about the Barrackman's, other than the four members of this family are buried in Greenwood. No records exist about who they were, when they may have lived here or even about what they may have accomplished in life. We simply know their names, father, mother, son and his wife, as they are inscribed on the identical tombstones. As mentioned, two of the stones bear the names of the Barrackman women, and although no one really knows for sure... it may be one of these two women who still haunts this burial plot!

According to many accounts, collected over the years from dozens of people who never knew one another, a visitor who remains in the cemetery as the sun is going down may be treated to an eerie, and breathtaking sight. According to the story, the visitor is directed to the Barrackman staircase as dusk falls on the graveyard. It is said that a semi-transparent woman in a long dress appears on the stone steps. She sits there on the staircase with her head bowed and appears to be weeping, although she has never been heard to make a sound. Those who do get the chance to see her, never see her for long. She always inexplicably vanishes as the sun dips below the horizon. She has never been seen in the daylight hours and never after dark... only just at sunset.

Who is this lonely woman and why does she haunt the staircase and the Barrackman graves? There are some who suggest she may have been a member of the family buried here, but what could have brought her back to her burial site? I tend to favor the idea that she may have been another person entirely, who found peace on this staircase and came to the place during her lifetime to weep for someone who died and was buried nearby.

Most likely, we will never know for sure just who she is or what brings her here, although she is still seen today. Perhaps one day she will break her silence and speak to some unsuspecting passerby, who just manages to get a glimpse of her before she fades away into the night.

Located on a high, desolate hill in the far southwest corner of Greenwood Cemetery is a collection of identical stone markers, inscribed with the names of the local men who served, and some who died, during the brutal days of the Civil War. The silence of this area is deafening. Visitors stand over the remains of some of the city of Decatur's greatest heroes and the bloody victors of the war. But not all of the men buried here served under the Stars and Stripes of the Union Army....

There are dark secrets hidden here.....

During the years of the Civil War, a great many trains passed through the city of Decatur. It was on a direct line of the Illinois Central Railroad, which ran deep into the south. The line continued north to Chicago and ran near the prison camp that was located there, Camp Douglas. Many trains came north carrying Union troops bound for Decatur and beyond. Soldiers aboard these trains were often wounded, sick and dying. Occasionally, deceased soldiers were taken from the trains and buried in Greenwood Cemetery, which was very close to the train tracks. These men were buried in the cemetery and the citizens of Decatur marked their graves with honor. But that wasn't always the case....

On many occasions, trains came north bearing Confederate prisoners who were on their way to the camp near Chicago. These soldiers were not treated so honorably. Often, Confederates who died were unloaded from the train and buried in shallow, unmarked graves in forgotten locations. Most of these soldiers were unknown victims of gunshot and disease and many were past the point of revealing their identity. These men will never be known and their families will never have discovered what became of them after they departed for the battlefields of war. Those men are now silent corpses scattered about the confines of Greenwood Cemetery.

Why was there such a hatred for the Confederacy in Decatur? Besides being the home of the 116th Illinois Regiment, it seemed that nearly everyone in the city had a friend or relative in the Union army. A number of places in Decatur were also used as stations on the 'Underground Railroad', which means that the abolitionists also had a stronghold here. This was the reason, in 1863, when a prison train holding southern prisoners pulled into Decatur, it was given the kind of reception that it was. The stories say the train was filled with more than 100 prisoners and that many of them had contracted yellow fever in the diseased swamps of the south.

The Union officers in charge of the train had attempted to separate the Confederates who had died in transit, but to no avail. Many of the other men were close to death from the infectious disease and it was hard to tell which men were alive and which were not. They called for wagons to come to a point near the cemetery but no one would answer the summons. Several soldiers were dispatched and a group of men and wagons were commandeered in the city. The bodies were removed from the train and taken to Greenwood Cemetery. They were unloaded here and their bodies were stacked at the base of a hill in the southwest corner of the graveyard. This location was possibly the least desirable spot in the cemetery. The hill was so steep that many of the grave diggers had trouble keeping their balance. It was the last place that anyone would want to be buried and for this reason, the enemies of the Union were placed there.

Ironically, years later, the top of this same hill would be fashioned into a memorial for Union soldiers who died in battle and for those who perished unknown.

The men from the city hastily dug shallow graves and tossed the bodies of the Confederates inside. It has been said that without a doctor present, no one could have known just how many of the soldiers had actually died from yellow fever.... were all of those buried here actually dead? Many say they were not, some of them accidentally buried alive, and this is why the area is the most haunted section of Greenwood.

To make matters worse, many years later, spring rains and flooding would cause the side of the hill itself to collapse in a mudslide and further disturb the bodies of these men. Not only did the Confederate remains lie scattered about in the mud, but the disaster also took with it the bodies of Union men who had been laid to rest in the memorial section at the top of the hill. This further complicated matters, as now, no had any idea how to identify the bodies. In the end, the remains were buried again and the hill was constructed into terraces to prevent another mudslide in the future. The bodies were placed in the Civil War Memorial section and the graves were marked with stones bearing the legend of "Unknown US Soldier". Sadly, it will never be known just who these men may be.

But what causes this section of the cemetery to be considered as haunted? Psychic impressions from the past or angry spirits? Some people believe that it may be both as investigations, and reports from eight decades, have revealed unexplainable tales, and strange energy, lingering around this hill. Visitors who have come here, many of them knowing nothing about the bizarre history of this place, have told of hearing voices, strange sounds, footsteps in the grass, whispers, cries of torment and some even claim to have been touched or pushed by unseen hands.

There are also the reports of the soldiers themselves returning from the other side of the grave. Accounts have been revealed over the years that tell of visitors to the cemetery actually seeing men in uniform walking among the tombstones... men that are strangely transparent.

The most stunning tale was reported a few years ago and was told to me first-hand. It happened that a young man was walking along the road in the back corner of the cemetery. He saw a man standing on the top of the hill, who beckoned to him. The boy walked up to him and was surprised to see that he was wearing tattered gray clothing which was very dirty and spotted with what looked like blood. The man looked at the boy oddly and he wore an expression of confusion on his face.

"Can you help me?", the man asked softly of the boy. "I don't know where I am..... and I want to go home."

Before the boy could answer, the man simply vanished.

MYSTERIES OF WILLIAMSBURG HILL

One of the strangest mystery spots in Central Illinois is undoubtedly Williamsburg Hill. It is located in the south central part of the region, near the small communities of Tower Hill and Shelbyville. The hill is not hard to find, for it rises to its highest point at 810 feet, making it the highest elevation in that part of the state. To drive across the hill today, you would see no evidence of the history that is hidden in this remote spot. Williamsburg Hill just seems to rise out of nowhere on the prairie and is covered by a heavy stand of trees.

The village of Williamsburg, which was also called Cold Spring for a time, was laid out in 1839 by Dr. Thomas Williams and William Horsman. It was located on the south side of the large hill and for about 40 years, was a bustling community of about four square blocks. At one time, there were two churches, a doctor's office, a saloon, a post office, a blacksmith shop and a number of modest homes. The Main Street of the community was once part of the "Old Anglin' Road", a stage route that ran from Shelbyville to Vandalia. It was this stage line that brought prosperity to the village for many years. Some say the community died out when the Beardstown, Shawneetown and Southeastern Railroad bypassed the village in 1880. However, others believe that the town was abandoned for much darker reasons, attributed to the strangeness of Williamsburg Hill itself.

Today, there is nothing left of the village, save for a few old gravel pits. The land where it once stood has long been plowed under and trees have covered the area where homes once stood. It has become another of Illinois' lost towns although to look back with a critical eye, it's hard to believe a settlement ever existed here anyway. Life would have not have been easy on the hills and ridges of this strange place, although a scattering of people do live here today.

One of the strangest locations on the hill is a place called Ridge Cemetery. This rugged graveyard can be found on the highest summit of Williamsburg Hill. The desolate burial ground has many tilted stones, thanks to the sharp hills, and also bears evidence of both vandalism and unmarked graves. The cemetery can be found by watching for a massive microwave tower, located just east of the burial ground.

Ridge Cemetery has been part of the lore that makes up Williamsburg Hill for many years and has long been considered a frightening place. It is located back off the main road and down a wooded lane that is very dark for those curiosity-seekers who venture down it at night, braving the sheriff's deputies who regularly patrol the road and graveyard. Cases of vandalism, and some say darker things, have forced the authorities to close the place after dark. There have been reports of cultists using the cemetery and this has sparked both gossip and concern in small, surrounding towns. As far as I know, there is little evidence to suggest these stories are true, but once such rumors get started, they are hard to stop.

Other stories of the burial ground are more ghostly in nature. Many of these tales speak of strange lights and apparitions in the vicinity of the graveyard and the woods beyond it. In the forest, there are a number of forgotten graves that have been hidden by time. There are also anecdotes concerning the old road that leads back to the cemetery, namely stories of a bobbing red light and a spectral old man who vanishes if anyone tries to approach him.

Paul Smith (not his real name) is one of those who claims to have encountered the unusual light. About 13 years ago, he and three friends made a nighttime trip to Williamsburg Hill and Ridge Cemetery. They decided to park the car on the main road and then walk back to the cemetery. They used no light, to avoid being spotted by anyone who lived nearby or who might be driving past. In this complete darkness, they were surprised to see a round red light appear ahead of them at the edge of the woods. The light hovered and shimmered about three feet above the ground.

"It looked as if someone was carrying it," Paul told me. "We stopped walking because we were sure we had been caught trespassing back there." Then, as the three young men watched, the light seemed to curve outward and start away from them and towards the cemetery.

"We were pretty scared by then, "Paul added. "We still weren't sure if the light belonged to somebody who lived around there. Then, one of my friends turned on his flashlight and pointed it toward the light."

To the shock of the trio, the light was not a lantern being carried by a person, but was actually floating in the air! A few seconds after the flashlight beam swept over it, the red light vanished. This marked an abrupt ending to the young men's late night trek to Ridge Cemetery!

In addition to the many stories told by visitors to Williamsburg Hill, there are also the incidents that occur involving those who still live here. Many of them will state that strange things happen here on a daily basis, as if the landmark that rises from nowhere out of the prairie acts as some sort of signal beacon, or magnet, for strange activity. Past accounts tell of ghostly figures on the roadways, animal mutilations and unexplained lights in the sky. So what makes Williamsburg Hill so strange and haunted and why has it been the source for so many legends over the years?

It's possible that the huge microwave tower on the hill could offer some clues, even if some of the stories were already being told before the tower was ever built. Could some of the phenomena be attributed to the tower? Is it possible that the strange lights, glowing balls of energy and eerie apparitions are some sort of side effect from the magnetic field around this structure? It has also been suggested that the tower may be attracting the paranormal phenomena, instead of creating it. Perhaps lost spirits are feeding off the energy given off by the tower, resulting in the myriad of stories that plague the place?

Or maybe, as was suggested earlier, the strangeness was already here, attracted by the natural landscape of the hill? Who knows? Regardless, if any of the numerous stories about Williamsburg Hill have even a semblance of truth to them, then the place is infested with ghosts! And would not be the sort of place where anyone in his right mind would want to venture after the sun goes down!

CHICAGO'S PHANTOM FIGURES

Without a doubt, the most famous ghostly hitchhiker in the Chicago area is the young girl who has been connected to Resurrection Cemetery for a number of decades. Her story will appear later in the chapter, but there are other restless and roaming ghosts of Chicago cemeteries as well.

One such spirit, a sort of "sister ghost" to Resurrection Mary, haunts the vicinity of Jewish Waldheim Cemetery, located at 1800 South Harlem Avenue in Chicago. This is perhaps one of the more peaceful and attractive of the city's downtown graveyards and is easily recognizable from the columns that are mounted at the front gates. They were once part of the old Cook County Building, which was demolished in 1908. This cemetery would most likely go quietly on through its existence if not for the tales of the "Flapper Ghost". While little background can be discovered about this spirit, it remains a fascinating story.

The story of the ghost states that she was a young Jewish girl who attended dances at the Melody Mill Ballroom, formerly on Des Plaines Avenue. She was said to be a very attractive brunette with bobbed hair and a dress right out of the Roaring 20's, hence the spirit's nickname of the "Flapper Ghost". This fetching phantom has been known to hitch rides on Des Plaines Avenue and most often has been seen near the cemetery gates. Some travelers passing the cemetery even claimed to see her entering a mausoleum that is located off Harlem Avenue.

Although recent sightings have been few, the ghost was most active in 1933, during the Century of Progress Exhibition, and again in 1973. In the years before World War II, she was often reported at the Melody Mill Ballroom, where she would dance with young men and often ask for a ride home. After they drove her to the cemetery, the girl would explain that she lived in the caretaker's house (since demolished) and then get out of the car. Often with her admirers in pursuit, she would then run out into the cemetery and vanish among the tombstones.

More sightings took place in 1973 and one report even occurred during the daylight hours. A family was visiting the cemetery one day and was startled to see a young woman dressed like a "flapper" walking toward a crypt, where she suddenly disappeared. The family hurried over to the spot, only to find no girl and nowhere to which she could have vanished so quickly.

According to author Dale Kaczmarek, another strange sighting took place in 1979 when a police officer saw a beautiful girl walking near the ballroom on a rainy night. He asked her where she was going and she replied "home". He offered her a ride and she directed him to an apartment building near the cemetery entrance. After the girl got out of the car, she vanished near a covered doorway and the policeman, shocked, got out and went after her. He was sure that she could not have gotten into the building so quickly and was even more surprised to see no wet footprints on the dry sidewalk below the building's awning.

Since that time, sightings of the "Flapper" have been few, but we should take into account that she appeared often back in the 1930's and then didn't show up again with any frequency until the 1970's. Perhaps she is just waiting round and will soon come back for a return engagement!

Another phantom hitcher haunts the roadways near the Evergreen Cemetery in Evergreen Park, a Chicagoland community. For more than two decades, an attractive teenager has been roaming out beyond the confines of the cemetery in search of a ride. A number of drivers claim to have spotted her and in the 1980's a flurry of encounters occurred when motorists in the south and western suburbs reported picking up this young girl. She always asked them for a ride to a location in Evergreen Park and then mysteriously vanished from the vehicle at the cemetery.

According to the legends, she is the spirit of a child buried within the cemetery, but there is no real folklore to explain why she leaves her grave in search of travelers, nor what brings her to the suburbs and so far from home. She is what some would call the typical "vanishing hitchhiker" but there is one aspect to this ghost that sets her apart from the others. In addition to seeking rides in cars, she is resourceful enough to find other transportation when it suits her.

In recent years, encounters with this phantom have also taken place at a bus stop that is located directly across the street from the cemetery. Many have claimed to see a dark-haired young girl here who mysteriously vanishes. On occasion, she has also climbed aboard a few Chicago Transit Authority buses as well.

One evening, a young girl climbed aboard a bus and breezed right past the driver without paying the fare. She walked to the back portion of the vehicle and sat down, seemingly without a care in the world. Irritated the driver called out to her, but she didn't answer. Finally, he stood up and walked back toward where she was seating. She would either pay, he thought, or have to get off the bus! Not surprisingly though, before he could reach her, she vanished before his eyes!

According to reports, other shaken drivers have had the same eerie experience at this bus stop. He has spoken with others who have also seen this young girl and every single one of them have seen her disappear as if she had never been there in the first place!

Another figure, this time much more menacing, reportedly haunts the region around St. Casimir's Cemetery in southwest Chicago. In the middle 1970's, people passing near the cemetery on Pulaski Road began to tell of a strange figure who was seen standing inside of the cemetery fence and wearing a long, black cape. It was said that the man was sickly thin, unkempt and had a ghastly white complexion. To make matters worse, his face wore such an expression of utter malevolence that people who reported seeing him often said that the shock of the encounter stayed with them for days.

One young man, who spied the figure in his automobile headlights one evening, saw the man bent over and facing away from him in the cemetery. When he slowed down to get a better look, the figure spun around and bared his teeth at him, sending the young man quickly on his way.

The stories continued and each witness reported a similar creature but even when the accounts varied slightly, they always mentioned the look of hatred on the figure's face. In June 1978, a "grotesque figure in a top hat and cape" was seen by local children. Alsip police officials reported that "the person was described as being six feet tall, extremely thin with broken teeth and wearing dirty, muddy clothing." They also noted that witnesses told of a disgusting odor coming from the black-clothed figure.

Similar reports of this same person still take place in the area today. Many of them have occurred while people are traveling southbound on Kostner Avenue and pause at the stoplight on 111th Street. As their headlights illuminate the front gates of the cemetery, they are often stunned to see the pale apparition of the man in black behind the fence. He is usually standing just within the gates, seemingly staring at the passing motorist. Within a few moments, he vanishes. Unfortunately though, a few passersby have had closer encounters with the creature. In these circumstances, the figure appears suddenly to those who are walking or riding a bicycle past the cemetery gates. These witnesses say that they have heard the sneering phantom growl at them as if in warning! This is a sure way to get them to pick up their pace, they say.

Who is this strange creature and why does he appear here? No one can say for sure, but author Dale Kaczmarek researched the story and discovered that, around the time of the original sightings, there was a mildly retarded young man who lived near the cemetery. He often jogged and walked alongside the road at night and one evening was killed by a passing car. Could this young man have been the thin "man in black" who was reported here in the 1970's? He could have been playing a prank on people who passed by the cemetery... and perhaps that "prank" continues after his death. Perhaps it is his ghost who appears at St. Casimir's now?

Whether it is or not, keep a watchful eye out when passing these gates by night for those who have encountered this unnerving phantom have never been the same again!

A "woman in white" haunts one of the area's most foreboding graveyards, a place called Archer Woods Cemetery. For years, the female phantom has been reported at this wooded burial ground, especially back in the days when it was a desolate spot along Kean Road. She does not wander the roadway flagging down passing motorists however, although she is usually spotted by those who drive by the cemetery at night.

Those unwitting travelers, passing along Kean Road, are often greeted by the sound of a woman loudly sobbing in despair. When they stop their vehicles for a closer look, they see a woman in a white gown wandering near the edge of the graveyard. She is always said to be weeping and crying and covering her face with her hands. She is normally only seen for a matter of seconds before she disappears.

In addition to the "Weeping Woman", Archer Woods is also said to be home to the another, more terrifying, specter, an old-fashioned hearse. This black coach is said to be driverless but pulled by a team of mad horses. The hearse itself is made from black oak and glass and carries the glowing coffin of a small child as cargo. Residents of the area have been reporting this bizarre "ghost hearse" for years and it is often seen along nearby Archer Avenue. The origins of the hearse vary, but one thing is sure... no one wants to encounter it while traveling through the shadows along Kean Road after dark!

PHANTOMS OF ROSEHILL

In earlier portions of the book, we mentioned some ghostly happenings connected to Chicago's Rosehill Cemetery but those stories barely scratched the surface of the cemetery's lore. You see, Rosehill, in addition to being one of the city's most historic graveyards is also one of the most haunted!

Rosehill Cemetery began in 1859, taking its name from a nearby tavern keeper named Roe. The area around his saloon was known for some years as 'Roes Hill'. In time, the name was slightly altered and became 'Rosehill'. After the closure of the "dreary" Chicago City Cemetery, where Lincoln Park is now located, Rosehill became the oldest and the largest graveyard in Chicago and serves as the final resting place of more than 1500 notable Chicagoans, including a number of Civil War generals, mayors, former millionaires, local celebrities and early founders of the city. There are also a number of deceased Chicagoans who are not peacefully at rest here and they serve to provide the cemetery with its legends of ghosts and strange happenings.

Perhaps the most famous ghostly site on the grounds is the tomb belonging to Charles Hopkinson, a real estate tycoon from the middle 1800's. In his will, he left plans for his mausoleum to serve as a shrine to the memory of he and his family. When he died in 1885, a miniature cathedral was designed to serve as the tomb. Construction was started and then halted when the property owners behind the Hopkinson site took the family to court. They claimed that the cathedral tomb would block the view of their own burial sites. The case proceeded all of the way to the Illinois Supreme Court, which ruled that the other family had no say over what sort of monument the Hopkinson family built and that they should have expected that something could eventually block the view of their site. Shortly after, construction on the tomb continued and was completed. Despite the fact that the courts ruled in the favor of Hopkinson, it is said that on the anniversary of the real estate investor's death, a horrible moaning sound can be heard coming from the tomb, followed by what appears to be sound of rattling chains.

Ghost lore is filled with stories of the dead returning from the grave to protest wrongs that were done to them in their lifetime, or to continue business and rivalries started while they were among the living. Such events have long been a part of the lore of Rosehill's community mausoleum.

The Rosehill Cemetery Mausoleum was proposed in 1912 and the cemetery appealed to the elite businessmen of the city for the funds to begin construction. These men were impressed with the idea and enjoyed the thought of entire family rooms in the mausoleum that could be dedicated to their families alone and could be decorated to their style and taste. The building was designed Sidney Lovell and is a massive, multi-level structure with marble passageways and row after row of the dead. It is filled with a number of Chicago notables from the world of business and even architect Sidney Lovell himself.

One of the funding subscribers for the mausoleum was John G. Shedd, the president of Marshall Field from 1909 to 1926 and the man who donated the wonderful Shedd Aquarium to Chicago. He guaranteed himself immortality with the development of what he dreamed would be the world's largest aquarium. Even though Shedd died in 1926, four years before the aquarium would open, his directors remained loyal to his plans and created an aquatic showplace. A little of that extravagance can be found in the Rosehill mausoleum, as Shedd's family room is one of the most beautiful portions of the building. The chapel outside the room features chairs that are carved in images depicting shells and sea horses and the window inside bathes the room with a blue haze that makes the place appear to be under water. For this window, Shedd commissioned the artisan Louis Comfort Tiffany and made him sign a contract that said he would never create another window like it.

There have been no ghost stories associated with John Shedd, but there are others entombed in the structure who may not have found the peace that Shedd found. Two of them men also laid to rest in the building are Aaron Montgomery Ward and his bitter business rival, Richard Warren Sears. One has to wonder if either of these men could rest in peace with the other man in the same structure, but it is the ghost of Sears who has been seen walking through the mausoleum at night. The business pioneer has been spotted, wearing a top hat and tails, leaving the Sears family room and walking the hallways from his tomb to that of Ward's. Perhaps the rivalry that plagued his life continues on after death.....

CHICAGO'S MOST HAUNTED PLACE?

Located near the southwest suburb of Midlothian is the Rubio Woods Forest Preserve, an island of trees and shadows nestled in the urban sprawl of the Chicago area. The rambling refuge creates an illusion that it is secluded from the crowded city that threatens its borders, and perhaps it is. On the edge of the forest is a small graveyard that many believe may be the most haunted place in the region. The name of this cemetery is Bachelor's Grove and this ramshackle burial ground may be infested with more ghosts than most can imagine. Over the years, the place has been cursed with more than one hundred documented reports of paranormal phenomena, from actual apparitions to glowing balls of light.

There have been no new burials here for many years and as a place of rest for the departed, it is largely forgotten. But if you should ask any ghost hunter just where to go to find a haunting, Bachelor's Grove is usually the first place in Chicago to be mentioned!

The history of Bachelor's Grove has been somewhat shadowy over the years but most historians agree that it was started in the early part of the 1800's. The name of the cemetery came from a settlement that was started in the late 1820's that consisted of mostly German immigrants and settlers from the East Coast. One family who moved into the area was named "Batchelder" and their name was given to the timberland where they settled. It's likely the settlement and (later) the cemetery took its name from this family in the form of "Batchelor".

Other accounts state that the cemetery's name comes from the fact that the settlement was called "Bachelor" because of a number of single men who came to live there. This part of the lore dates back to 1833 or 1834 when a man named Stephen H. Rexford settled in the region with some other single men and began calling the place "Bachelor's Grove". Some historians dispute this, stating that the name of "Batchelor's Grove" was already in use at that time.

Regardless, the small settlement continued for some years as Bachelor's Grove, until 1850, when it was changed to "Bremen" by postmaster Samuel Everden in recognition of the new township name where the post office was located. In 1855, it was changed again to "Bachelder's Grove" by postmaster Robert Patrick but the post office closed down just three years later. Officially, the settlement ceased to exist and was swallowed by the forest around it.

The cemetery itself has a much stranger history. The land for the burial ground was first set aside in 1844 by Samuel Everden and was named "Everden" in his honor. The first burial took place in that year and as time passed, the eighty-two lots slowly began to fill. Burials continued here on a regular basis until around 1965, when things began to drop off. It should be noted that the last actual internment here was in 1989 when the ashes of a local resident were buried on the grounds. However, up until that point, the cemetery had been largely abandoned.

The last independent caretaker of the cemetery was a man named Clarence Fulton, whose family were early settlers in the township. According to Fulton, Bachelor's Grove was like a park for many years and people often came here to fish and swim in the adjacent pond. Families often visited on weekends to care for the graves of the deceased and to picnic under the trees. Things have certainly changed since then!

Problems began in and around the cemetery in the early 1960's, at the same time that the Midlothian Turnpike was closed to vehicle traffic in front of the cemetery. Even before that, the cemetery had become a popular "lover's lane" and when the road closed, it became even more isolated. Soon it began to show signs of vandalism and decay and a short time later, became considered haunted. Although the amount of paranormal activity that actually occurs in the cemetery has been argued by some, few can deny that strange things do happen here. When the various types of phenomenon really began is unclear but it has been happening for more than three decades now. Was the burial ground already haunted? Or did the haunting actually begin with the destructive decades of the 1960's and 1970's?

The vandals first discovered Bachelor's Grove in the 1960's and probably because of its secluded location, they began to wreak havoc on the place. Gravestones were knocked over and destroyed, sprayed with paint, broken apart and even stolen. Police reports later stated that markers from Bachelor's Grove turned up in homes, yards and even as far away as Evergreen Cemetery! Worst of all, in 1964, 1975 and 1978, graves were opened and caskets removed. Bones were sometimes found to be strewn about the cemetery.

Desecrated graves are still frequently found in the cemetery.

Was the haunting first caused by these disturbances? Most believe so, but others cite another source for the activity. Near the small pond that borders the cemetery, forest rangers and cemetery visitors have repeatedly found the remains of chickens and other small animals that have been sliced and mutilated in a ritualistic fashion. Officers that have patrolled the woods at night have reported seeing evidence of black magic and occult rituals in and around the graveyard. In some cases, inscriptions and elaborate writings have been carved in and painted on trees and grave markers and on the cemetery grounds themselves. This has led many to believe that the cemetery has been used for occult activities.

If you combine this sorted activity with the vandalism that has nearly destroyed the place, you have a situation that is ripe for supernatural occurrences. Could this be what has caused the blight on Bachelor's Grove? Even the early superstitions of the tombstone give credence to the idea that man has always felt that desecration of graves causes cemeteries to become haunted. Grave markers began as heavy stones that were placed on top of the graves of the deceased in the belief that the weight of it would keep the dead person, or their angry spirit, beneath the ground. Those who devised this system believed that if the stone was moved, the dead would be free to walk the earth.

There is no question that vandals have not been kind to Bachelor's Grove, but then neither has time. The Midlothian Turnpike bypassed the cemetery and even the road leading back to the graveyard was eventually closed. People forgot about the place and allowed it to fade into memory, just like the poor souls buried here.

Today, the cemetery is overgrown with weeds and is surrounded by a high, chain-link fence, although access is easily gained through the holes that trespassers have cut into it. The cemetery sign is long since gone. It once hung above the main gates, which are now broken open and lean dangerously into the confines of Bachelor's Grove.

The first thing noticed by those who visit here is the destruction. Tombstones seem to be randomly scattered about, no longer marking the resting places of those whose names are inscribed upon them. Many of the stones are missing, lost forever and perhaps carried away by thieves. These macabre crimes gave birth to legends about how the stones of the cemetery move about under their own power. The most disturbing things to visitors though are the trenches and pits that have been dug above some of the graves, as vandals have attempted to make off with souvenirs from those whose rest they disturb.

Near the front gate is a broken monument to a woman whose name was heard being called repeatedly on an audio tape. Some amateur ghost hunters left a recording device running while on an excursion to Bachelor's Grove and later, upon playback of the tape, they discovered that the recorder had been left on the ruined tombstone of a woman that had the same name as that being called to on the tape. Coincidence? Perhaps, but it hardly seems likely.

Just beyond the rear barrier of the cemetery is a small, stagnant pond that can be seen by motorists who pass on 143rd Street. This pond, while outside of the graveyard, is still not untouched by the horror connected to the place. One night in the late 1970's, two Cook County forest rangers were on night patrol near here and claimed to see the apparition of a horse emerge from the waters of the pond. The animal appeared to be pulling a plow behind it that was steered by the ghost of an old man. The vision crossed the road in front of the ranger's vehicle, was framed for a moment in the glare of their headlights, and then vanished into the forest. The men simply stared in shock for a moment and then looked at one another to be sure that had both seen the same thing. They later reported the incident and since that time, have not been the last to see the old man and the horse.

Little did the rangers know, but this apparition was actually a part of an old legend connected to the pond. It seems that in the 1870's, a farmer was plowing a nearby field when something startled his horse. The farmer was caught by surprise and became tangled in the reins. He was dragged behind the horse and it plunged into the small pond. Unable to free himself, he was pulled down into the murky water by the weight of the horse and the plow and he drowned. Since that time, the vivid recording of this terrible incident has been supernaturally revisiting the surrounding area.

In addition to this unfortunate phantom, the pond was also rumored to be a dumping spot for murder victims during the Prohibition era in Chicago. Those who went on a "one-way ride" were alleged to have ended the trip at the pond near Bachelor's Grove. Thanks to this, their spirits are also said to haunt the dark waters.

Strangely though, it's not the restless spirits of gangland execution victims that have created the most bizarre tales of the pond. One night, an elderly couple was driving past the cemetery and claimed to see something by the bridge at the edge of the pond. They stopped to get a closer look and were understandably terrified to see a huge, two-headed man come out from under the bridge and cross the road in the light from their headlights! Whatever this creature may have been, it quickly vanished into the woods.

Incredibly, even the road near Bachelor's Grove is reputed to be haunted. Could there be such a taint to this place that even the surrounding area is affected? The Midlothian Turnpike is said to be the scene of vanishing "ghost cars" and phantom automobile accidents. No historical events can provide a clue as to why this might be, but the unexplained vehicles have been reported numerous times in recent years. The stories are all remarkably the same too. People who are traveling west on the turnpike see the tail lights of a car in front of them. The brake lights go on, as if the car is planning to stop or turn. The car then turns off the road. However, once the following auto gets to the point in the road where the first vehicle turned, they find no car there at all! Other drivers have reported passing these phantoms autos, only to see the car vanish in their rearview mirrors.

One young couple even claimed to have a collision with one of these phantom cars in 1978. They had just stopped at the intersection of Central Avenue and the Midlothian Turnpike. The driver looked both ways, saw that the road was clear in both directions, then pulled out. Suddenly, a brown sedan appeared from nowhere, racing in the direction of the cemetery. The driver of the couple's car hit the brakes and tried to stop, but it was too late to avoid the crash. The two vehicles collided with not only a shuddering impact, but with the sound of screeching metal and broken glass as well. To make the event even more traumatic, the couple was then shocked to see the brown sedan literally fade away! They climbed out of their car, which had been spun completely around by the impact, but realized that it had not been damaged at all. They had distinctly heard the sound of the torn metal and broken glass and had felt the crush of the two cars coming together, but somehow it had never physically happened!

It remains a mystery as to where these phantom cars come from, and where they vanish to. Why do they haunt this stretch of roadway? No one knows...

For those searching for Bachelor's Grove, it can be founding by leaving the roadway and walking up an overgrown gravel track that is surrounded on both sides by the forest. The old road is blocked with chains and concrete dividers and a dented "No Trespassing" sign that hangs ominously near the mouth to the trail. The burial ground lies about a half-mile or so beyond it in the woods.

It is along this deserted road where other strange tales of the cemetery take place. One of these odd occurrences is the sighting of the "phantom farm house". It has been seen appearing and disappearing along the trail for several decades now. The reports date back as far as the early 1960's and continue today. The most credible thing about many of the accounts is that they come from people who originally had no idea that the house shouldn't be there at all.

The house has been reported in all weather conditions and in the daylight hours, as well as at night. There is no historical record of a house existing here but the descriptions of it rarely vary. Each person claims it to be an old frame farm house with two-stories, white, wooden posts, a porch swing and a welcoming light that burns softly in the window. Popular legend states that should you enter this house though, you would never come back out again. As witnesses approach the building, it is reported to get smaller and smaller until it finally just fades away, like someone switching off an old television set. No one has ever claimed to set foot on the front porch of the house.

But the story gets stranger yet! In addition to the house appearing and disappearing, it also shows up at a wide variety of locations along the trail. On one occasion it may be sighted in one area and then at an entirely different spot the next time. Author Dale Kaczmarek, who also heads the *Ghost Research Society* paranormal investigation group, has interviewed dozens of witnesses about the paranormal events at Bachelor's Grove. He has talked to many who say they have experienced the vanishing farm house. He has found that while all of their descriptions of the house are identical, the locations of the sightings are not. In fact, he asked the witnesses to place an "X" on the map of the area where they saw the house. Kaczmarek now has a map of the Bachelor's Grove area with "X's" all over it!

Also from this stretch of trail come reports of "ghost lights". One such light that has been reported many times is a red, beacon-like orb that has been seen flying rapidly up and down the trail to the cemetery. The light is so bright, and moves so fast, that it is impossible to tell what it really looks like. Most witnesses state that they have seen a "red streak" that is left in its wake.

Others, like Jack Hermanski from Joliet, have reported seeing balls of blue light in the woods and in the cemetery itself. These weird lights have sometimes been reported moving in and around the tombstones in the graveyard. Hermanski encountered the lights in the early 1970's and chased a number of them. All of the lights managed to stay just out of his reach. However, a woman named Denise Travers did manage to catch up with one of the blue lights in December 1971. She claimed to pass her hand completely through one of them but felt no heat or sensation.

Besides the aforementioned phenomena, there have been many sightings of ghosts and apparitions within Bachelor's Grove Cemetery itself. The two most frequently reported figures have been the "phantom monks" and the so-called "Madonna of Bachelor's Grove".

The claims of the monk-like ghosts are strange in themselves. These spirits are said to be clothed in the flowing robes and cowls of a monastic order and they have been reported in Bachelor's Grove and in other places in the Chicago area too. There are no records to indicate that a monastery ever existed near any of the locations where the "monks" have been sighted though, making them one of the greatest of the area's enigmas.

The most frequently reported spirit though is known by a variety of names from the

"Madonna of Bachelor's Grove" to the "White Lady" to the affectionate name of "Mrs. Rogers". Legend has it that she is the ghost of a woman who was buried in the cemetery next to the grave of her young child. She is reported to wander the cemetery on nights of the full moon with an infant wrapped in her arms. She appears to walk aimlessly, with no apparent direction and completely unaware of the people who claim to encounter her. There is no real evidence to say who this woman might be but, over the years, she has taken her place as one of the many spirits of this haunted burial ground.

And there are other ghosts as well. Legends tell more apocryphal tales of a ghostly child who has been seen running across the bridge from one side of the pond to the other, a glowing yellow man and even a black carriage that travels along the old road through the woods.

Many of these tales come from a combination of stories, both new and old, but the majority of first-hand reports and encounters are the result of literally hundreds of paranormal investigations that have been conducted here over the last forty years. Many of the ghost hunters who come to this place are amateur investigators, looking for thrills as much as they are looking for evidence of the supernatural, while others, like Dale Kaczmarek and the *Ghost Research Society*, are much more on the serious side.

Kaczmarek and his investigators have turned up many clues and pieces of evidence that seem to fit randomly into the mystery of Bachelor's Grove. These mysterious bits of evidence, while showing that strange things do happen here, never really seem to provide the hard evidence that these researchers look for. Even the photographs collected during their outings tantalize the investigators. For example, a series of photos taken by the group in 1979 show a monk-like figure standing near the cemetery fence. The figure appeared to be wearing a hooded robe and holding a baby in its arms. Oddly, this was three years before the *Ghost Research Society* collected any accounts of the "White Lady"!

Perhaps the most stunning photograph from Bachelor's Grove was taken in August 1991, during a full-fledged investigation of the cemetery. *Ghost Research Society* members came to the burial ground in the daytime and covered the area with the latest in scientific equipment, cameras, tape recorders and video cameras. All of the members were given maps of the cemetery and instructed to walk through and note any changes in electro-magnetic readings or atmosphere fluctuations. After the maps were compared, it was obvious that several investigators found odd changes in a number of distinct areas. A number of photos were taken in those areas, using both standard and infrared film. Nothing was seen at the time the photographs were taken, but once they were developed, the investigators learned that something had apparently been there!

In a photo, taken by Mari Huff, there appeared the semi-transparent form of a woman, who was seated on the remains of a tombstone. Was this one of the ghosts of

Bachelor's Grove? Skeptics immediately said "no", claiming that it was nothing more than a double exposure or an outright hoax.

Curious, I asked for and received a copy of the photograph and had it examined by several independent photographers. Most of them would have liked to come up with a reason why the photograph could not be real, but unfortunately they couldn't. They ruled out the idea of a double exposure and also the theory that the person in the photo was a live woman who was placed in the photo and made to appear like she was a ghost. One skeptic also claimed that the woman in the photo was casting a shadow, but according to the photographers who analyzed the image, the "shadow" is actually nothing more than the natural shading of the landscape. Besides that, one of them asked, if she is casting a shadow in that direction, then why isn't anything else in the frame?

Genuine or not (and I think it is), this photograph is just one of the hundreds of photos taken here that allegedly show supernatural activity. While many of them can be ruled out as nothing more than atmospheric conditions, reflections and poor photography, there are others that cannot.

In the end, we have to ask, what is it about Bachelor's Grove Cemetery? Is it as haunted as we have been led to believe? I have to leave that up to the reader to decide, but strange things happen here and there is little reason to doubt that this one of the most haunted places in the Midwest.

But haunted or not, Bachelor's Grove is still a burial ground and a place that should be treated with respect as the final resting place of those interred here. It should also be remembered that the cemetery is not a private playground for those who are intrigued by ghosts and hauntings. It is first and foremost a repository for the dead and should be protected as such by those who hope to enjoy it, and possibly learn from it, in the years to come.

Thanks to the efforts of local preservation groups, it appears that Bachelor's Grove is not beyond restoration, but it should still be protected against the abuses that it has suffered in the past. It is a piece of our haunted history that we cannot afford to lose.

HAUNTED ARCHER AVENUE

Perhaps the greatest cemetery ghost story of all time (and one that I have saved for the final entry in this book) is centered around a stretch of roadway on the south side of Chicago called Archer Avenue. It appears that this road may be the perfect location for a haunting as there are a number of locations along its route that boast more than their share of ghosts. The paranormal activity on the roadway seems to be anchored at both ends by cemeteries, both of which have their own ghost stories. One of them is the famous Resurrection Cemetery and the other, lesser-known, burial ground is St. James-Sag.

But what makes Archer Avenue so haunted? In her book, *Chicago Haunts*, author Ursula Bielski explains the history of Archer Avenue and its connections to strangeness. In the early days of Chicago, the road was an Indian trail and some have suggested that the original inhabitants forged a path here because of some mystical, magnetic force that connected it to the next world. They say that paranormal energies would also be attracted to this magnetism and this would explain the hauntings in the area. The author also mentions that the area may be so haunted because of its proximity to water. Archer Avenue is nearly surrounded by water sources like the Cal-Sag Channel, the Des Plaines River, the Illinois-Michigan Canal, the Chicago Sanitary and Shipping Canal and even Maple Lake, which reportedly is the scene of "ghost lights" activity.

But no matter what the reason, Archer Avenue may be the most haunted street in Chicago! The Indian trail that it used to be was turned into an actual road in the 1830's. Irish workers on the Illinois-Michigan Canal completed the construction. Most of them lived near Lemont, at the southern end of Archer Avenue. Here is located the St. James-Sag Church and burial ground, which dates back to around 1817, a few years before Archer Avenue was built to follow the route of the canal. Most of the men who worked on the road and canal moved out of Chicago and became parishioners of the church.

Legend has it that they settled into a small, nearby community, which was cursed by an early rector of St. James-Sag because the residents were lax in their attendance at services. The story has it that the curse caused the community to die out and no trace of it can be found today.

Supernatural events have been reported at St. James-Sag since the middle 1800's. It was around this time when the first sightings of the "phantom monks" took place here. These stories continued for decades and there were many reliable witnesses to the strange activity. One of them, a former rector of the church, admitted on his deathbed that he had seen ghosts roaming the cemetery grounds for many years.

One winter night in 1977, a Cook County police officer was passing the cemetery and happened to turn his spotlight up past the cemetery gates. He claimed to see eight hooded figures floating up the cemetery road toward the rectory. He pursued what he first thought were pranksters into the graveyard but while he stumbled and fell over the uneven ground and tombstones, the monk-like figures eerily glided past without effort. He said that he nearly caught up with them when "they vanished without a trace".

Another, earlier legend of the graveyard concerns a phantom hearse that is possibly the same vehicle seen on Kean Road and at nearby Archer Woods Cemetery. The description of the vehicle is the same, from the black horses to the glowing coffin of a child, and was first reported back in 1897. According to a report in the *Chicago Tribune*, two musicians spent the night in a recreation hall that is located at the bottom of the hill below the St. James-Sag rectory. They were awakened in the early morning hours by the sound of a carriage on the stones outside. They looked out and saw the macabre hearse. They became the first to report the eerie vehicle, but they would not be the last.

What is it about this strange and haunted place called Archer Avenue? Is it really connected to the world beyond, or is there a natural explanation for the ghost sightings linked to the region? Are they truth or legend? That remains to be seen, but there may be more to this seemingly innocent roadway than meets the eye!

RESURRECTION MARY

It is a cold night in late December on the south side of Chicago. A taxicab travels along Archer Avenue as rain and sleet pelt the windshield. The driver reaches over to crank the heater up one more notch. It is the kind of night, he thinks, that makes your bones ache.

As the car rolls past the Willowbrook Ballroom, a pale figure, blurry though the wet and icy glass of the window, appears along the roadside. The driver cranes his neck and sees a young woman walking alone. She is strangely dressed for such a cold and wet night, wearing only a white cocktail dress and a thin shawl over her shoulders. She stumbles along the uneven shoulder of the road and the cabbie pulls over and stops the car. He rolls down the window and the young girl approaches the taxi. She is beautiful, he sees, despite her disheveled appearance. Her blond hair is damp from the weather and plastered to her forehead. Her light blue eyes are the color of ice on a winter lake.

He invites her into the cab and she opens the back door and slides across the seat. The cabbie looks into the rearview mirror and asks her where she wants to go. He offers her a free ride. It's the least that he can do in this weather, he tells her.

The girl simply replies that he should keep driving down Archer Avenue, so the cabbie puts the car into gear and pulls back onto the road. He notices in his mirror that the girl is shivering so he turns up the heater again. He comments on the weather, making conversation, but she doesn't answer him at first. He wonders if she might be a little drunk because she is acting oddly. Finally, she answers him, although her voice wavers and she sounds almost fearful. The driver is unsure if her whispered words are directed to him or if she is speaking to herself. "The snow came early this year," she murmurs and then is silent once more.

The cabbie agrees with her that it did and attempts to make more small talk with the lovely young girl. He soon realizes that she is not interested in conversation. Finally, she does speak, but when she does, she shouts at him. She orders him to pull over to the side of the road. This is where she needs to get out!

The startled driver jerks the steering wheel to the right and stops in an open area in front of two large, metal gates. He looks up and realizes where they have stopped. "You can't get out here," he says to the young woman, "this is a cemetery!"

When he looks into the rearview mirror, he realizes that he is in the cab alone... the girl is no longer in the backseat. He never heard the back door open or close, but the beautiful girl has simply disappeared.

One must wonder if it finally dawned on him just who he had taken for a ride in his cab. She is known all over the Chicago area as the region's most enigmatic and sought after ghost. Her name is "Resurrection Mary".

Chicago is a city filled with ghosts, from haunted houses to ghostly graveyards. But of all of the tales, there is one that rises above all of the others. I like to think of Resurrection Mary as Chicago's most famous ghost. It is also probably my favorite ghost story of all time. It has all of the elements of the fantastic from the beautiful female spirit to actual eyewitness sightings that have yet to be debunked. There is much about the story that appeals to me and I never tire of hearing or talking about Mary, her sightings and her mysterious origins.

Although stories of "vanishing hitchhikers" in Chicago date back to the horse and buggy days, Mary's tale begins in the 1930's. It was around this time that drivers along Archer Avenue started reporting strange encounters with a young woman in a white dress. She always appeared to be real, until she would inexplicably vanish. The reports of this girl began in the middle 1930's and started when motorists passing by Resurrection Cemetery began claiming that a young woman was attempting to jump onto the running boards of their automobiles.

Not long after, the woman became more mysterious, and much more alluring. The strange encounters began to move further away from the graveyard and closer to the O

Henry Ballroom, which is now known as the Willowbrook. She was now reported on the nearby roadway and sometimes, inside of the ballroom itself. On many occasions, young men would meet a girl at the ballroom, dance with her and then offer her a ride home at the end of the evening. She would always accept and offer vague directions that would lead north on Archer Avenue. When the car would reach the gates of Resurrection Cemetery, the young woman would always vanish.

More common were the claims of motorists who would see the girl walking along the road. They would offer her a ride and then witness her vanishing from their car. These drivers could describe the girl in detail and nearly every single description precisely matched the previous accounts. The girl was said to have light blond hair, blue eyes and was wearing a white party dress. Some more attentive drivers would sometimes add that she wore a thin shawl, or dancing shoes, and that she had a small clutch purse.

Others had even more harrowing experiences. Rather than having the girl vanish for their car, they claimed to actually run her down in the street. They claimed to see a woman in a white dress bolt in front of their car near the cemetery and would actually describe the sickening thud as she was struck by the front of the car. When they stopped to go to her aid, she would be gone. Some even said that the automobile passed directly through the girl. At that point, she would turn and disappear through the cemetery gates.

Bewildered and shaken drivers began to appear almost routinely in nearby businesses and even at the nearby Justice, Illinois police station. They told strange and frightening stories and sometimes they were believed and sometimes they weren't. Regardless, they created an even greater legend of the vanishing girl, who would go on to become Resurrection Mary.

But who is this young woman, or at least who was she when she was alive?

According to Dale Kaczmarek, the most accurate version of the story concerns a young girl who was killed while hitchhiking down Archer Avenue in the early 1930's. Apparently, she had spent the evening dancing with a boyfriend at the O Henry Ballroom. At some point, they got into an argument and Mary (as she has come to be called) stormed out of the place. Even though it was a cold winter's night, she thought, she would rather face a cold walk home than another minute with her boorish lover.

She left the ballroom and started walking up Archer Avenue. She had not gotten very far when she was struck and killed by a passing automobile. The driver fled the scene and Mary was left there to die.

Her grieving parents buried her in Resurrection Cemetery, wearing a white dress and her dancing shoes. Since that time, her spirit has been seen along Archer Avenue, perhaps trying to return to her grave after one last night among the living.

It has never been known just who the earthy counterpart of Mary might have been, but several years ago, a newspaper report confused things so badly that a number of writers and researchers ended up creating their own "Mary". She was another girl who was tragically killed, but had nothing to do with the woman who haunts Archer Avenue. In the quest to learn Mary's identity, speculation fell onto a woman named Mary Bregovy, who is also buried in Resurrection Cemetery. Unfortunately, there are too many factors that prevent her from being Resurrection Mary.....

Even though Bregovy was killed in an auto accident in 1934, it is unlikely that she was returning home from the O Henry Ballroom, as some have claimed. The accident in which she was killed took place on Wacker Drive in downtown Chicago. The car that she was riding in collided with an elevated train support and she was thrown through the windshield. This is a far cry from being killed by a hit-and-run driver on Archer Avenue.

Bregovy also did not resemble the phantom that has been reported either. According to memory and photographs, she had short, dark hair, which is the opposite of the fair-skinned blond ghost. Besides that, the undertaker who prepared Bregovy for her funeral, John Satala, recalled that she was buried in an orchid-colored dress, not the white one of legend.

However, John Satala does add an interesting note to the story. In fact, he may have been the person who caused the confusion between spectral "Mary's" in the first place. In a newspaper interview many years ago, Satala mentioned a caretaker at Resurrection Cemetery who told him that he had seen a ghost on the cemetery grounds. The caretaker believed the ghost was that of Mary Bregovy.

So, if Resurrection Mary was not Mary Bregovy, who was she? Some have speculated that she never really existed at all. They have disregarded the search for her identity, believing that she is nothing more than an "urban legend" and a piece of fascinating folklore. They believe the story can be traced to nothing more than Chicago's version of the "vanishing hitchhiker".

While the story of Resurrection Mary does bear some resemblance to the tale (as can be seen in an earlier chapter), the folklorists have forgotten an important thing that Mary's story has, that the many versions of the other stories do not... credible eyewitness accounts. Many of these reports are not just stories that have been passed from person to person and rely on a "friend of a friend" for authenticity. In fact, some of the encounters with Mary have been chillingly up close and personal and remain unexplained to this day.

Besides that, as you will soon see, Mary is one of the few ghosts to ever leave physical evidence behind!

Aside from harried motorists who encountered Mary along Archer Avenue, one of the first people to ever meet her face to face was a young man named Jerry Palus. His experience with Mary took place in 1939 but would leave such an impression that he would never forget it until his death in 1992. Palus remained an unshakable witness and appeared on a number of television shows to discuss his night with Resurrection Mary. Regardless, he had little to gain from his story and no reason to lie. He never doubted the fact that he spent an evening with a ghost!

Palus met the young girl at the Liberty Grove and Hall, a dance hall that was near 47th Street and Mozart. He had apparently seen her there on several occasions and finally asked her to dance one night. She accepted and they spent several hours together. Strangely though, she seemed a little distant and Palus also noticed that her skin was very cold, almost icy to the touch. When he later kissed her, he found her lips were also cold and clammy.

At the end of the evening, the young woman asked Palus for a ride home and she gave him an address and then directed him down Archer Avenue. As they approached the gates to the Resurrection Cemetery, she asked him to pull over. She had to get out here, she told him. The beautiful girl then turned in her seat and faced Palus. "This is where I have to get out," she spoke softly, "but where I'm going, you can't follow."

Palus was a little confused by her statement, but before he could respond, the girl got out of the car and ran toward the cemetery gates. She vanished before she reached them... right before Jerry's eyes! That was the moment when he knew that he had danced with a specter!

Determined to find out what was going on, Palus visited the address the girl had given him on the following day. The woman who answered the door told him that he couldn't have possibly been with her daughter the night before because she had been dead for several years. However, Palus was able to correctly identify the girl from a family portrait in the other room

This was only the beginning for Mary and from that point on, she began making regular appearances on Archer Avenue. Stories like the one told by Jerry Palus have become commonplace over the years, but his account remains among the most convincing. Since that time, dozens of other young men have told of picking up the same girl, or meeting her at the ballroom, only to have her disappear from their car. The majority of the reports seem to come from the cold winter months, like the account passed on by a cab driver. He picked up a girl who was walking along Archer Avenue one night in 1941. It was very cold outside, but she was not wearing a coat. She jumped into the cab and told him that she needed to get home very quickly. She directed him along Archer Avenue and a few minutes later, he looked back and she was gone. He realized that he was passing in front of the cemetery when she disappeared.

The stories continued but perhaps the strangest account of Mary was the one that occurred on the night of August 10, 1976. This event has remained so bizarre after all this time because on this occasion, Mary did not just appear as a passing spirit. It was on this night that she left evidence behind!

A driver was passing by the cemetery around 10:30 that night when he happened to see a girl standing on the other side of the gates. He said that when he saw her, she was wearing a white dress and grasping the iron bars of the gate. The driver was considerate enough to stop down the street at the Justice police station and alert them to the fact that someone had been accidentally locked in the cemetery at closing time. An officer responded to the call but when he arrived there was no one there. The graveyard was dark and deserted and there was no sign of any girl.

But his inspection of the gates, where the girl had been seen standing, did reveal something. The revelation chilled him to the bone! He found that two of the bars in the gate had been pulled apart and bent at sharp angles. To make things worse, at the points on the green-colored bronze where they had been pried apart were blackened scorch marks. Within these marks was what looked to be skin texture and handprints that had been seared into the metal with incredible heat.

The marks of the small hands made big news and curiosity-seekers came from all over the area to see them. In an effort to discourage the crowds, cemetery officials attempted to remove the marks with a blowtorch, making them look even worse. Finally, they cut the bars off and installed a wire fence until the two bars could be straightened or replaced.

The strange marks on the bars at Resurrection Cemetery.. handprints of a ghost? (courtesy of Dale Kaczmarek)

The cemetery emphatically denied the supernatural version of what happened to the bars. They claimed that a truck backed into the gates while doing sewer work at the cemetery and that grounds workers tried to fix the bars by heating them with a blowtorch and bending them. The imprint in the metal, they said, was from a workman trying to push them together again. While this explanation was quite convenient, it did not explain why the marks of small fingers were clearly visible in the metal.

The bars were removed to discourage onlookers, but taking them out had the opposite effect and soon, people began asking what the cemetery had to hide. The events allegedly embarrassed local officials, so they demanded that the bars be put back into place.

Once they were returned to the gate, they were straightened and painted over with green paint so that the blackened area would match the other bars. Unfortunately though, the scorched areas continued to defy all attempts to cover them and the twisted spots where the handprints had been impressed remained obvious until just recently, when the bars were removed for good.

During the 1970's and 1980's, Mary sightings reached their peak. People from many different walks of life, from cab drivers to ministers said they had picked her up and had given her rides. It was during this period that Resurrection Cemetery was undergoing some major renovations and perhaps this was what caused her restlessness.

Other accounts also began to surface at this time, which had Mary being struck by passing cars. Drivers started reporting a young girl in white who ran out in front of their automobile. Occasionally, the girl would vanish when she collided with the car and at other times, would crumple and fall to the road as if seriously injured. When the motorist stopped and went to help the girl, she would disappear.

On August 12, 1976, Cook County police officers investigated an emergency call about an apparent hit and run victim near the intersection of 76th Street and Roberts Road. The officers found a young female motorist in tears at the scene and they asked her where the body was that she had allegedly discovered beside the road? She pointed to a wet grass area and the policemen could plainly see a depression in the grass that matched the shape of a human body. The girl said that just as the police car approached the scene, the body on the side of the road vanished!

In May 1978, a young couple was driving down Archer when a girl suddenly darted out in the road in front of their car. The driver swerved to avoid her but knew when he hit the brakes that it was too late. As they braced for impact, the car passed right through the girl! She then turned and ran into Resurrection Cemetery, melting right past the bars in the gate. Another man was on his way to work in the early morning hours and spotted the body of a young girl lying directly in front of the cemetery gates. He stopped his truck and got out, quickly discovering that the woman was apparently badly injured, but still alive. He jumped into his truck and sped to the nearby police station, where he summoned an ambulance and then hurried back to the cemetery. When he came back, he found that the body was gone! However the outline of her body was still visible on the dew-covered pavement.

On the last weekend in August 1980, Mary was seen by dozens of people, including the Deacon of the Greek Church on Archer Avenue. Many of witnesses contacted the Justice police department about their sightings. Squad cars were dispatched and although the police could not explain the mass sightings of a young woman who was not present when they arrived, they did find the witnesses themselves. Many of them flagged down the officers to tell them what they had just seen.

On September 5, a young man was leaving a softball game and driving down Archer Avenue. As he passed the Red Barrel Restaurant, he spotted a young woman standing on the side of the road in a white dress. He stopped the car and offered her a ride and she accepted, asking that he take her down Archer. He tried to draw her into conversation, even joking that she looked like "Resurrection Mary", but she was not interested in talking. He tried several times to get her to stop for a drink, but she never replied. He was driving past the cemetery, never having stopped or even slowed down, when he looked over and saw that the girl was gone. She had simply vanished!

In October 1989, two women were driving past Resurrection Cemetery when a girl in a white dress ran out in front of their car. The driver slammed on the brakes, sure that she was going to hit the woman, but there was no impact. Neither of the women could explain where the apparition had disappeared to.

During the 1990's, reports of Mary slacked off, but they have never really stopped altogether. Many of the roadside encounters happened near a place called Chet's Melody Lounge, which is located across the road and a little south of the cemetery gates. Because it is open into the early morning hours, it often becomes the first place where late night drivers look for the young girl who vanished before their eyes!

A number of shaken drivers have stumbled into the bar after their strange encounters, as did a cab driver in 1973. He claimed that his fare, a young woman, jumped out of the back seat of his cab without paying. She ran off and he came into Chet's because it was the closest place that she could have gone to. He told the bartender that she was an attractive blond and that she had skipped out on her fare, but imagine his surprise when staff members told him that no young woman had come in.

Another bizarre encounter took place in the summer of 1996 when the owner of the lounge, the late Chet Prusinski, was leaving the bar at around four in the morning. A man came running inside and told Chet that he needed to use the telephone. He excitedly explained that he had just run over a girl on Archer and now he couldn't find her body. Chet was skeptical about the man's story until a truck driver came in and confirmed the whole thing. He had also seen the girl but stated that she had vanished, "like a ghost". The police came to investigate but, not surprisingly, they found no trace of her.

So, who is Mary and does she exist? Many remain skeptical about her, but I have found that this doesn't really seem to matter. You see, people are still seeing Mary walking along Archer Avenue at night. Drivers are still stopping to pick up a forlorn figure who seems inadequately dressed in the winter months, when encounters are most prevalent. Curiosity-seekers still come to see the gates where the twisted and burned bars were once located and some even roam the graveyard, hoping to stumble across the place where Mary's body was laid to rest.

Who is she? No one knows but that has not stopped the stories, tales and even songs from being spun about her. She remains an enigma and her legend lives on, not content to vanish, as Mary does when she reaches the gates to Resurrection Cemetery.

You see, our individual belief, or disbelief, does not really matter. Mary lives on anyway. I doubt that we will ever know who she really was, or why she haunts this peculiar stretch of roadway.

In all honesty, I don't suppose that I ever really want to know who she was. I guess that prefer Mary to remain just as she is, a mysterious, elusive and romantic spirit of the Windy City.

SELECT BIBLIOGRAPHY & RECOMMENDED READING FOR CEMETERY & GHOST BUFFS

Adams, Norman - Dead and Buried? (1972)

Alexander, John - Ghosts! Washington Revisited (1998)

Amsler, Kevin - Final Resting Place (1997)

Aries, Phillipe - The Hour of Our Death (1981)

Baker, Ronald - Hoosier Folk Legends (1982)

Baltimore New America (newspaper)

Baltimore Sun (newspaper)

Bettenhausen, Brad - "Batchelor Grove Cemetery": Where the Trails Cross (1995)

Bielski, Ursula - Chicago Haunts (1998)

Bielski, Ursula - More Chicago Haunts (2000)

Bingham, Joan & Dolores Riccio - More Haunted Houses (1991)

Bingham, Joan & Dolores Riccio - Haunted Houses USA (1989)

Blue & Gray Guide to Haunted Places of the Civil War (1996)

Brown, John Gary - Soul in the Stone (1994)

Brown, Alan - "Seeing is Believing" (Ghosts of the Prairie Magazine 1999)

Brunvand, Jan Harold - The Vanishing Hitchhiker (1981)

Brunvand, Jan Harold - Curses! Broiled Again (1989)

Brunvand, Jan Harold - The Mexican Pet (1986)

Buscher, David - "In the Statue's Grip" (unpublished)

Canning, John - Great Unsolved Mysteries (1984)

Carlson, Bruce & Lori Erickson - Ghosts of Johnson County, Iowa (1987)

Citro, Joseph A. - Passing Strange (1996)

Coleman, Loren - Mysterious America (1983 / 2000)

Courtaway, Robbi - Spirits of St. Louis (1999)

Davies, Rodney - The Lazarus Syndrome (1998)

Dengler, John - "Ghosts of South Main" (St. Charles Living Magazine)

Drake, Samuel Adams - New England Legends and Folklore (1883)

Duffey, Barbara - Banshees   Bugles and Belles: True Ghost Stories of Georgia (1995)

Edwards, Frank - Strange World (1964)

Enright, D.J. - Oxford Book of Death (1983)

Farris, David - Mysterious Oklahoma (1995)

Fate Magazine (various issues)

Florence, Robert - New Orleans Cemeteries (1997)

Floyd, E. Randall - Great American Mysteries (1990)

Gay, John & Felix Barker - Highgate Cemetery: Victorian Valhalla (1984)

Genge, N.E. - Urban Legends (2000)

Ghosts of Paramount Studios (internet website)

Ghosts of the Prairie Magazine and Internet Website

Guiley, Rosemary Ellen - Encyclopedia of Ghosts and Spirits (2000)

Hauck, Dennis William - Haunted Places: The National Directory (1996)

Heitz, Lisa Hefner - Haunted Kansas (1997)

Henson, Michael Paul - More Kentucky Ghost Stories (1996)
Hucke, Matt & Ursula Bielski - Graveyards of Chicago (1999)
Iserson, Kenneth V. - Death to Dust (1994)
Jackson, Kenneth T. & Camilo Jose Vergara - Silent Cities (1989)
Jacobson, Laurie & Marc Wannamaker - Hollywood Haunted (1994)
Jarvis, Sharon - Dead Zones (1992)
Jarvis, Sharon - Dark Zones (1992)
Jarvis, Shaorn - True Tales of the Unknown: The Uninvited (1989)
Jarvis, Sharon - True Tales of the Unknown: Beyond Reality (1991)
Jenkins, Tommy - Graphic History of St. Simon's Island (1994)
Jones, Barbara - Design for Death (1967)
Kaczmarek, Dale - Windy City Ghosts (2000)
Keister, Douglas - Going Out in Style (1997)
Kutz, Jack - Mysteries and Miracles of New Mexico (1988)
Kutz, Jack - Mysteries and Miracles of Colorado (1993)
Lamb, John J. - San Diego Specters (1999)
Linehan, Edward - National Geographic magazine article
Macrorie, K.T. - Hoosier Hauntings (1997)
Marimen, Mark - Haunted Indiana (1997)
Martin, Maryjoy - Twilight Dwellers: Ghosts, Ghouls and Goblins of Colorado (1985)
McNeil, W.K. - Ghost Stories of the American South (1985)
Melton, J. Gordon - The Vampire Book (1999)
Meyer, Richard E. - Cemeteries and Gravemarkers: Voices of American Culture (1989)
Mitford, Jessica - American Way of Death (1963)
Montell, William Lynwood - Ghosts Across Kentucky (2000)
Montgomery, Kate - "Black Angel of Oakland Cemetery" and correspondence
Munn, Debra D. - Ghosts on the Range (1989)
Murphy, Edwin - After the Funeral (1995)
Murray, Earl - Ghosts of the Old West (1998)
Myers, Arthur - Ghostly Register (1986)
Myers, Arthur - A Ghost Hunters Guide (1993)
Myers, Arthur - Ghostly Gazetteer (1990)
Neely, Charles - Tales and Songs of Southern Illinois (1938)
Nickell, Joe - Looking for a Miracle (1993)
Norman, Michael & Beth Scott - Haunted America (1994)
Norman, Michael & Beth Scott - Historic Haunted America (1995)
Pohlen, Jerome - Oddball Illinois (2000)
Preik, Brooks Newton - Haunted Wilmington (1995)
Robinson, David - Saving Graces (1995)
Robinson, Charles Turek - True New England Mysteries   Ghosts   Crimes & Oddities (1997)
Robson, Ellen & Diane Halicki - Haunted Highway (1999)
Rondina, Christopher - Vampire Legends of Rhode Island (1997)
Russell, Randy & Janet Barnett - Granny Curse (1999)
Saxon, Lyle - Fabulous New Orleans (1928)
Schechter, Harold - A to Z Encyclopedia of Serial Killers (1996)

Scott, Beth & Michael Norman - Haunted Heartland (1985)
Steiger, Brad & Sherry Hansen-Steiger - Montezuma's Serpent (1992)
Taylor, Troy - Haunted New Orleans (2000)
Taylor, Troy - Haunted Decatur Revisited (2000)
Taylor, Troy - Haunted Illinois (1999)
Taylor, Troy - Dark Harvest (1997)
Taylor, Troy - Where the Dead Walk (1997)
Taylor, Troy - The Ghost Hunter's Guidebook (1999)
Taylor, LB - Ghosts of Fredericksburg (1991)
Terjung, Shara - various articles and correspondence
Walsh, John Evangelist - Midnight Dreary: The Mysterious Death of Edgar Allan Poe (2000)
Weekly Retriever (newspaper)
Weitzman, David - Underfoot (1976)
Wilkins, Robert - Death: A History of Man's Obsessions and Fears (1990)
Williams, Ben and Jean & John Bruce Shoemaker - The Black Hope Horror (1991)
Windham, Kathryn Tucker - Jeffrey Introduces 13 More Southern Ghosts (1971)
Windham, Kathyrn Tucker - 13 Tennessee Ghosts and Jeffrey (1977)
Windham, Kathryn Tucker - 13 Georgia Ghosts and Jeffrey (1973)
Winer, Richard - Houses of Horror (1983)
Winer, Richard & Nancy Osborn - Haunted Houses (1979)
Winer, Richard & Nancy Osborn Ishmael - More Haunted Houses (1981)
Woodyard, Chris - Haunted Ohio (1991)
Woodyard, Chris - Haunted Ohio IV (1994)
Yankee Magazine - Mysterious New England (1979)
Young, Richard and Judy Dockery - Ozark Ghost Stories (1995)

Personal Interviews and Correspondence

ABOUT THE AUTHOR: TROY TAYLOR

Troy Taylor is the author of 16 previous books about ghosts and hauntings in America, including HAUNTED ILLINOIS, SPIRITS OF THE CIVIL WAR, THE GHOST HUNTER'S GUIDEBOOK. He is also the editor of GHOSTS OF THE PRAIRIE Magazine, a travel guide to haunted places in America. A number of his articles have been published here and in other ghost-related publications.

Taylor is the president of the "American Ghost Society", a network of ghost hunters, which boasts more than 450 active members in the United States and Canada. The group collects stories of ghost sightings and haunted houses and uses investigative techniques to track down evidence of the supernatural. In addition, he also hosts a National Conference each year in conjunction with the group which usually attracts several hundred ghost enthusiasts from around the country.

Along with writing about ghosts, Taylor is also a public speaker on the subject and has spoken to well over 100 private and public groups on a variety of paranormal subjects. He has appeared in literally dozens of newspaper and magazine articles about ghosts and hauntings. He has also been fortunate enough to be interviewed over 300 times for radio and television broadcasts about the supernatural. He has also appeared in a number of documentary films like AMERICA'S MOST HAUNTED, BEYOND HUMAN SENSES, GHOST WATERS, NIGHT VISITORS and in one feature film, THE ST. FRANCISVILLE EXPERIMENT.

Born and raised in Illinois, Taylor has long had an affinity for "things that go bump in the night" and published his first book HAUNTED DECATUR in 1995. For six years, he was also the host of the popular, and award-winning, "Haunted Decatur" ghost tours of the city for which he sometimes still appears as a guest host. He also hosts the "History & Hauntings Tours" of Alton, Illinois.

In 1996, Taylor married Amy Van Lear, the Managing Director of Whitechapel Press, and they currently reside in a restored 1850's bakery in Alton.

WHITECHAPEL PRODUCTIONS PRESS
HISTORY & HAUNTINGS BOOK CO.

Whitechapel Productions Press was founded in Decatur, Illinois in 1993 and is a publisher and purveyor of books on ghosts and hauntings. We also produce the "Ghosts of the Prairie" Magazine and the "Ghosts of the Prairie" Internet web page. We are also the distributors of the "Haunted America Catalog", the largest specialty catalog of ghost books in the United States.

<u>Our current titles include</u>
Haunted Illinois by Troy Taylor
Spirits of the Civil War by Troy Taylor
The Ghost Hunter's Guidebook by Troy Taylor
Haunted Alton by Troy Taylor
Haunted Decatur Revisited by Troy Taylor
Haunted New Orleans by Troy Taylor
Season of the Witch by Troy Taylor

and Windy City Ghosts by Dale Kaczmarek

<u>Upcoming Titles include</u>
Haunted History: Ghosts of the Prairie
A New Series Begins with Hauntings Across the Midwest by Troy Taylor

Ghosts Along the River Road
A Search for Hauntings along the Mississippi River by Troy Taylor

Ghost Lights and Grease Paint
History & Hauntings of American Theaters by Troy Taylor

Call us Toll-Free for More Information at 1-888-Ghostly

Or visit us On-line at the Ghosts of the Prairie Web Page at
www.prairieghosts.com